Oliver Optic

Outward bound: Young America afloat

A story of travel and adventure

Oliver Optic

Outward bound: Young America afloat
A story of travel and adventure

ISBN/EAN: 9783337109134

Printed in Europe, USA, Canada, Australia, Japan

Cover: Foto ©Andreas Hilbeck / pixelio.de

More available books at **www.hansebooks.com**

SHUFFLES IN TROUBLE.

OUTWARD BOUND:

OR,

YOUNG AMERICA AFLOAT.

A STORY OF TRAVEL AND ADVENTURE.

BY

WILLIAM T. ADAMS

OLIVER OPTIC

Entered according to Act of Congress, in the year 1866, by
WILLIAM T. ADAMS,
In the Clerk's Office of the District Court of the District of Massachusetts.

ELECTROTYPED AT THE
Boston Stereotype Foundry,
No. 4 Spring Lane.

GEORGE WEBSTER TERRILL

This Volume

IS RESPECTFULLY DEDICATED.

YOUNG AMERICA ABROAD.

BY OLIVER OPTIC.

A Library of Travel and Adventure in Foreign Lands. First and Second Series; six volumes in each Series. 16mo. Illustrated.

First Series.

I. *OUTWARD BOUND;* OR, YOUNG AMERICA AFLOAT.
II. *SHAMROCK AND THISTLE;* OR, YOUNG AMERICA IN IRELAND AND SCOTLAND.
III. *RED CROSS;* OR, YOUNG AMERICA IN ENGLAND AND WALES.
IV. *DIKES AND DITCHES;* OR, YOUNG AMERICA IN HOLLAND AND BELGIUM.
V. *PALACE AND COTTAGE:* OR, YOUNG AMERICA IN FRANCE AND SWITZERLAND.
VI. *DOWN THE RHINE;* OR, YOUNG AMERICA IN GERMANY.

Second Series.

I. *UP THE BALTIC;* OR, YOUNG AMERICA IN DENMARK AND SWEDEN.
II. *NORTHERN LANDS;* OR, YOUNG AMERICA IN PRUSSIA AND RUSSIA.
III. *VINE AND OLIVE;* OR, YOUNG AMERICA IN SPAIN AND PORTUGAL.
IV. *SUNNY SHORES;* OR, YOUNG AMERICA IN ITALY AND AUSTRIA.
V. *CROSS AND CRESCENT;* OR, YOUNG AMERICA IN GREECE AND TURKEY.
VI. *ISLES OF THE SEA;* OR, YOUNG AMERICA HOMEWARD BOUND.

PREFACE.

OUTWARD BOUND is the first volume of "A Library of Travel and Adventure in Foreign Lands," and contains the voyage of the Academy Ship "Young America" across the Atlantic. The origin and progress of this aquatic institution are incidentally developed, and the plan is respectfully submitted to the consideration of those who are interested in the education and moral training of the class of young men who are the characters in the scenes described in this work. Besides a full description of the routine and discipline of the ship, as an educational and reformatory institution, the volume contains a rather free *exposé* of the follies and frailties of youth, but their vices are revealed to suggest the remedy.

The story includes the experience of the officers and crew of the Young America, eighty-seven in number, though, of course, only a few of them can appear as prominent actors. As the ship has a little world, with all the elements of good and evil, within her wooden walls, the story of the individual will necessarily be interwoven with that of the mass; and the history of "The Chain League," in the present volume, of which Shuffles is the hero, will, it is hoped, convey an instructive lesson to young men who are disposed to rebel against reasonable discipline and authority.

In the succeeding volumes of this series, the adventures, travels, and "sight-seeing," as well as the individual and collective experience of the juvenile crew of the Academy Ship, will be narrated. They will visit the principal ports of Europe, as well as penetrate to the interior; but they will always be American boys, wherever they are.

The author hopes that the volumes of the series will not only be instructive as a description of foreign lands, and interesting as a record of juvenile exploits, but that they will convey correct views of moral and social duties, and stimulate the young reader to their faithful performance.

HARRISON SQUARE, MASS.,
    November 2, 1866.

CONTENTS.

CHAPTER		PAGE
I.	The Idea suggested.	11
II.	The Young America.	27
III.	The Ensign at the Peak.	43
IV.	Officers and Seamen.	59
V.	Our Fellows.	75
VI.	The Fourth of July.	91
VII.	Heaving the Log.	106
VIII.	Outward Bound.	122
IX.	The Watch Bill.	138
X.	Making a Chain.	154
XI.	The Gamblers in No. 8.	170
XII.	The Root of all Evil.	186
XIII.	Piping to Mischief.	202
XIV.	All Hands, Reef Topsails!	218
XV.	After the Gale.	233

CONTENTS.

CHAPTER		PAGE
XVI.	THE WRECK OF THE SYLVIA.	248
XVII.	PEAS AND BEANS.	263
XVIII.	THE RESULT OF THE BALLOT.	280
XIX.	MAN OVERBOARD!	299
XX.	THE END OF THE CHAIN LEAGUE.	318

OUTWARD BOUND.

OUTWARD BOUND;

OR,

YOUNG AMERICA AFLOAT.

CHAPTER I.

THE IDEA SUGGESTED.

THERE are no such peaches this side of New Jersey; and you can't get them, for love or money, at the stores. All we have to do is, to fill our pockets, and keep our mouths closed — till the peaches are ripe enough to eat," said Robert Shuffles, the older and the larger of two boys, who had just climbed over the high fence that surrounded the fine garden of Mr. Lowington.

"What will Baird say if he finds it out?" replied Isaac Monroe, his companion.

"Baird," the gentleman thus irreverently alluded to, was the principal of the Brockway Academy, of which Shuffles and Monroe were pupils in the boarding department.

"What will he say when he finds out that the King of the Tonga Islands picks his teeth with a pitchfork?" added Shuffles, contemptuously. "I don't intend that he shall find it out; and he won't, unless you tell him."

"Of course, I shall not tell him."

"Come along, then; it is nearly dark, and no one will see us."

Shuffles led the way down the gravelled walk till he came to a brook, on the bank of which stood the peach tree whose rich fruit had tempted the young gentlemen to invade the territory of Mr. Lowington with intent to plunder.

"There they are," said the chief of the young marauders, as he paused behind a clump of quince bushes, and pointed at the coveted fruit. "There's no discount on them, and they are worth coming after."

"Hark!" whispered Monroe. "I heard a noise."

"What was it?"

"I don't know. I'm afraid we shall be caught."

"No danger; no one can see us from the house."

"But I'm sure there's some one near. I heard something."

"Nonsense! It was only a dagger of the mind, such as Baird talks about," answered Shuffles, as he crawled towards the peach tree. "Come, Monroe, be quick, and fill your pockets."

This peach tree was a choice variety, in whose cultivation the owner had been making an elaborate experiment. Mr. Lowington had watched it and nursed it with the most assiduous care, and now it bore about a dozen remarkably large and beautiful peaches. They were not quite ripe enough to be gathered, but Shuffles was confident that they would "mellow" in his trunk as well as on the tree. The experiment of the cultivator had been a success, and he had already prepared, with much care and labor, a paper explanatory of the process, which he intended to read before the Pomological Society, exhibiting the fruit as the evidence of the practicability of his method. To Mr. Lowington, therefore, the peaches had a value far beyond their intrinsic worth.

Shuffles gathered a couple of the peaches, and urged his companion to use all possible haste in stripping the tree of its rich burden.

"Hallo, there! What are you about?" shouted some one, who hastened to make his presence known to the plunderers.

Monroe began to retreat.

"Hold on!" interposed Shuffles. "It's no one but Harry Martyn."

"He can tell of us just as well as anybody else."

"If he does, he will catch it."

"What are you doing?" demanded Harry Martyn, — who was a nephew of Mr. Lowington, and lived with him, — as he crossed the rustic bridge that spanned the brook.

"Don't you see what I'm doing?" replied Shuffles, with an impudent coolness which confounded Harry.

"Stop that, Shuffles!" cried Harry, indignantly. "My uncle wouldn't take ten dollars apiece for those peaches."

"That's more than he'll get for them," added Shuffles, as he reached up and gathered another peach.

"Stop that, I tell you!" said Harry, angrily, as he

stepped up, in a menacing attitude, before the reckless marauder.

"Shut up, Harry! You know me, and when I get all these peaches, I've got something to say to you."

Shuffles was about to gather another of the peaches, when Harry, his indignation overcoming his prudence, grasped his arm, and pulled him away from the tree.

"What do you mean, Harry Martyn?" exclaimed Shuffles, apparently astonished at the temerity of the youth. "I can't stop to lick you now; but I'll do it within twenty-four hours."

"Well, don't you touch those peaches, then."

"Yes, I will touch them. I intend to have the whole of them; and if you say a word to your uncle or any one else about it, I'll pulverize that head of yours."

"No, you won't! You shall not have those peaches, anyhow," replied the resolute little fellow, who was no match, physically, for Shuffles.

"If you open your mouth——"

"Hallo! Uncle Robert! Help, help! Thieves in the garden!" shouted Harry, who certainly had no defect of the lungs.

"Take that, you little monkey!" said Shuffles, angrily, as he struck the little fellow a heavy blow on the side of the head with his fist, which knocked him down. "I'll fix you the next time I see you."

Shuffles consulted his discretion rather than his valor, now that the alarm had been given, and retreated towards the place where he had entered the garden.

"What's the matter, Harry?" asked Mr. Lowington,

as he rushed over the bridge, followed by the gardener and his assistants, just as Harry was picking himself up and rubbing his head.

"They were stealing your peaches, and I tried to stop them," replied Harry. "They have taken some of them now."

Mr. Lowington glanced at the favorite tree, and his brow lowered with anger and vexation. His paper before the "Pomological" could be illustrated by only nine peaches, instead of thirteen.

"Who stole them, Harry?" demanded the disappointed fruit-grower.

The nephew hesitated a moment, and the question was repeated with more sternness.

"Robert Shuffles; Isaac Monroe was with him, but he didn't take any of the peaches."

"What is the matter with your head, Harry?" asked his uncle, when he observed him rubbing the place where the blow had fallen.

"Shuffles struck me and knocked me down, when I called out for you."

"Did he? Where is he now?"

"He and Monroe ran up the walk to the back of the garden."

"That boy shall be taken care of," continued Mr. Lowington, as he walked up the path towards the point where the marauders had entered. "The Academy is fast becoming a nuisance to the neighborhood, because there is neither order nor discipline among the students."

The thieves had escaped, and as it would be useless to follow them, Mr. Lowington went back to the house; but he was too much annoyed at the loss of his splendid peaches, which were to figure so prominently before the " Pomological," to permit the matter to drop without further notice.

" Did he hurt you much, Harry?" asked Mr. Lowington, as they entered the house.

" Not much, sir, though he gave me a pretty hard crack," answered Harry.

" Did you see them when they came into the garden?"

" No, sir; I was fixing my water-wheel in the brook when I heard them at the tree. I went up, and tried to prevent Shuffles from taking the peaches. I caught hold of him, and pulled him away. He said he couldn't stop to lick me then, but he'd do it within twenty-four hours. Then he hit me when I called for help."

" The young scoundrel! That boy is worse than a pestilence in any neighborhood. Mr. Baird seems to have no control over him."

Suddenly, and without any apparent reason, Mr. Lowington's compressed lips and contracted brow relaxed, and his face wore its usual expression of dignified serenity. Harry could not understand the cause of this sudden change; but his uncle's anger had passed away. The fact was, that Mr. Lowington happened to think, while his indignation prompted him to resort to the severest punishment for Shuffles, that he himself had been just such a boy as the plunderer of his cherished fruit. At the age of fifteen he had been the pest of the town in which he resided. His father was a very wealthy man, and resorted to many expedients to cure the boy of his vicious propensities.

Young Lowington had a taste for the sea, and his father finally procured a midshipman's warrant for him to enter the navy. The strict discipline of a ship of war proved to be the "one thing needful" for the reformation of the wild youth; and he not only became a steady young man, but a hard student and an accomplished officer. The navy made a man of him, as it has of hundreds of the sons of rich men, demoralized by idleness and the absence of a reasonable ambition.

When Mr. Lowington was thirty years old, his father died, leaving to each of his three children a quarter of a million; and he had resigned his position in the navy, in order to take care of his property, and to lead a more domestic life with his wife and daughter than the discipline of the service would permit.

He had taken up his residence in Brockway, the early home of his wife. It was a large town on the sea shore, only a few miles from the metropolis of New England, thus combining all the advantages of a home in the city and in the country. For several years he had been happy in his peaceful retirement. But not wealth, nor even integrity and piety, can bar the door of the lofty mansion against the Destroyer of the race. His wife died of an hereditary disease, which gave no indication of its presence till she had passed her thirtieth year. Two years later, his daughter, just blooming into maturity, followed her mother down to the silent tomb, stricken in her freshness and beauty by the same insidious malady.

The husband and father was left desolate. His purest and fondest hopes were blighted; but, while he was submissive to the will of the Father, who doeth all things well, he became gloomy and sad. He was not seen to smile for a year after the death of his daughter, and it was three years before he had recovered even the outward semblance of his former cheerfulness. He was rich, but alone in the world. He continued to reside in the home which was endeared to him by the memories of his loved and lost ones.

When his wife's sister died in poverty, leaving two children, he had taken them to his home, and had become a father to them. Harry Martyn was a good boy, and Josephine Martyn was a good girl; but they were not his own children. There was something wanting — an aching void which they could not fill, though Mr. Lowington was to them all that could be asked or expected of a parent.

Mr. Lowington busied himself in various studies and experiments; but life had ceased to be what it was before the death of his wife and daughter. He wanted more mental occupation; he felt the need of greater activity, and he was tempted to return to the navy, even after his absence of ten years from the service; but this step, for many reasons, was not practicable. At the time when his garden was invaded by the vandal students from the Brockway Academy, he was still thinking what he could do to save himself from the inglorious life of ease he was leading, and, at the same time, serve his country and his race.

Shuffles had robbed his garden of some of his choicest fruit; had struck his nephew a severe blow on the head, and threatened to inflict still greater chastisement upon him in the future. Mr. Lowington was justly indignant; and his own peace and the peace of the neighborhood demanded that the author of the mischief should be punished, especially as he was an old transgressor. It was absolutely necessary that something should be done, and the retired naval officer was in the right frame of mind to do it. Just then, when he was wrought up to the highest pitch of indignation, his anger vanished. Shuffles at sixteen was the counterpart of himself at fifteen.

This was certainly no reason why the hand of justice should be stayed. Mr. Lowington did not intend to stay it, though the thought of his own juvenile depravity modified his view, and appeased his wrath. He put on his hat and left the house. He walked over to the Academy, and being shown to the office of the principal, he informed him of the depredations committed in his garden.

"Who did it, Mr. Lowington?" demanded the principal, with proper indignation in his tones and his looks.

"Shuffles."

"I need not have asked. That boy gives me more trouble than all the others put together," added Mr. Baird, with an anxious expression. "And yet what can I do with him?"

"Expel him," replied Mr. Lowington, laconically.

"I don't like to do that."

"Why not?"

"It would be an injury to me."

"Why so?"

"It would offend his father, who is a person of wealth and influence. When Shuffles came to Brockway, ten other boys came with him. He was expelled from another institution, which so incensed his father that he induced the parents of ten others to take their sons out, and send them to me. If I expel Shuffles, I shall lose about a dozen of my students, and I can't afford to do that."

"But must the neighborhood suffer from his depredations?"

"I will talk with the boy; I will keep him in his room for a week."

"I'm afraid the boy needs severer measures. If this were the first, or even the third time, I would not say so much."

"My dear sir, what can I do?"

"The boy needs strict discipline. If I were still in the navy, and had him aboard my ship, I could make a man of him."

"I don't think anything can be done."

"Something must be done, Mr. Baird. My garden shall not be robbed with impunity."

"I will do what I can, Mr. Lowington."

But the owner of the stolen fruit was by this time satisfied that nothing would be done. The principal of the Brockway Academy had not force nor influence enough to control such a boy as Shuffles. Mr. Lowington took his leave, determined to apply to another tribunal for the correction of the evil. That night the peach thieves were arrested, and put in the lock-up. The next day they were tried, found guilty, and sentenced to pay a fine and costs, which Mr. Baird promptly paid. Within a week Mr. Lowington's stable was burned to the ground. Shuffles was seen near the building just before the fire broke out; but it could not be proved that he was the incendiary, though no one doubted the fact. He was arrested, but discharged on the examination.

"You see how it is, Mr. Lowington," said the principal of the Academy, as the two gentlemen met after the examination. "It would have been better for you if you had not prosecuted the boy for stealing the peaches."

"I don't think so," replied Mr. Lowington. "I must do my duty, without regard to consequences; and you will pardon me if I say you ought to do the same."

"If I expel the boy he would burn the house over my head."

"Then you think he burned my stable?"

"I don't know; it cannot be proved that he did."

"I have no doubt of the fact. I have no ill will against the boy. I only desire to protect myself and my neighbors from his depredations."

"I think you were very unfortunate in the method you adopted, Mr. Lowington," replied the principal of the Academy. "It has reacted upon yourself."

"Shall this boy steal my fruit and burn my buildings with impunity?" added Mr. Lowington, with considerable warmth.

"Certainly not."

"I applied to you for redress, Mr. Baird."

"I told you I would talk with the boy."

"Such a reprobate as that needs something more than talk."

"What would you do with him, sir?" demanded Mr. Baird, earnestly.

"I hardly know. I should certainly have expelled him; but that, while it protects the Academy, does not benefit the boy."

"It would only harden the boy."

"Very likely; and his remaining will harden a dozen more by his influence. Mr. Baird, I shall be obliged to take my nephew out of your institution," added Mr. Lowington, seriously.

"Take him out?"

"I must, indeed."

"Why so?" asked Mr. Baird, who was touched in a very tender place.

"Because I am not willing to keep him under the influence of such an example as this Shuffles sets for his companions. As the matter now stands, the young rascal has more influence in the Academy than you have. You cannot manage him, and you dare not expel him. The boy knows this, and he will not leave his advantage unused."

"I hope you won't take Harry out of the school," said Mr. Baird.

"I must."

"Others may do the same."

"I cannot help it; with my view of the matter, they can hardly do otherwise."

"But you see, sir, what the effect of this step must be."

"Mr. Baird, I must be frank with you. You have declined to expel Shuffles, while you know that his influence is bad. You asked me what you should do; and I told you. Now, you prefer to retain Shuffles, but you must lose others. Permit me to say that you should do your duty without regard to consequences."

"I cannot afford to lose my scholars."

"Your position is a difficult one, I grant, Mr. Baird; but without discipline you can do nothing for yourself or the boys."

Mr. Lowington went home, Harry was taken from the Academy, and a dozen parents and guardians followed the example of the advocate for discipline. Mr. Baird was in despair. The institution was falling to pieces for the want of discipline. The principal had not the nerve to enforce order, even with the limited means within his reach. He went to see Mr. Lowington, and begged him to assist in stemming the tide which was setting against the Brockway Academy. The retired naval officer became deeply interested in the subject of school discipline in general, especially in its connection with the education of rich men's sons given to insubordination. He pitied poor Mr. Baird in his perplexities, for he was a good man and an excellent teacher.

In the mean time Shuffles grew worse instead of better. Finding that he could have his own way, that the principal was no match for him, his influence for evil was stronger than Mr. Baird's for good. The worthy schoolmaster had finally resolved to expel his troublesome student, when Mr. Lowington one day surprised him by offering to buy out the Academy at a price far exceeding its value. He gladly accepted the offer as the best solution of the problem, and the naval officer became principal of the Brockway Academy.

Mr. Lowington did not expel the refractory pupil at once. He waited for an overt act; but Shuffles found the anaconda of authority tightening upon him. He attempted to vindicate himself before his fellow-students by setting fire to a haystack on the marsh, belonging to the new principal. A searching investigation followed, and Shuffles was convicted. Mr. Lowington wrote to the boy's father, announcing his expulsion. Mr. Shuffles went to Brockway full of wrath, and threatened the new head of the institution with the loss of a large number of his scholars if he disgraced his son by expelling him. If the boy had done wrong, — and he supposed he had, — let him be talked to; let him be confined to his room for a day or two; but he must not be expelled; it was a disgrace to the boy.

The principal was as firm as a rock, and Mr. Shuffles was calm when he found that threats were unavailing. Mr. Lowington pointed out to his visitor the perils which lay in the path of his son. Mr. Shuffles began to be reasonable, and dined with the principal. A long and earnest consideration of the whole matter took place over the dessert. The fiat of expulsion was revoked, and young Shuffles was turned over to the ex-naval officer, with full power to discipline him as he thought best. Mr. Lowington had converted the father, and he hoped he should be able to convert the son.

After dinner, Mr. Shuffles went down the bay with his host in the yacht. On the way they passed the school ship Massachusetts, to which boys are sentenced by the courts for crime and vagrancy, and on board of which they are disciplined and educated. Mr. Lowington explained the institution to his guest.

"An excellent idea," said Mr. Shuffles.

"It is just the place for your son," replied Mr. Lowington.

"But it is for criminals."

"Very true."

"Robert is not a criminal."

"If he is not now, he soon will be, if he continues in his present course. If I had him on shipboard, I could make a man of him."

"Then I wish you had him on shipboard."

"Perhaps I may yet," replied the principal, with a smile. "I did not purchase the Academy with the intention of becoming a pedagogue, in the ordinary sense of the word. I have no intention of remaining in it."

"I hope you will."

"I have been thinking of fitting up a vessel like the school ship, that rich men's sons may have the benefit of such an institution without the necessity of committing a crime. I could do more for the boys in a month on board ship than I could in a year at Brockway."

This was the first mention which Mr. Lowington made of his plan, though he had been considering it for several weeks. Mr. Shuffles hoped that this idea of a nautical academy would be reduced to practice; for he now felt that it was just what his son needed. The project was discussed during the rest of the trip.

The history of the scheme, from its inception, need not be followed in detail. Many persons were consulted in regard to it; there were plenty to approve, and plenty to disapprove; but in October the keel of a four hundred ton ship was laid down. The object of this marine institution was thoroughly explained, and before the ship was ready for launching there were applications for every berth on board of her.

The idea was exceedingly popular among the boys, all of whom were anxious to be students on board, especially as it was already hinted that the ship would visit Europe. To parents it held out for their sons all the benefits of a sea voyage, with few of its disadvantages. It would furnish healthy exercise and a vigorous constitution to its pupils.

In March of the following year the ship was at anchor in Brockway harbor, ready to receive her juvenile crew.

CHAPTER II.

THE YOUNG AMERICA.

WITH Mr. Lowington, the Academy Ship, which was the name he usually applied to the idea he had matured, and thus far carried into effect, was not a speculation; he did not intend to see how much money could be made by the scheme. It was an experiment in the education of rich men's sons, for only rich men could pay for scholarships in such an expensive institution.

The Brockway Academy was to be continued, under the management of a board of trustees. An accomplished teacher had been selected by Mr. Lowington, and the school, under its present administration, was in a highly prosperous condition. Only ten of its pupils had been transferred to the Academy Ship, for it required no little nerve on the part of parents to send their sons to school on the broad ocean, to battle with the elements, to endure the storms of the Atlantic, and to undergo the hardships which tender mothers supposed to be inseparably connected with a life on shipboard.

For six months Mr. Lowington had studied upon his plan, and it was hardly matured when the new ship came to anchor in Brockway harbor. During this period he had visited the principal cities of the Northern States, those of the southern section being closed against his operations by the war of the rebellion, then raging at the height of its fury. He had interested his friends in his bold enterprise, and boys with whom the experiment was to be inaugurated were gathered from all parts of the country.

The securing of the requisite number of pupils was the first success, and what he had regarded as the most difficult part of the enterprise. More than half of them had been obtained before it was deemed prudent to lay the keel of the ship. The details of the plan had been carefully considered during the winter, and when the ship was moored at Brockway, the organization of the school, its rules and regulations, had all been written out. The boys began to arrive about the first of March, and by the first of April all of them, eighty-seven in number, were on board.

Mr. Lowington was naturally very anxious for the success of his experiment, and for months he had labored with unceasing diligence in perfecting his plan, and carrying it into operation. In this occupation he had found the activity he needed; and he may not be blamed for believing, all the time, that he was laboring for his country and his race.

If it has been inferred from what has been said of Mr. Lowington, of his domestic afflictions, and of his views on the subject of discipline, that he was an austere, cold, and unsympathizing man, a wrong impression has been conveyed. The boys of the Brockway Academy, when they came to know him, loved him as much as they respected him. He was not the man needlessly to abridge the harmless enjoyment of youth, or to repress its innocent hilarity. He watched the sports of the students with interest and pleasure, and encouraged them by all the means in his power. He was fond of humor, enjoyed a harmless joke, and had a keen appreciation of juvenile wit. He was a good companion for the boys, and when they understood him, he was always welcome to the play-ground.

The new ship had been duly christened Young America at the launching, by Miss Josey Martyn — a name which was rapturously applauded by the boys. She was one hundred and eighteen feet in length, and of about four hundred tons burden. She had been built as strong as wood, iron, and copper could make her. For a ship, she was small, which permitted her to be light sparred, so that her juvenile crew could handle her with the more ease. She had a flush deck; that is, it was unbroken from stem to stern. There was no cabin, poop, camboose, or other house on deck, and the eye had a clean range over the whole length of her. There was a skylight between the fore and the main mast, and another between the main and mizzen masts, to afford light and air to the apartments below. There were three openings in the deck by which entrance could be obtained to the interior of the ship: the fore hatch, the main hatch, and the companion-way, the two former being used by the crew, and the latter by the officers.

The between-decks, which is the space included between the upper and the lower deck, was fitted up for the accommodation of the officers and crew. Descending by the companion-way — which in the

Young America extended athwartships — on the right, at the foot of the stairs, was the officers' cabin, occupying the part of the ship nearest to the stern. This apartment was twenty-eight feet long, by fifteen in breadth at the widest part, with four state rooms on each side. The mizzen mast passed up through the middle of it. This cabin was richly but plainly fitted up, and was furnished well enough for a drawing-room on shore. It was for the use of the juvenile officers of the ship, fifteen in number, who were to hold their positions as rewards of merit. The captain had a room to himself, while each of the other apartments was to accommodate two officers.

On the left of the companion-way, descending the stairs, was the " old folks' cabin," as it was called by the students. It was in the locality corresponding to that occupied by the ward room of a man-of-war. Though the after cabin is the place of honor on board a ship, Mr. Lowington had selected the ward room for himself and the teachers, in preference to the after cabin, because it was next to the steerage, which was occupied by the larger portion of the pupils, and because the form of the ship did not contract the dimensions of the state rooms. This cabin was twenty-two feet long and fifteen feet wide, with no waste room, as in the after cabin, caused by the rounding in of the ship's counter. On the sides were five state rooms, besides a pantry for the steward, and a dispensary for the surgeon.

The forward room on the starboard side was occupied by Mr. Lowington alone; the next on the same side by the chaplain and doctor; and each of the three on the port side by two of the teachers. This cabin was elegantly finished and furnished, and the professors were delighted with its cheerful and pleasant aspect.

From the main cabin, as that of the "faculty" was called, were two doors, opening into the steerage, fifty-two feet in length by fifteen feet in width of clear space between the berths, which diminished to nine feet abreast of the foremast. This apartment was eight feet high, and was lighted in part by a large skylight midway between the fore and main mast, and partly by bull's eyes in the side of the ship. There were seventy-two berths, placed in twelve rooms, opening from passage-ways, which extended athwartships from the main steerage, and were lighted by the bull's eyes. There were no doors to these dormitories, each of which contained six berths, in two tiers of three each. It was intended that the six boys occupying one of these rooms should form a mess. Between the gangways, or passages, were mess tables, which could be swung up against the partition when not in use.

The steerage was neatly and tastefully fitted up, and furnished, though not so elegantly as the cabins. It was to be the school room, as well as the parlor and dining room of the boys, and it would compare favorably with such apartments in well-ordered academies on shore. There was plenty of shelves, pouches, and lockers, under the lower berths, and beneath the bull's eyes at the head of the main gangways, for clothing and books, and each boy had a place for every article which the regulations allowed him to possess.

Forward of the foremast there were two large state rooms; that on the starboard side having four berths, for the boatswain, carpenter, sailmaker, and head steward; and the one on the port side with six, for the two cooks and the four under stewards, all of whom were men skilful and experienced in their several departments. Forward of these was the kitchen, from which opened the lamp room, a triangular closet in the bow of the ship. Mr. Lowington had taken the idea of locating the cooking apartment in the extreme forward part of the vessel from the Victoria and Albert, the steam yacht of the Queen of England.

The hold beneath the berth deck contained the water tanks, bread room, chain lockers, and a multitude of store rooms for provisions, clothing, and supplies of every description needed on board during a long voyage.

The Young America was to be officered and manned by the students. They were to work the ship, to make and take in sail, to reef, steer, and wash down decks, as well as study and recite their lessons. They were to go aloft, stand watch, man the capstan, pull the boats; in short, to do everything required of seamen on board a ship. Mr. Lowington was to lure them into the belief, while they were hauling tacks and sheets, halyards and braces, that they were not at work, but at play. The labor required of them was an essential element in the plan, by which the boys were to obtain the necessary physical exercise, and the discipline they so much needed.

By the first of April the last of the students had reported to the principal on board, and the professors, as the boys insisted upon calling them, had taken possession of their state rooms. Though some of the pupils had been on board nearly a month, the organization of the ship had not been commenced; but classes had been formed in some of the studies, by the teachers, and the pupils recited every day. The boatswain had instructed the boys in rowing, and some temporary regulations had been adopted for the eating and sleeping departments. But not a boy had been allowed to go aloft, and nothing more than ordinary school discipline had been attempted.

The boys, as boys always are, were impatient at this delay. They wanted to be bounding over the ocean — to be on their way to some foreign port. They were anxious to work, to climb the rigging, and stand at the wheel. As yet they knew very little of the purposes of the principal, and had but a faint perception of the life they were to lead in the Academy Ship. It was understood that the officers were to be selected for their merit, and that the ship, some time or other, was to cross the ocean; but beyond this, all was darkness and uncertainty.

"To-morrow will be the first day of April," said George Wilton, as he walked the deck of the Young America with Richard Carnes, a dignified young gentleman of seventeen. "Mr. Lowington said we should go to work on that day."

"If he said so, then of course we shall go to work," replied Carnes.

"I'm tired of waiting," added Wilton. "I think this is a stupid kind of life. We are not even tied to a bell rope here."

"You will get discipline enough as soon as the crew are organized."

"I suppose we shall. Do you think we shall go to sea to-morrow?"

"Go to sea to-morrow!" exclaimed Carnes.

"Shuffles said so."

"How can we go to sea to-morrow? The crew don't know the mainmast from a handspike. They couldn't do anything with the ship now; they don't know the ropes."

"You do, Carnes."

"Well, I know something about a ship," replied the dignified young gentleman, who had made one voyage up the Mediterranean with his uncle.

"I was pretty sure we should get out into blue water by to-morrow."

"Nonsense!"

"Shuffles said so."

"He is mistaken."

"What are we going to do?"

"I don't know; I'm content to wait till orders come."

"I don't want to wait any longer," added Wilton.

"What are you talking about, fellows?" asked Shuffles, joining them, as they walked forward.

"Didn't you say we were going to sea to-morrow, Shuffles?" asked Wilton.

"Of course we are."

"Who says so?" demanded Carnes.

"All the fellows say so."

"It can't be true."

"Why not? We are not going to stay here forever."

"In my opinion, we shall stay here some weeks, if not some months," added Carnes.

"What for?"

"To pursue our studies, in the first place, and to learn our duty as seamen, in the second."

"I don't believe I shall stay here a great while longer," said Shuffles, with evident disgust. "There's no fun lying here."

"You can't help yourself," added Wilton.

"Perhaps I can't, but I can try," said Shuffles, as he glanced towards the shore.

"All hands ahoy!" shouted Peaks, the boatswain, as his shrill whistle rang through the ship.

The boys had been taught the meaning of this call, and they gathered in the waist, eager to know what was to be required of them.

Mr. Lowington stood on the raised hatch over the main scuttle, where all the students could see him. It was evident that he had some announcement to make, especially as the following day had been assigned for organizing the ship's company. The boys were silent, and their faces betrayed the curiosity which they felt.

"Young gentleman," the principal began, "this ship will go into commission to-morrow."

"Don't know what you mean, sir," said Paul Kendall, as Mr. Lowington paused to observe the effect of his announcement.

"I did not suppose that many of you would understand the expression. In the navy, a ship is said to go into commission when the captain takes his place on board, and the crew are organized for duty. When this takes place, the ensign is hoisted. To-morrow, at twelve o'clock, we shall display the colors at the peak. With us, going into commission will only mean the organization of our school. From that time, we shall observe the discipline of a man-of-war, so far as the ship and crew are concerned."

"Shall we go to sea then?" asked Wilton.

"I think not," replied Mr. Lowington, laughing. "We shall not leave the harbor till every officer and seaman knows his duty. You shall have enough to do to-morrow, young gentlemen."

"When shall we be able to go to sea?"

"I don't know. There are many ropes in the ship, and you have a great deal to learn before I shall be willing to trust you with the anchor at the cat-head."

"What is the cat-head, sir?" asked Kendall.

"Do you wish to go to sea without knowing what the cat-head is?" replied the principal. "You shall know in due time. To-morrow we shall select the officers, fifteen in number, who are to occupy the after cabin."

This announcement created a decided sensation among the eighty-seven boys gathered in the waist, for the subject had been full of interest to them. The after cabin had thus far been a sealed book; the door was locked, and they had not even seen the inside of the apartment. They were curious to visit this cabin, and to know who were to occupy it.

"After the organization of the school, it is my intention to give these offices to those who obtain the highest number of merit marks, which will be given for good conduct, good lessons, and progress in seamanship. The best boy, who is at the same time the best scholar and the best seaman, shall be captain. We have no marks now by which to make the selection, and I intend to have you elect him the first time, reserving to myself the right to veto your choice if it is obviously an improper one."

As Mr. Lowington uttered this last remark, he glanced, perhaps unconsciously, at Shuffles, who stood directly in front of him.

"Young gentlemen, the ballot will take place to-morrow morning, at nine o'clock. I have given you this notice, that you may be able to consider the matter, and, if you choose, to make nominations for the several offices," continued the principal.

"What are the offices, sir?"

"The first and most important one, of course, is the captain. The others are four lieutenants, four masters, two pursers, and four midshipmen."

"What are they to do?" asked Kendall.

"I will not explain their duties now; it would require too much time. I mentioned them in the order of their importance. Now, young gentlemen, you should select your candidates for these offices by merit, not by favor. I am aware that a few of you have been to sea, but probably none of you are competent to handle a ship; and your choice should be based mainly on good character and good conduct. I hope I shall be able to approve the choice you may make. You are dismissed now."

"Three cheers for the principal!" shouted one of the boys.

"Silence, young gentleman! Let me say now, that no expressions of approbation or disapprobation are to be allowed."

The boys separated into groups, and immediately gave their attention to the important subject suggested to them by Mr. Lowington. It must be acknowledged that violent symptoms of "log-rolling" began to be exhibited. There were fifty, if not eighty-seven young men who wished to be captain, and sit at the head of the table in the after cabin. Some of them went down into the steerage, and in five minutes there was a confused jabbering in every part of the ship.

"For whom shall you vote, Wilton?" asked Shuffles, in a group of half a dozen which had gathered around one of the mess tables.

"I don't know; whom do you go for?" replied Wilton.

"I rather think I shall go for Bob Shuffles. In my opinion, he is the best fellow on board," replied the owner of that name.

"That's modest," laughed Wilton.

"Do you know of any fellow that would make a better captain than I should?"

"You don't know the first thing about a ship."

"What odds does that make? I can learn as fast as anybody else."

"Do you expect every fellow to vote for himself?" asked Howe, another of the group.

"Of course I don't; I expect them to vote for me," answered Shuffles, with great good-nature.

"You are rather cheeky, Shuffles."

"What's the use of mincing the matter? Here we

are, half a dozen of the best fellows in the ship. We can't all be captain; but one of us can be just as well as not."

"That's so," added Howe, approvingly. "But who shall that one be?"

"I am the one, without a doubt," said Shuffles.

"I don't see it," interposed Monroe, shaking his head; and he was the young gentleman who had assisted the aspirant for the captaincy to rob Mr. Lowington's favorite peach tree.

"What have you got to say about it, Ike Monroe? Do you expect us to go for you?"

"I didn't say so."

"That's what you meant."

"I've just as much right to the place as you have, Bob Shuffles."

"Do you think you could make the fellows stand round as I can? But hold on; fellows, don't let us fight about it. We are just the best six fellows on board, and if we have a mind to do so, we can have this thing all our own way," continued Shuffles.

"I don't see how," said Philip Sanborn.

"Don't you know how the politicians manage these things?"

"I don't."

"I'll tell you, then."

"But the principal said we must go according to merit, and elect the fellows who were the best fitted for the offices," interposed Howe.

"Exactly so; that's just what we are going to do. I'm going to be captain; can you tell me of any better fellow for the place?" demanded Shuffles, who, putting aside the jesting manner in which he had commenced the discussion, now assumed an earnest and impudent tone.

"Didn't you hear what Lowington said when he wound up his speech?" asked Wilton.

"What?"

"About vetoing our choice if it was not a proper one."

"What of it?" asked Shuffles, innocently.

"Don't you think he would veto you?"

"Me! Not he! Lowington knows that I'm smart; I was too smart for him once, and he knows it. He won't veto me. We have been the best of friends lately."

"I don't believe he'll have a chance to veto you," said Wilton.

"What do you mean?"

"I don't believe you will be elected."

"I know I shall, if we manage it right. Let us look at it," continued Shuffles, as he took a pencil from his pocket. "Got a piece of paper?"

Monroe gave him a piece of paper, and the wire-puller began to make his calculations.

"Eighty-seven votes," said he, writing the number on the paper. "Necessary to a choice, forty-four. Here are six votes to start with."

"For whom?" asked Monroe.

"For me, for captain, first, and for each of the others for whatever place he wants; say for Wilton for first lieutenant; Howe for second, Sanborn for third, Monroe for fourth, and Adler for first master. What do you say to that, fellows?"

As with the political "slate," there was some difference of opinion in regard to the minor officers, even after Shuffles' claim to the captaincy had been conceded. But this disposition of the spoils was finally agreed to.

"Now we want thirty-eight more votes," Shuffles proceeded.

"Just so; and you might as well attempt to jump over the main royal yard as to get them," added Adler, who, having been assigned to the office lowest in rank, was least satisfied with the "slate."

"Hold on; we haven't done yet. There are nine more offices. Now we will pick out some good fellow, that will work for us, for each of these places; then we will promise him six votes if he will go our ticket, and do what he can for us."

"That will give us only fifteen votes," said Adler.

"I think that will be doing very well to start with. Then you five fellows can electioneer for me, and I'll do the same for you."

"I think we have made one mistake," added Sanborn. "Most of the fellows will go for Carnes for captain. He is an old salt, and has more influence than any other student in the ship. We ought to offer him some place."

"Make him purser, if you like," said Shuffles, contemptuously.

"That won't go down. Make him first lieutenant."

"And shove me out?" demanded Wilton, indignantly. "I don't see it!"

"Nor I," added Shuffles. "I won't vote for Carnes, any how. He's a snob and a flunky."

It was useless to resist the fiat of the chief wire-puller; the ticket remained as it had been originally prepared; and the young gentlemen proceeded to distribute the rest of the offices.

CHAPTER III.

THE ENSIGN AT THE PEAK.

THE students on board of the Young America were between the ages of fourteen and seventeen. By the regulations, no boy under fourteen or over seventeen could be admitted, and they averaged about fifteen. They had, therefore, reached the years of discretion. Among them were a great many who were disposed to be wild boys, and not a few who had found it difficult to remain in similar institutions on shore. They were not criminal or depraved, but simply wild; with a tendency to break through reasonable restraint; with a taste for mad pranks, and a contempt for authority.

Of this class, who were a trial and a torment to the teachers of the ordinary high schools and academies, the larger proportion would have scorned to steal, or commit any wanton outrage upon the persons or property of others. There were many high-minded, noble-hearted young men, who could not tamely submit to authority, and were prone to insubordination, and who only needed the right kind of discipline to make them earnest and faithful men and useful citizens. There were few, if any, dunces or blockheads among them, for a life on shipboard had no attractions for such boys. They were, almost without an exception, wide-awake, bold, daring fellows, who had a taste for stirring events; fellows who wanted to climb the Rocky Mountains, visit the North Pole, and explore the Mammoth Cave. They were full of fun and mischief, and it would have been easy at any time to get up a party among them to march the principal's cow into the parlor of the Academy; to climb to the belfry on a winter's night, and fill the inverted bell with water, where it would freeze solid before morning; or to convey the occupants of the hen-coop to the recitation room.

It was Mr. Lowington's task to repress the mischief in these boys, to keep them occupied with work and play, and to develop their moral and mental capacities. He had doubtless taken a heavy load upon himself, but he felt that he was to labor for his race and his country. At least one half of his students were too wild to attend the ordinary public or private schools, or to profit by them if admitted. With such material, his work could not be a sinecure. But he had a taste for it, and he gave his whole heart and soul to the performance of his duties.

When the students were gathered on board the Young America, they were mostly strangers to him, though he had communicated personally or by letter with the parents of all of them. He had read and listened to the stories of their pranks and peccadilloes, but when they came together, he hardly knew one from another, and was not prejudiced against any individual by the terrible accounts of him related by parents, guardians, or teachers. He purposed to give them the opportunity to select their own officers at first, in order to win a more cheerful obedience from them, and because the students knew each other better than he knew them.

After the announcement of the principal that the voting would commence on the following morning, nothing else was talked of on board. The qualifications of various members of the school were discussed by groups of excited voters; and we must do them the justice to say that most of them considered the matter unselfishly and with a single eye to the public good. Perhaps it is a little remarkable that not a single student, outside of the little group of wire-pullers that gathered in the steerage, thought of Shuffles for the position of captain; and the "log-rollers" were likely to have up-hill work in electing themselves to the six principal offices. But they went to work, and labored very diligently till bed-time in carrying their point.

While none thought of Shuffles in connection with the highest position, many mentioned the dignified young gentleman, who had made one voyage up the Mediterranean — Richard Carnes. He had been on board a fortnight, and had won and retained the respect of all his companions.

Before the little band of wire-pullers in the steerage had made up the "slate" to suit their minds, the crowd on deck had agreed upon Richard Carnes for captain, and were busy in discussing the qualifications of others for the subordinate offices, when the log-rollers separated, and went to work upon their mission.

"How are you going to vote for captain, Kendall?" said Wilton, stepping up to the young gentleman who had proposed so many questions to the principal, and who had been so honest in confessing his ignorance of nautical matters.

"For Carnes, of course."

"Humph! I wouldn't vote for him," sneered the wire-puller.

"Why not?"

"He's too stiff; he'll put on airs, and be a tyrant over us."

"No, he won't."

"You see if he don't. I say, Kendall, are you up for any office?" continued Wilton, with a certain appearance of slyness which the straightforward young gentleman did not exactly like.

"Am I?"

"Yes, you. Wouldn't you like a room in the after cabin?"

"Perhaps I would," answered Kendall, thoughtfully; and the place was certainly very inviting to him.

"They say the after cabin is a perfect little palace."

"I dare say it is."

"You can just as well go in there, if you like."

"I don't see how that can be. I don't think I'm fit to be an officer. I am from Cincinnati, and I never saw a ship till I came east three weeks ago."

"None of the fellows know anything about a ship. All of us will have to learn."

"Carnes knows all about one."

"No, he don't. He made one voyage, and knows

just enough to talk salt. He's a good fellow enough, but he isn't fit for captain. If you want to be an officer, Kendall, and have a berth in the after cabin, you can, just as well as not."

"Well, I would like such a place; I can't deny it; but I don't think the fellows will go for me."

"They will, if you say so."

"If I say so! I'm not going to ask them to vote for me," replied Kendall, warmly; for he was no politician, and had a vein of modesty in his composition.

"You needn't say a word to any one. If you will go for our ticket, it will be all right. Half a dozen of us have talked this matter over, and we have concluded that you would be the best fellow for second master."

"Have you?" asked Kendall, who could not help being gratified to learn that even half a dozen of his companions had thought him worthy to be an officer of so high a rank as second master. "I'm very much obliged to you."

"All you have to do, is to go for our ticket."

"What do you mean by your ticket?" demanded Kendall, who was rather confused by the technical terms of the wire-puller.

Wilton explained that his little party had selected a candidate for each of the offices; and if all the fellows agreed to it, there would be fifteen votes for their ticket, to begin with.

"Well, what is your ticket?" demanded Kendall, impatiently. "If they are all good fellows, I will go for them. Of course you mean to vote for Carnes for captain."

"Not exactly," replied Wilton, with evident disgust. "We shall put up a better fellow than he is for captain."

"Why, all the boys are going for him," added Kendall, astonished to find there were any who did not believe in Carnes.

"No, they are not."

"I thought they were."

"He will not be elected, and you need not throw your vote away upon him, because, if you don't want a place in the after cabin, there are plenty of fellows who do," added the wire-puller, with apparent indifference.

"But I do want it."

"Then all you have to do, is to go for our ticket."

"I think Carnes will make the best captain."

"Very well; if you think so, you have a right to your own opinion. I haven't any mortgage on it."

"Whom are you going to run for captain?"

"It's no use to talk any more about it, if you are going for Carnes," replied Wilton, as he turned to move away.

The wire-puller was playing a part. Paul Kendall was a noble little fellow, and was already a great favorite on board, not only with the boys, but with the principal and the professors. Wilton knew that he had a great deal of influence, and it was important to secure him for their ticket. If he could tell others that Kendall was going for their men, it would induce many to join their party. The "favorite," though he was an honest, noble-hearted fellow, was still human, and a berth in the after cabin was a strong temptation to him.

"I'm not going to say I'll vote for a fellow till I know who he is," added Kendall. "If he's the right person, perhaps I'll go for him, though I wanted to see Carnes captain."

"Carnes can't be elected, I tell you. We are going against him."

"Whom are you going for, then?"

"For Bob Shuffles," replied Wilton, desperately, for he did not wish to mention his candidate till he had won the assent of his companion.

"Shuffles!" exclaimed Kendall, with something like horror mingled with his astonishment; "I shall not go for him, anyhow."

"Why not?"

"I don't think he is the right person for the place."

"I do; he's a first-rate fellow — none of your milk and water chaps, that swallow camels and strain at gnats."

Kendall had some decided objections to Shuffles, and he positively refused to vote for him, even to obtain the coveted position in the after cabin. Wilton argued the matter with much skill and cunning; but his logic and his eloquence were both wasted.

"Well, if you won't go for Shuffles, you must be content with your place in the steerage," added Wilton.

"I won't go for him, any how," said Kendall, firmly.

"You are making a mistake."

"I don't think so. I'm bound to vote for the best fellow, and I'm sure Shuffles isn't the right one."

"See here, Kendall; don't say a word to the others

that I spoke to you of this little matter. I thought you would go with us, or I shouldn't have said anything to you."

"Not say anything? Why not?"

"Because it will be better to keep still."

"I shall not do anything of the kind. You have got up a plan to defeat Carnes, by giving the offices to fellows who will vote against him. You wish me to keep still, while you carry out your plan. I can see through a cord of wood, when there's a hole big enough."

"I mentioned this thing to you in confidence."

"You didn't say a word about confidence; and I didn't promise to keep still. I won't keep still. I think it is a mean trick to buy up the votes of the fellows, and I'll blow the whole thing higher than a kite."

"You'll catch it if you do," said Wilton, in a threatening tone.

"Catch what?" demanded Kendall, with a very pretty exhibition of dignity.

"Bob Shuffles will give it to you."

"Give what to me?"

"Give you the biggest licking you ever had in your life," answered Wilton, angrily. "You are so stupid, you can't understand anything."

"I think I can understand the licking, when it comes. That's a game that two can play at."

"What do you mean. you little bantam? Do you think you can whip Bob Shuffles?"

"I had no idea of whipping him; and I have no idea of his whipping me, either."

Kendall was spunky; Wilton could make nothing of him by threats or persuasion; and he turned away from him to seek a more promising field of labor. Kendall took off his cap, scratched his head as he reflected upon the event which had just transpired, and made up his mind that it was an insult to an independent elector to attempt to buy his vote with the paltry consideration of an office. He was sorry that he had been even tempted by the proposition of the wire-pullers, and thankful that his sense of honor and decency had prompted him to decline it when asked to vote for an improper person. True to his promise, he made all haste to expose the conspiracy, as he regarded it, against Carnes.

When the students turned in that night, the wire-pullers had found a sufficient number of candidates for all the offices on the terms set forth in the compact, each of whom had promised to use his influence for the entire ticket. Shuffles had made a very pretty calculation, to the effect that each of the fifteen candidates could influence at least two votes besides his own for the ticket, which would inevitably elect it. But during all this time Paul Kendall had been laboring like a Trojan for Carnes, and had induced his friends to do the same.

At nine o'clock in the morning, the polls were opened for the election of officers. A box was placed on the fife-rail, at the mainmast, in which the ballots were deposited, under the inspection of Professor Mapps.

"Have all the students voted?" called the professor,

when the voting was suspended. "If so, I declare the poll closed."

It was a moment of intense excitement on the spar deck of the Young America when Mr. Lowington stood up on the hatch to announce the vote. There was a pleasant smile upon his face, which indicated that it would not be his painful duty to veto the choice of the independent electors.

"Young gentlemen, your balloting appears to have been conducted with entire fairness," said he, "and I will proceed to declare the result. Whole number of votes, eighty-seven; necessary to a choice, forty-four. Paul Kendall has five; Charles Gordon has seven; Robert Shuffles has twenty-two; Richard Carnes has fifty-three, and is elected captain of the Young America for the succeeding three months."

The party who had worked and voted for Carnes applauded the result most lustily, and gave three cheers for the new captain, which, on this exciting occasion, were not objected to by the principal. Shuffles's jaw dropped down, and his lip quivered with angry emotion.

"That little whipper-snapper of a Kendall did that," said Wilton, in a low tone, to the disappointed candidate. "I was afraid of this when I saw him blowing about the deck."

"I'll settle it with him when I get a good chance," growled Shuffles, as he went to the rail and looked over into the water, in order to conceal his disappointment and chagrin.

"Young gentlemen will bring in their votes for first

lieutenant," said Professor Mapps, as he placed the box on the fife-rail again.

The boys marched around the mainmast, and deposited their ballots for the second officer, as they had done before. The friends of Shuffles rallied again, hoping that something might yet come of the compact they had made with him, and gave him their votes for first lieutenant, though, in his chagrin, he declared that he would not accept the position. Fortunately for him, he was not called upon to do so; for Charles Gordon was elected by a very large majority. As the election proceeded, it became evident that there was no office for Shuffles. Paul Kendall was elected fourth lieutenant, and the announcement of the vote was greeted by even more hearty applause than had been bestowed upon the captain.

At the conclusion of the balloting, Shuffles found that not a single one of the wire-pullers, or of the candidates nominated by them, had been elected. The attempt to bribe the independent voters, by giving them office, had been a signal failure; and it is to be hoped that Young America, when fully developed, will stick to his principles.

"Captain Richard Carnes," said Mr. Lowington, as he stepped upon the hatch, after the voting had been concluded.

The young gentleman thus addressed came forward, blushing beneath the honors which had been bestowed upon him. The principal took his hand.

"Captain Carnes, I congratulate you upon your election to the highest office in the gift of your companions; and I congratulate your fellow-students also upon having so good a young man to handle the ship. You have been modest, and they have been wise. I congratulate you both. Young gentlemen, I am satisfied that your captain will be just, courteous, and gentlemanly, in his relations with you; and I hope you will yield a willing and cheerful obedience to his orders, and to those of all your superiors. Let me say that this business is not a farce; it is not mere boys' play; for as soon as the officers and crew are fully trained and instructed, all ship duty will be carried on without assistance from me or others. When necessary, I shall advise the captain what to do, but I shall not do it myself; neither shall I needlessly interfere with the discipline of the ship.

"This is the last time an election of officers will be permitted, for it is liable to many objections, not the least of which are the bribery and corruption by which some have attempted to obtain office."

Mr. Lowington looked at Shuffles, as though he knew all about the method to which he had resorted to secure an election; but we are quite sure that Paul Kendall had never lisped a word of it to him, or to any of the instructors.

"On the first day of July, young gentlemen, all the offices will be vacant; and they will be awarded strictly in accordance with the marks you may obtain. There will be no veto upon the result of the merit roll. These places, therefore, are open to all. We have no aristocracy on board. Every student in the ship is a candidate for the captaincy. Now, if the officers elect will follow me to the after cabin, I will install them into their new positions; after which I will proceed to organize the crew."

The door of the after cabin, which had hitherto been a mystery to all the boys, was unlocked by the head steward, and Mr. Lowington, followed by the officers, entered. The students on deck were ordered forward, and were not even permitted to look down the companion-way, for the principal intended to keep the after cabin exclusively for the officers; and no one not entitled to admission was to be allowed to cross its threshold. He believed that this mystery, and this rigid adherence to the division line between officers and crew, would promote the discipline of the ship, and enhance the value of the offices — the prizes for good conduct, and general fidelity to duty.

"Captain Carnes, this is your state room," continued Mr. Lowington, opening the door of the room farthest forward on the starboard side. "As the commander of the ship you are entitled to an apartment by yourself."

"Thank you, sir," replied the captain, as he stepped into the room.

"You will find on the hooks your uniform as captain. There are three suits, from which you will select one that fits you."

Captain Carnes entered and closed the door. If he did not feel like a king, he ought to have felt so.

Mr. Lowington then gave the next room to the first and second lieutenants, who were to occupy it together; and they were also directed to clothe themselves in the uniforms deposited there for their use. The third state room was given to the third and fourth lieutenants, and the fourth to the first and second midshipmen. The forward room of the port side was assigned to the first and second masters; the next to the third and fourth; the third to the two pursers, and the last to the third and fourth midshipmen.

In a short time the officers came out of their rooms clothed in their uniforms, which consisted of a blue frock coat, with brass buttons, and blue pants. The cap was of the same material, with a gold band around it. Thus far the uniforms were all alike; but there were distinguishing insignia to indicate the rank of each. All the officers had shoulder-straps, by which their positions were designated. The captain had two anchors; the first lieutenant had one anchor, with four stars, one above, one below, and one on each side; the second lieutenant had the anchor with three stars — none above; the third lieutenant, one star on each side of the anchor; and the fourth lieutenant one star below the anchor. The captain also wore five narrow gold bands on each of his coat sleeves; the first lieutenant four, and so on, the fourth wearing but one band.

The shoulder-straps of the masters contained no anchor; only the stars, one for each grade, the first master having four stars; the fourth only one. The rank of the pursers was indicated by the outline of a parallelogram for the second, and two of the same figure, one within the other, for the first. The straps of the midshipmen contained gilt numbers, from one to four, designating their grade.

The officers presented a very elegant and dashing appearance in their new uniform; and if some of them did not feel a little vain, it was because they were less human than boys usually are.

"What are we to do, sir?" asked Kendall of the principal, after the uniforms had been duly criticised.

"Nothing, at present."

"Nothing! Why, I feel like a counterfeit gold dollar, in this rig, when I know no more about a ship than I do about the inside of the moon."

"You will learn in due time. You will go on deck now, young gentlemen; and remember that, as officers, you are not to be familiar with the crew while you are on duty."

"Can't we speak to them?" asked Kendall, who was not disposed to be so exclusive as naval discipline required him to be.

"Not while you are on duty, except when it is necessary to do so. We will now assign the berths in the steerage to the crew."

As the boys came on board, they had taken the berths as they pleased. Shuffles had selected a room, and invited his "cronies" to occupy the bunks it contained with him. The berths were now to be distributed by lot. Professor Mapps had provided seventy-two slips of paper, on each of which he had written a number. The boys were mustered into line, and drew out these numbers from the package. As each student drew his slip, the purser wrote down his name in a book, with the number he had drawn.

In the steerage, each berth had its own number, which was also applied to a locker, and a seat at one of the mess tables. When the drawing was completed, each student had his berth, his clothes locker, and his seat at meals. Many of them were extremely dissatisfied when they found that they had been separated from their " cronies;" but the principal was firm, and would not allow a single change to be made.

By this time it was twelve o'clock, and Boatswain Peaks piped all hands to muster. The ensign was hoisted, and saluted with three cheers, in which all hands, young and old, joined. When this ceremony was finished, the crew were piped to dinner, and the officers went to their cabin, where the steward had set the table for them for the first time. They dined like lords, though upon the same fare as their companions in the steerage.

CHAPTER IV.

OFFICERS AND SEAMEN.

AFTER dinner the organization of the crew was continued. All hands were "piped to muster," and by this time most of those who had been disaffected at the drawing of berths had recovered their natural equanimity, and all were intensely interested in the arrangement of the details. None of the boys knew what was coming, and their curiosity kept them in a continuous state of excitement.

"All who have drawn even numbers will take the starboard side of the ship," said Mr. Lowington from his perch on the hatch. "All who have drawn odd numbers will take the port side."

"This is the starboard side, my lads," added Mr. Fluxion, the instructor in mathematics — who, like the principal, had been a naval officer, — as he pointed to the right, looking forward.

Some had already forgotten their numbers, and there was considerable confusion before the order could be obeyed.

"Young gentlemen, the books will be opened to-day; and a student who forgets his number again will lose a mark," said Mr. Lowington. "Are they all in their places, Mr. Fluxion?"

"They are, sir," replied the instructor, who had just counted them.

"Young gentlemen, you are thus divided into two equal parts — the starboard and the port watches. Now form a straight line, toe the crack, and call your numbers in order, beginning with the starboard watch."

The boys eagerly followed this direction, though some assistance was required from the instructors in repressing their superfluous enthusiasm.

"Very well," continued Mr. Lowington, when the students were formed in two lines. "Every boy in the starboard watch whose number is divisible by four, step forward one pace. Number three in the port watch, do the same. Mr. Mapps, oblige me by seeing that every alternate boy in the line steps forward."

"The line is formed, sir," replied the instructor, when he had carried out the direction of the principal.

"Each watch is now divided into two parts — the first and second parts, as they will be called. Now, young gentlemen, the clothing will be distributed, and each student will put on his uniform at once."

The four lines were then marched down into the steerage, each under the charge of an instructor, to a particular locality, where the head steward and his assistants had deposited the clothing for each watch and quarter watch. The uniform consisted of blue seaman's pants and a heavy flannel shirt or frock, such as is worn in the United States navy. To each student, the following articles were served out: —

    1 pea-jacket.
    1 blue cloth jacket.

1 pair blue cloth pants.
1 pair blue satinet pants.
1 blue cap.
1 straw hat, of coarse, sewed straw.
1 Panama hat, bound.
2 knit woollen shirts.
2 pair knit woollen drawers.
2 white frocks.
2 pair white duck pants.
4 pair socks.
2 pair shoes.
2 black silk neck-handkerchiefs.

These articles were given to the boys, and they were required to put on the every-day uniform; after which they were directed to arrange the rest of the clothing in the lockers belonging to them. The contractor who had furnished the goods was present with four tailors, to attend to the fitting of the clothes, which were all numbered according to the size. In a short time the students began to come out of their rooms, clothed in their new rig. They looked intensely "salt," and there was no end to the jokes and smart things that were said on this interesting occasion. Even Shuffles hardly knew himself in his new dress.

The frock had a broad rolling collar, in each corner of which was worked an anchor in white. The black silk neck-handkerchief was worn under the collar, and not many of the boys had acquired the art of tying the regular sailor's knot. Boatswain Peaks not only stood up as a model for them, but he adjusted the "neck gear" for many of them. Bitts, the carpenter, and

Leech, the sailmaker, who were also old sailors, cheerfully rendered a valet's assistance to such as needed help.

Agreeably to the directions of Mr. Lowington, the shore suits of the students were done up in bundles, each marked with the owner's name, and the head steward took them to Mr. Lowington's house for storage.

Rigged out in their "sea togs," the students began to feel salt, as well as to look salt. Some of them tried to imitate the rolling gait of the boatswain when they walked, and some of them began to exhibit an alarming tendency to indulge in sea slang.

"There, my hearty, you look like a sailor now," said Peaks, when he had rolled over the collar and tied the square knot in the handkerchief of Wilton.

"Shiver my timbers, but I feel like one," laughed the embryo seaman.

"What's that, young gentleman?" demanded Mr. Lowington, who happened to be within hearing; "what did you say?"

"I said I felt like a sailor, sir."

"What was the expression you used?"

"I only said shiver my timbers, sir."

"You stole that expression from a yellow-covered novel. Did you ever hear Mr. Peaks, who has been a sailor all his lifetime, use such language?"

"I'll be bound he never did," added Peaks.

"No, sir, I don't know that I ever did."

"Some sailors do use such expressions; but it is gross affectation for these young gentlemen, who never saw a blue wave, to indulge in them. If you please,

Wilton, you will not use such language. It is simply ridiculous. Mr. Peaks, you will pipe all hands to muster again."

The shrill whistle of the boatswain sounded through the ship, and the boys tumbled up the ladders, eager to learn what was to be done next. As they formed in lines, they presented a novel and picturesque appearance in their jaunty uniform. Most of them had already learned to wear their caps canted over on one side, and not a few of them, perhaps as much from necessity as because it was a sailor's habit, hitched up their trousers, and thrust their hands deep down into the side pockets.

The students were again formed in watches and quarter watches, each of which classes and sub-classes was indicated on the uniforms. All the starboard watch wore a small silver star on the right arm, above the elbow, and the port watch the same emblem on the left arm. The first part of each watch had a figure 1, under the star, and the second part a figure 2 in the same position.

The rest of the day was spent in the organization for ship's duty, which was far from completed when the sun went down. The next day every boy was kept so busy that he had no time to grumble. The instructors attended to the lessons in the steerage with one watch, while the other was on deck acquiring seamanship. In the course of the month, as the boys learned their duties, and the capabilities of each were ascertained, they were assigned to their stations in the various evolutions required in working the vessel.

Boatswain Peaks had taught the boys, a few at a

time, how to set a sail, reef and furl it. They had been gradually accustomed to going aloft, until the giddy height of the main royal did not appall them, and they could lay out on the yards without thinking of the empty space beneath them. By the first of June, all the petty officers had been appointed, and every student had his station billet. When the order was given to unmoor ship, to make sail, or to furl the sails, every one knew where to go and what to do. The station billets were cards on which the various evolutions of the ship had been printed in a column on the left, while the particular duty of the owner of the card was written against it. The card was kept by the student, and he was expected to learn its contents, so that he could take his place without stopping to consult it, when an order was given. Here is a specimen of the cards:—

PORT WATCH, NO 21. Second Part.	WILLIAM FOSTER, Captain of the Forecastle.
Reefing.	Head Bowlines.
Tacking or Wearing.	Forecastle. Let go head bowlines. Let go and shorten in foretack and belay it.
Getting under Way.	Head Bowlines. Downhauls and head-sheets.
Anchoring.	Head Bowlines, Sheets and Tacks. Downhauls.
Loosing Sails.	Foretopmast Staysail.
Furling.	Head Bowlines and Downhauls, Staysail.
Mooring and Unmooring.	Forecastle.
Boat.	Professor's Barge, stroke-oar.
Mess.	No. 11.

The crew had been in training a month before an attempt was made to set more than one sail at once; but by this time the officers knew the orders, having practised every day since the organization. The petty officers had been appointed, and had, to some extent, become familiar with their duties.

The boys still continued to wonder when the Young America would go on a cruise, for they were very anxious to see the blue water, and to roll on the great waves of the Atlantic; but they were so constantly occupied with ship's duty and their studies, that the time did not hang heavily on their hands. Two months of constant practice had made tolerable seamen of them, and the discipline of the ship went on regularly. The young officers, as Mr. Lowington had promised, began to conduct the evolutions and give the orders.

On the 1st day of June, after breakfast, the students were thrown into a fever of excitement by an unusual order, and they ventured to hope that the ship was to leave her moorings.

"Mr. Gordon, you will pipe all hands to muster," said Captain Carnes to the first lieutenant.

"Pass the word for the boatswain," added Gordon to one of the midshipmen, who stood near him.

This call was answered, not by Peaks, who no longer performed the duties of boatswain, but by one of the students, who had been appointed to this position.

"Pipe all hands to muster, boatswain," said the first lieutenant, as the petty officer touched his cap to him.

6*

"All hands on deck, ahoy!" shouted the boatswain, as he piped the call.

This was an unusual order for that time of day, the forenoon being appropriated to study for each watch in turn; and those who were below hastened on deck to ascertain what was to be done.

"All hands, stations for loosing sail!" piped the boatswain, when ordered to do so by Gordon.

The first lieutenant was in charge of the ship, under the direction of the captain. The second lieutenant stood on the forecastle, where he was attended by the boatswain. The third lieutenant was in the waist, and the fourth on the quarter deck, near the mizzen-mast. These were the stations of the officers whenever all hands were called. Mr. Lowington and the instructors stood near the companion-way, watching with interest this first attempt to make sail all over the ship.

"Lay aloft, sail-loosers!" shouted Gordon; and his order was repeated by the officers at their several stations.

The little tars who belonged on the topsail and top-gallant yards sprang up the rigging like so many cats, excited beyond measure by the scene of activity around them.

"Lower yardmen in the chains!" continued Gordon; and his order was passed along by the officers. "Aloft, lower yardmen!"

In a moment the crew were in their places; the studding-sail booms were triced up with the usual system, so that the sails could be reached.

"Lay out!" continued the first lieutenant; and the

boys walked out on the foot-ropes to their stations on the yards. "Loose!"

The ropes by which the sails were secured to the yards were removed at this order, and the topmen held the sails in their places.

"All ready on the forecastle, sir," reported Foster, who was captain of that part of the ship.

"All ready in the foretop."

"All ready in the maintop."

"All ready in the mizzentop," reported the several captains of the tops, in their proper order.

These reports were passed to the first lieutenant in charge of the deck, by his subordinates.

"Let fall!" shouted Gordon, highly excited; and the sails dropped from the yard. "Overhaul your rigging aloft! Man sheets and halyards! Sheets home, and hoist away!"

These orders were passed from mouth to mouth among the officers, and return reports made, according to the strict discipline of the navy. They were promptly executed by the crew, though of course not without some blunders; and the Young America was covered with her cloud of canvas. Mr. Lowington commended the officers and crew for the promptness and skill they had displayed in their first concerted attempt at making sail. He then directed Captain Carnes to furl. Both evolutions were then repeated, until a proficiency satisfactory for one day was attained.

"Not going to sea, after all," said Shuffles, when the crew were dismissed from muster.

"No," replied Wilton. "I'm tired of lying here, and if we don't go to sea soon, I shall take myself off."

" I'm with you."

" I thought we were going to have some fun on board, but we don't do anything but study and shake out topsails."

" Do you know how you stand on marks, Wilton?" asked Shuffles.

" No; not very high, though."

" Don't you think you shall get into the cabin next term?"

" I know I shall not. I haven't tried for anything."

" On the first of next month, you know, new officers will be appointed, and I suppose the crew will be messed over again."

" I don't care. I'm getting tired of this thing. I had a better time at the Academy before we came on board."

" There isn't much chance for any sport. Hardly a fellow has been allowed to go on shore since we joined the ship."

" We'll get up a mutiny, if things don't improve."

" I was thinking of that very thing myself," said Shuffles, in a low tone.

" A mutiny!" exclaimed Wilton, who had used the word in jest.

" Just for fun, you know," laughed Shuffles.

" You don't mean any such thing."

" Not yet, of course."

" Do you at any time?"

" We want something more exciting than this kind of a life. Here we are, kept down and treated like common sailors. We have to touch our caps and make our manners to Dick Carnes and the rest of the flunkies in the after cabin. My father pays as much for me as Dick Carnes' father does for him, and I don't think it is fair that he should live in the cabin and I in the steerage."

"If you get marks enough, you can have a berth in the cabin," replied Wilton.

"Marks! Confound the marks! I'm not a baby. Do you think a fellow seventeen years old is going to be put up or put down by marks?" said Shuffles.

"I thought you had been working for a place in the cabin."

"So I have, but I don't expect to get it. I never studied so hard in my life, and I believe I haven't had a bad mark since I came on board. Lowington thinks I have reformed," laughed Shuffles. "And so I have."

"What do you want to get up a mutiny for, then?"

"I shall not, if I get a decent position; if I don't, I'm going in for some fun."

"But do you really think of getting up a mutiny?" asked Wilton, curiously.

"I was thinking the other day what a fine thing it would be if our fellows had the ship all to themselves."

"What could we do with her?"

"Go on a cruise in her."

"We couldn't handle her; there is hardly a fellow on board that knows anything about navigation."

"Of course, I don't mean to do anything yet a while; not this year, perhaps. One of these days, if we stay on board, we shall know all about a ship. Fifteen or twenty of the fellows are studying navigation. We are going to Europe some time or other. When we do, we can take the ship, and go it on our own hook."

"I don't believe you mean anything of the kind, Bob Shuffles."

"I've been thinking about it, anyhow. We can lock Lowington and the rest of the old folks into their cabin while they are at dinner; and there are enough of us to handle Peaks and Bitts."

"I think you are crazy, Shuffles."

"We should have a high old time if we could get possession of the ship. We wont say a word about it yet."

"I think you had better not."

"We might go round Cape Horn into the Pacific, and have a splendid time among the beautiful islands of the South Sea."

"Of course all the fellows wouldn't join you."

"We could put those ashore somewhere who did not agree with us."

"You know the penalty of mutiny on the high seas."

"Bah!" said Shuffles, contemptuously. "It would be nothing but a lark. No one would think of hanging us, or even sending us to prison for it. My father is rich enough to get me out of any scrape."

"So is mine; but I don't think it would be quite safe to go into a mutiny."

"Not yet, my dear fellow. You can think it over."

"But I'm tired of this kind of a life. I liked it first rate in the beginning. Do you think Lowington really intends to go to sea with the ship?"

"I know he does."

"If he don't go pretty soon, I shall run away, and go to sea in earnest."

"Don't say a word about the mutiny at present, Wilton. By and by, if things go right, or if they don't go right, we may want to take some stock in such an enterprise."

"I don't see it yet, but of course I shall keep still."

It is doubtful whether even so daring a young man as Shuffles, who had the temerity to do almost anything, seriously contemplated getting up a mutiny. Very likely his untamed and vicious imagination had revelled in such an enterprise; had pictured the delights of the rover's life at sea; but a boy of ordinary common sense could hardly think of engaging in such a mad scheme.

The last week of June, with which month ended the first school term on board of the Young America, was devoted to examinations and reviews in all the studies for which extra marks were given. On the last day the instructors made up the merit lists, and on the morning of the 1st of July all hands were mustered, and the result declared. Most of the officers, all of whom had studied with unremitting diligence, in order to retain their positions, were reinstated in their offices. The third lieutenant, however, fell out, having failed in his reviews, and to the astonishment of all, Robert Shuffles was found to be entitled to the place. The first and second lieutenants exchanged ranks, and Paul Kendall fell to the position of second master. Three of the tenants of the after cabin were compelled to move into the steerage, and three of the crew were transferred to the officers' quarters.

Many were disappointed, and perhaps some were disheartened, for the competition had been a severe struggle; and as much depended upon natural ability as upon energy and perseverance. But the Young America was a world by herself. She had all the elements of society within her wooden walls, and success and failure there followed the same rules as in the great world of which she was an epitome.

After the officers had been duly installed in their positions, the petty offices were given to those having the highest number of marks among the crew. It was certainly democratic for the late third lieutenant to become captain of the foretop, and for a second master to become coxswain of the professors' barge; but these young gentlemen, though disappointed, submitted with a good grace to their misfortune.

The student having the highest number of marks among the crew was allowed to have the first choice of berths in the steerage; the one having the next highest number had the second choice, and so on, until all the numbers had been appropriated. At the conclusion of the reorganization, Mr. Lowington made a speech, "comforting the mourners," and reminding all the students that, on the 1st of October, there would be another distribution of the places of honor. He hoped those who had failed to attain what they aspired to reach would not be discouraged, for, after all, they had been gaining knowledge, and thus the real end of the school had been reached.

"How about the mutiny?" said Wilton to the new third lieutenant, when both were off duty in the evening.

"It won't pay just now," replied Shuffles, with great good humor.

"I suppose not," sneered Wilton, who had not even won a petty office. "What would Lowington say if he knew the third lieutenant talked of getting up a mutiny on board?"

"What would he say?" repeated Shuffles, who was as much surprised at the high rank he had gained as his companion had been.

"Yes; what would he say if I should tell him of it?"

"He would say you were a mean pup for telling tales out of school; at least, he ought to say so, and I think he would. Lowington is a pretty good fellow, after all."

"No doubt he is, now you are third lieutenant."

"You needn't snuff at it, Wilton. If you want a place, why don't you sail in, and get one. Just look out for your marks; that's all you have to do."

"Marks! I thought a fellow seventeen years old was not to be put up or put down by marks," said Wilton, bitterly.

"That depends somewhat upon whether you get in or out," laughed Shuffles.

"I suppose you and Paul Kendall will be fast friends now," added the discontented student.

"Kendall behaves very well, and has treated me first rate since I went into the cabin."

"I suppose if I want to run away, you will stop me now."

"If you are going to do that, you musn't tell me of it, now I'm an officer," replied Shuffles, as he turned on his heel, and walked aft.

Wilton was disgusted, and felt that he had lost his best friend, now that Shuffles had worked his way into the cabin.

CHAPTER V.

OUR FELLOWS.

"I WOULD like leave of absence for to-morrow, Mr. Pelham," said Wilton, as he touched his cap to the first lieutenant of the Young America, on the day before the Fourth of July.

"I am sorry to inform you, Wilton, that no leave of absence will be granted to-morrow," replied Pelham, in accordance with the instructions given him by the captain, who, in turn, had received his orders from the principal.

"No leave!" exclaimed Wilton, his jaw dropping down.

"Such are the orders."

"I have always been in the habit of celebrating the Fourth of July," replied Wilton. "Are we to stay on board the ship, and mope all day?"

"I presume the day will be celebrated on board in a proper manner," added the first lieutenant.

"On board! What can a fellow do here? We might as well go to bed, and sleep off the day."

"No words are necessary, Wilton," replied Pelham, as he turned and walked away.

"That's a good one!" added Wilton, to the group of boys who had come with him to the mainmast, to request the same favor, if the spokesman was permitted to go on shore and celebrate the day.

"Not to celebrate!" exclaimed Monroe, with something like horror in his tones and looks.

"Work on the Fourth of July!" chimed in Adler.

"I won't stand it, for one!" said Wilton.

"Nor I, for another," added Monroe.

So said half a dozen others.

"Well, what are you going to do about it?" demanded Adler. "Here we are, and we can't get ashore."

"Perhaps we can," said Wilton, as he led the way to a retired part of the deck, where they could talk without being overheard. "Did any one ever hear of such a thing as keeping the fellows on board on the Fourth of July? Why, every little Greek in the city yonder has his liberty on that day; and we are to be cooped up here like a parcel of sick chickens! I suppose we shall have to recite history and French, and shake out topsails, as usual."

"It's outrageous. I don't believe the fellows will stand it," added Adler, who did not know how bad the case was, until it had been rehearsed by Wilton, who, in the absence of Shuffles, had become the leader of a certain clique on board, given to taking opposite views.

"But I don't see what we can do," said Monroe.

"We will do something. I won't stand it. If I stay on board the ship to-morrow, it will be as a prisoner," answered Wilton.

"It's a hard case; but what can we do about it?" asked Sanborn.

"Suppose we go to Lowington, and state the case to him," suggested Adler.

"What's the use of that? Of course the first lieutenant spoke by the card. He had his orders to say what he did, and I'm sure they came from Lowington."

"There can be no doubt of that; but it would be better to have it from him."

"I'm willing to ask Lowington for the day, if the fellows want me to do so; but it won't do any more good than it would to bark at the mainmast," continued Wilton. "I have an idea in my head, if the fellows will stand by me," he added, in a lower tone, as he looked over the rail at the swinging boom, to which the boats in constant use were made fast.

"What is it?" asked Monroe, eagerly.

"Keep shady, for a while. How many fellows can we muster?"

"I don't know."

"Well, don't stir the matter yet. Here comes Lowington, and we will talk to him first. Come, fellows, let's make a dive at him."

Wilton, attended by his companions, walked up to the principal, as he was going forward. Touching his cap respectfully, as the discipline of the ship required, he opened the case.

"Mr. Lowington, some of the students would like to go on shore to-morrow, to celebrate the Fourth. Can't we have liberty?"

"You know the rule; you should apply to the first lieutenant for leave of absence," replied Mr. Lowington.

"We have, sir, and been refused."

"Then there is nothing more to be said. The first lieutenant speaks with authority."

"I beg your pardon, sir, but are we to stay on board all day to-morrow?"

"That is certainly the arrangement, Wilton."

"Some of us would like to celebrate the day, sir, and we think it is rather hard to be obliged to do duty on the Fourth of July."

"I intend to have the day celebrated in a proper manner. I have made preparations for a gala day on board."

"If you please, sir, we would rather go on shore."

"I am very sorry, for your sake, that I shall be unable to reverse the answer of the first lieutenant. If I permit one or a dozen to go ashore, I cannot refuse any, and all must go. I think the boys will be satisfied with the arrangements I have made for the day."

"I never was kept in school on the Fourth of July before, sir," growled Wilton.

"Then this will be a new event in your experience," answered Mr. Lowington, coldly, as he turned from the petitioners, and went forward.

There were a great many wild boys on board of the Young America, and it was morally impossible for the whole crew to attend the celebration in the city, without more or less of them getting into a scrape. They had been kept on board for two months, and not allowed to go on shore, except under the supervision of one of the instructors; and to let any considerable number of them loose on such a day as the Fourth of July, would only be courting trouble, for they would be all the more disorderly after the long period of restraint.

Mr. Lowington did not willingly deprive the boys of any innocent gratification. He had faithfully considered the matter of celebrating the day, and taken the advice of the instructors on the subject. It had been proposed to procure a band of music, and visit the city in a body, under the usual discipline; but there were many difficulties attending such a plan. The boys were all the sons of rich men, and most of them were abundantly supplied with pocket money. As it would be impossible to prevent the escape of some of them from the procession, in the crowded streets, it was feared that their money would prove to be " the root of all evil." The project had finally been abandoned; and, as a substitute, a programme for a celebration on board had been arranged, for there the students would be entirely under the control of the instructors, who would check all excesses. It was anticipated that a few discontented spirits would grumble, but no rebellion was expected.

Wilton and his companions were dissatisfied, and disposed to be rash. They felt that they had been harshly and cruelly denied a reasonable privilege. The subject of celebrating the Fourth had been under consideration for a long time among the boys, and it had been generally believed that all hands would be permitted to go on shore, with perfect liberty, on that day; and many of them had already arranged their plans for the occasion.

"Well, what do you think now?" said Wilton, as Mr. Lowington walked forward.

"I think it's too bad," replied Adler. "It is meaner than dirt to make us stay on board on the Fourth of July."

"But I don't see how we are going to help ourselves," added Monroe, looking at Wilton for a solution of this difficult problem.

"I do."

"How?"

"Keep still; don't say a word here," continued Wilton. "Scatter, now, and I will be on the topgallant forecastle in a few minutes."

Wilton strolled about the deck a short time, and then went to the place of meeting, where he was soon joined by the rest of the discontented pupils.

"How many fellows can we muster?" asked he, when his associates in mischief had again gathered around him.

"I know at least a dozen, who are up to anything," replied Monroe; "but some of them are in the other watch. What are you going to do?"

"I'll tell you: There are the professors' barge and the third cutter at the swinging boom. We will drop into them when the instructors go down to supper, and make for the shore. All the rest of the boats are at the davits; and before they can get them into the water, we shall be out of their reach. What do you think of that for a plan!"

"I think it is a first-rate one. But hadn't we better wait till the instructors turn in?" suggested Adler.

"No; the boats will all be hoisted up to the davits at sunset. We must do it while the professors are at supper, or not at all. We want eight oars for the barge, and six for the third cutter; that makes fourteen fellows. Can we raise as many as that?"

"Yes, I think we can; we will try, at any rate."

"But you must look out, or some fellow will blow the whole thing," added Wilton. "Mind whom you speak to."

The trustworthiness of the various students was canvassed, and it was decided what ones should be invited to join the enterprise. The discontented boys separated, and went to work with great caution to obtain the needed recruits. Unfortunately, in such a crowd of young men, there are always enough to engage in any mischievous plot, and it is quite likely that twice as many as were wanted could have been obtained to man the boats in the runaway expedition.

Wilton missed Shuffles very much in arranging the details of the present enterprise. While at the Brockway Academy, they had plotted mischief so often that each seemed to be necessary to the other. But Shuffles had reformed; he was now third lieutenant of the ship, and it was not safe to suggest a conspiracy to him, for he would attempt to gain favor with the principal by exposing or defeating it.

Yet Shuffles was so bold in thought, and so daring in execution, that Wilton could hardly abandon the hope of obtaining his assistance; besides, the third lieutenant would be officer of the deck when the professors went to supper, and might wink at their departure in the boats, if he did not actually help them off.

"Would you say anything to Shuffles?" asked

Wilton, still in doubt, of Monroe, as they happened to meet again in the waist.

"To Shuffles!" exclaimed Monroe, in an energetic whisper.

"I mean so."

"Certainly not. I should as soon think of speaking to Lowington himself."

"But Shuffles may join us. He is always in for a good time."

"Why, you ninny, he is third lieutenant of the ship."

"No matter if he is. I think Shuffles would like to join us."

"Nonsense! He has been in office only three days, and it would break him. He would be degraded to the steerage," replied Monroe, who could not help thinking that Wilton was beside himself in proposing such a thing, and that the enterprise was doomed to failure in such incompetent hands.

"If he won't join us, perhaps he will help us off. He is officer of the deck, you know, in the second dog watch."

"I know he is; but don't you open your mouth to him. If you do, I'll back out at once."

"Back out?"

"Yes, back out. I believe you are crazy. Why don't you go to Captain Carnes, and done with it?" said Monroe, with energy.

"I haven't any hold on Carnes, and I have on Shuffles."

"What do you mean?" asked the prudent conspirator, curiously.

"If Shuffles won't join us, he won't blow on us, you may depend upon that. He wouldn't dare to do it. I could break him before sundown, if I chose," said Wilton, with conscious power.

"That alters the case."

"Of course, I shouldn't think of saying anything to him, if I did not know what I was talking about. I have him where the hair is short, and he knows it, as well as I do."

"What is it, Wilton?"

"No matter what it is. When a thing is told me in confidence, I keep it to myself; but if he turns traitor to his cronies, he must look out for breakers. He knows what it is."

"Well, if you can get him, he will be a first-rate fellow to have."

"I think I can get him. Here he comes; you keep out of the way, and I will see how deep the water is."

Monroe went forward to find a student to whom he had been deputed to speak in the interest of the enterprise, leaving Wilton to grapple with the old lion of mischief, whose teeth, however, seemed to have been worn out in the cause.

"What's up, Wilton?" demanded the third lieutenant, who was now off duty, and therefore allowed to speak to the crew, though it was a privilege of which the officers seldom availed themselves.

"Who said anything was up?" asked Wilton.

"You look as though you meant something. What were you and Ike Monroe talking about just now?" continued Shuffles. "About me, I'll be bound, for you kept looking at me, as though you meant something."

"What makes you think so? Have you heard anything?" asked Wilton, fearful that the plot had leaked out.

"Not a word; I only judged by your looks."

"I suppose if anything was up, you wouldn't have anything to do with it now."

"Most decidedly, I should not. I like my present position too well to fall out of it. I'm going to be captain next term, if I can fetch it any way in the world."

"You mean to be a flunky, just like the rest of them. You are not the same fellow you used to be."

"Yes, I am."

"You are getting too big for your boots."

"You wrong me, Wilton. I'm just as good a fellow as I ever was. I think I'm the best fellow in the ship, and for that reason I want to be captain. I'm ahead of Carnes so far on marks this month."

"Well, if you want to be the head flunky, I hope you'll get it. We are not going ashore to-morrow, they say," added Wilton, changing the topic to get nearer to the business of the hour.

"So Pelham told me."

"Are you willing to stay on board and study, and do ship's duty, on the Fourth of July?"

"We are going to celebrate."

"How?"

"I'm sure I don't know."

"We shall celebrate to-morrow just as we do every day — as close prisoners on board the ship. I, for one, don't like it, and I won't stand it."

"Won't you?" laughed Shuffles.

"When I say I won't, I mean so."

"O, you do — do you?"

"You better believe I do," added Wilton, shaking his head resolutely.

"What are you going to do?"

"I'm going ashore, by hook or by crook."

"Better not get into any scrape."

"You say that as one of the flunkies."

"Well, you had better not say anything to me, for I shall have to do my duty as an officer. Don't say anything to me, and then I shall not know anything about it."

"Humph!" sneered Wilton, not pleased with this non-committal policy.

"I don't want to do anything mean with any of our fellows; so don't say a word to me. I shall do my duty as an officer, as I promised to do when I was made third lieutenant."

"Do you mean to say you will stop me, Shuffles, if you see me going?" demanded Wilton.

"I do mean so; I promised faithfully to do my duty as an officer, and I shall do it."

"See here, Bob Shuffles; you needn't talk to me in that manner. I knew the ship's cable from a pint of milk, and you can't come the flunky over me."

"I'm going to do just as you would do if you were in my place. I won't hear a word about any of your plans."

"But will you interfere with them?"

"If it is my duty to do so, I shall. I intend to obey orders; and if I have the deck, I shall keep things straight, whatever happens."

"Lowington don't know you as well as I do."

"No matter if he don't; he shall have no fault to find with me this term, if I can help it."

"It's no use for me to mince the matter with you, Bob Shuffles. We understand each other too well for that. Something's up."

Shuffles turned on his heel, and was about to walk away.

"Hold on a minute, Shuffles," continued Wilton. "I won't tell you what's up, but I'll tell you this: if you interfere with what I do, or with what the fellows with me do, I'll tell Lowington about the mutiny — I will, as sure as your name is Bob Shuffles. Do you understand me?"

"Well, I do; and it seems to me that sounds very much like a threat."

"Call it what you like. If you turn traitor to our fellows, you must stand the racket of it. You are not a saint just yet, and those that live in glass houses musn't throw stones."

"I believe I haven't played false to any of our fellows. If I don't choose to get into any scrape with them, I have a right to keep out. That's all I've got to say."

"But what are you going to do, Shuffles? Our fellows will want to know."

"I'm going to do my duty," replied the third lieutenant, as he walked away, regardless of the efforts of his companion to detain him.

Shuffles was experiencing the truth of the old maxim, that honesty is the best policy. It is to be regretted that his present devotion to duty had no higher incentive than mere policy; but it may be hoped of those who do their duty from low motives, that they may gather inspiration even from their politic fidelity to obey its behests from higher motives. The third lieutenant of the Young America intended to keep the promise he had made in accepting his office, simply because it would pay best.

Wilton and his confederates had no difficulty in making up the required number of discontents and malcontents before six o'clock, which was the time fixed for carrying out the enterprise they had planned. Some of the recruits joined because they anticipated a good time in the city in celebrating the Fourth, and others from a mere love of mischief and excitement. The details of the scheme had been carefully elaborated by Monroe and Wilton, after the ranks of the conspirators were full. Having learned a valuable lesson from the daily discipline of the ship, the mischief was certainly well planned. Each boy was assigned to a particular position in the boats, and knew on what thwart he was to sit, and which oar he was to pull.

Wilton and Monroe, as the master spirits of the enterprise, were to run out first on the swinging boom, and slide down the painters, each into the boat he was to command. The others were to follow in the same way, descending from the boom, for it was not considered prudent to run the boats up to the gangway, where some enthusiastic officer might easily interfere with the plan, which was to depend for its success upon the celerity of its execution.

When four bells struck, the professors went down to

their evening meal, as usual, and the boatswain piped the port watch to supper, the starboard watch having taken theirs at three bells, or half past five. Wilton gave a low whistle, when Shuffles, officer of the deck, was abaft the mizzenmast, with his back to the runaways, who had gathered in the waist, and were waiting for the signal.

"Be lively, fellows," said the leader of the enterprise, as he sprang over the rail, and ran out on the boom, followed by Monroe.

The others, in the order in which they had been instructed, did the same. About half of them were on the boom, when the movement was reported to the officer of the deck by the midshipman on duty in the waist. Shuffles rushed forward, now understanding, for the first time, the intentions of Wilton; and true to the inspiration of fidelity, he set about defeating the object of "our fellows."

The studding-sail boom, to which the boats were fastened, was supported by a topping-lift from above, and kept in position, at right angles with the side of the ship, by guys extending forward and aft.

"Stand by that fore guy!" shouted Shuffles, as he sprang upon the rail. "Cast off!"

"Lively, fellows!" said Wilton, when he saw that the third lieutenant intended to swing in the boom to the ship's side.

"Stand by the after guy of the studding-sail boom!" continued Shuffles, with becoming energy.

Both his orders were promptly obeyed; but seeing that his movement would be too late, he rushed to the topping-lift, and cast it off, causing the swinging boom to drop into the water, just as the last boy was about to slide down into the professors' boat. Of course the luckless fellow went into the water; but he was promptly picked up by his companions in mischief.

"If I'm caught, Bob Shuffles, you look out for breakers!" cried Wilton, as the third lieutenant appeared at the gangway again.

The tide was coming in, and the boats swung so far abaft the boom that it had fallen clear of them when it dropped into the water. Wilton and Monroe were prompt to avail themselves of their present success, and the boys sat in the boats, with their oars up, ready to pull as soon as the order was given.

"Let fall!" said Wilton; and the eight oars of the professors' barge dropped into the water, and the rowers placed them in readiness for the first stroke.

Monroe, in the third cutter, followed the example of his principal, and was hardly a second behind him.

"Give way!" added Wilton.

"Give way!" repeated Monroe; and the two boats gathered way and darted off towards the nearest point of the shore.

Thus far the enterprise of "our fellows" was entirely successful, and Shuffles stood on the gangway, chagrined at the defeat which had attended his efforts to prevent the escape of the runaways.

"Stand by to clear away the first cutter!" shouted he, suddenly and with energy, as he made his way to the davits, where the boat indicated was suspended.

"Cast off the gripes, and man the falls!" he continued, when the watch were collected at the scene of action. "Mr. Kendall, you will inform the captain what has happened."

Within three minutes, the first cutter was in the water, for the crew had been frequently exercised in the evolution of lowering boats, and performed it with remarkable facility for boys. Before the first cutter touched the water, the captain, the principal, and all the professors, came on deck.

Mr. Lowington was entirely cool, though everybody else appeared to be intensely excited. The crew of the first cutter were piped away, and at the principal's suggestion, the third lieutenant was sent off in the boat to prevent the landing of the rebellious pupils.

"Up oars! Let fall! Give way!" said Shuffles, in the boat, delivering his orders in rapid succession; and the first cutter darted off in chase of the runaways.

CHAPTER VI.

THE FOURTH OF JULY.

THE first cutter was manned by her regular crew, who had been trained with the utmost care to pull together, while Wilton, in the professors' barge, which was of the same size, had some very indifferent oarsmen. The runaways had made up their force of such material as they could obtain, and though all were somewhat accustomed to rowing, they had not been drilled to work together; they were not the unit of power in pulling a boat. Shuffles, therefore, had a manifest advantage, and he was determined to bring back the fugitives.

The second cutter, in charge of Paul Kendall, was cleared away, and, with Mr. Lowington and Mr. Fluxion on board, left the ship to take part in the pursuit. The chase promised to be an exciting one, for Wilton and Monroe were straining every nerve to reach the shore before they were overtaken. They were making for the nearest land, and having just the number of hands required to pull the boat, each of them was obliged to use an oar himself. They had no coxswains, and Wilton, at the bow oar of the professors' barge, could not see what was ahead, though he kept the pursuing boats in full view.

The nearest land, not more than half a mile from the ship, was a point covered with salt marsh, above which was a cove, whose opening was about ten rods in width. Wilton was making for the point below the cove, but his calculations were made without judgment or discretion. If he reached the land, his party would be obliged to walk a mile in order to get round the cove, on a narrow strip of marsh, where they might be intercepted. But the fatal defect in his plan of operations was a failure to consider the depth of water between the ship and the point. The flow of the tide from the cove, while it kept a clear channel through the entrance, had formed a bar off the tongue of land on the seaward side of it, which was bare at half tide, and was now just covered. Wilton was pulling for this bar, with all the strength of his crew.

Shuffles was prompt to observe the mistake of his late crony, and just as prompt to profit by it. The first cutter was gaining rapidly on the chase; but Shuffles, as she reached the border of the main channel, ordered his coxswain to keep the boat's head towards the entrance of the cove.

"We shall never catch them on this tack," said the coxswain of the cutter, who knew nothing about the bar.

"I think we shall," replied the third lieutenant, confidently.

"We are not going towards the point."

"That's very true, and the professors' barge will not go much farther in that direction. Pull steady, my lads; don't hurry yourselves. There is plenty of time."

The coxswain thought his superior officer was taking the matter very coolly, and knowing of the intimacy which had formerly subsisted between Shuffles and Wilton, he was ready to conclude that the third lieutenaut was willing to permit the escape of "our fellows." While he was putting this construction on the conduct of his superior, the professors' barge "took the ground," and stuck fast.

"They're aground, Mr. Shuffles," said the coxswain.

"There's just where I expected them to be," answered Shuffles, quietly.

"Shall I run towards them?"

"No; keep her as she is. There isn't more than a foot of water anywhere between them and the point."

The third cutter, being a smaller boat than the professors' barge, did not touch the bar as soon as her consort; but Monroe saw that his craft could not land her party on the point at that stage of the tide, and he ordered his crew first to lay on their oars, and then to back water. Wilton's boat was aground at the bow, and when he had sent part of his crew aft, she was easily pushed off the bar. By this delay he had lost the chance of landing at the point, and his only alternative was to pull up to the cove; but in doing so, it would be impossible to avoid the first cutter, which had now secured a position off the mouth of the little bay.

"Stand by to lay on your oars," said the coxswain of the first cutter, as directed by the lieutenant in command. "Oars!"

The crew ceased rowing, and laying on their oars, waited the next movement of the runaways. In the mean time the second cutter was well away from the ship, and Mr. Lowington, promptly comprehending the intentions of the third lieutenant, directed the officer in command to pull towards the boats on the bar, keeping well to seaward, in order to prevent them from escaping in that direction.

Wilton realized that he was cornered, and hoping that Shuffles would not be over-zealous in the discharge of his duty, directed his course towards the opening of the cove. A few strokes brought him within hailing distance of the first cutter.

"No use, Wilton," said Shuffles, laughing. "You may as well pull for the ship. It's all up with you."

But the leader of the runaways, instead of heeding this good advice, attempted to push by astern of the first cutter.

"Stern, all! Give way!" shouted Shuffles, sharply. "Coxswain, stand by with your stern line!"

It was generally understood that the third lieutenant of the Young America was a fighting character, and that he could whip any officer or seaman in the ship, though his prowess had not been practically demonstrated. Shuffles took the stern line himself, instead of intrusting the duty to the coxswain. He intended to grapple the bow of the professors' barge, and make fast to it with the rope; but the cutter did not gather way enough in season to do this. As she backed, she fouled the oars of the barge, and Shuffles secured a firm hold of her stern.

"What are you doing, Bob Shuffles?" demanded Wilton, angry, when he saw that his late crony was fully in earnest.

THE NEW YORK
PUBLIC LIBRARY

ASTOR, LENOX AND
TILDEN FOUNDATIONS
R   L

The Escape from the Ship.

The third lieutenant made no reply; but passing his rope through a ring in the stern of the barge, he made it fast, and then pushed the cutter off from her. When the line had run out about a fathom, he secured the end he held in his hand to the after thwart of his own boat. Thus the first cutter and the barge were lashed together, stern to stern.

"Cast off that rope!" shouted Wilton to the stroke oarsman in the barge.

"Don't you touch it, my lad," interposed Shuffles, when the boy attempted to obey the order of his leader. "If you attempt it, you will purchase a sore head."

The third lieutenant had picked up a boat-hook, and stood ready to rap any of the barge's crew who might attempt to cast off the line by which the boats were fastened together. No one was disposed to cross the purposes of so formidable a person as Shuffles, and the stroke oarsman did not obey the order of Wilton. It would not be safe to do so.

"Now, Wilton, what do you say?" demanded Shuffles, a smile of triumph playing upon his face, which was very aggravating to the leader of the runaways. "Will you go back to the ship, or not?"

"No, of course I won't," replied the discomfited chief of the malcontents.

"You had better, my dear fellow. There comes Mr. Lowington."

"I didn't think this of you, Bob Shuffles," said Wilton, reproachfully.

"I told you I should do my duty; and I shall, to

the end. If you will return, all right; if not, I shall take you back."

"No, you won't."

"I think I will," added the third lieutenant, quietly. "Stand by to give way!" he continued, to the coxswain.

"Two can play at that game," said Wilton, as he gave the same order to his crew.

"Give way!" shouted the coxswain of the first cutter, with energy.

"Give way!" repeated Wilton, in the barge.

The rope straightened; Shuffles stood up in the stern-sheets of the cutter, to prevent the line from being cast off, and the contest began, to ascertain which should drag the other. It was rather ludicrous, in spite of the serious question of discipline involved in the affair, and the boys in the cutter were intensely amused, as well as excited. Both crews struggled with all their might, and each leader urged his followers to renewed exertions.

The discipline of the first cutter was on the point of carrying the contest in favor of law and order, when Monroe, seeing that his friend was nearly worsted, backed the third cutter up to the bow of the barge, and took her painter on board, which he made fast at the stern. Resuming his oar, he ordered his crew to give way together. Then law and order appeared to be at a discount, for the eight oarsmen in the first cutter were not a match, even in the cause of discipline, against the fourteen in the barge and third cutter.

Shuffles did not give it up, notwithstanding the

great odds against him. Letting out the stern line far enough to allow space for a new manœuvre, he directed the starboard oarsmen to lay on their oars, while those on the port side pulled the boat round. Then all gave way together, and the barge was dragged round sideways, until her oars fouled with those of Monroe's boat. At this stage of the exciting proceedings, the second cutter came up with the principal.

Mr. Fluxion sat in the stern-sheets, shaking his sides with laughter at the singular contest which was going on; but Mr. Lowington, though evidently amused, maintained his gravity, and was as dignified as usual. The appearance of the principal ended the struggle. A glance from him was quite sufficient to take all the stiffening out of the runaways, and even Wilton, though he talked valiantly behind Mr. Lowington's back, and neglected even to give him the simple title of "mister," had not the courage to resist the strong arm of his authority. As the second cutter backed up to the barge, the principal stepped on board of her, and took a seat in the stern-sheets.

"Young gentlemen, you will return to the ship," said Mr. Lowington, sternly, as he took the tiller-ropes in his hands. "Give way!"

The malcontents had no thought of further resistance. The presence of the principal was sufficient to overcome all insubordination; they did not dare to disobey him. Mechanically they bent to their oars, and without a word pulled back to the ship.

Mr. Fluxion, by direction of Mr. Lowington, had taken his place in Monroe's boat, and followed the barge, the two cutters bringing up the rear. This was the first instance of flagrant insubordination which had occurred since the organization of the ship's company, and the students were not a little anxious to learn how it would be treated. It was singular that Shuffles, who on shore had always been the ringleader in enterprises of mischief, had been the means of defeating the scheme of the runaways.

The boats were hoisted up at the davits, and the boatswain was ordered to pipe all hands on deck. The principal looked calm, but stern, as he took the position on the hatch which he usually occupied when he addressed the students.

"Wilton and Monroe," said he.

The culprits came forward, hanging their heads with shame.

"I learn that you are the ringleaders in this movement. Is it so?"

"I suppose we are," replied Wilton.

"Who proposed the plan?"

"Wilton first spoke to me about it," answered Monroe.

"And you induced the others to join you?"

"Yes, sir."

"As the ringleaders, Wilton and Monroe will lose twenty marks each, and remain in their mess rooms to-morrow. The other twelve lose ten marks each," continued Mr. Lowington. "Young gentlemen, those who have engaged in this scheme are not to be trusted. I have nothing further to say."

The crew were dismissed, and all the students were disposed to laugh at the mildness of the punishment compared with the enormity of the offence.

"Mr. Shuffles," said the principal, as he stepped down from the hatch, "I am very much obliged to you for the zeal and energy which you have exhibited in the discharge of your duty. Not only was your disposition to do your duty highly commendable, but your plans displayed skill and forethought."

"Thank you, sir," replied the third lieutenant; "I am very glad to have pleased you."

Mr. Lowington bowed, and descended to the cabin to finish his supper, which had been interrupted by the event described. What the professors said about the affair was not known to the boys; but Shuffles was warmly praised for the moderate but skilful measures he had used in the capture of the rebels.

At sundown, a shore boat came alongside with an abundant supply of fireworks, which had been ordered by Mr. Lowington. They were hoisted on board, and deposited in a safe place. At the usual hour, the boys turned in to dream of the good time which these squibs and crackers suggested to them — all but Monroe and Wilton, who had something else to think about. The latter was disappointed and surly, while the former congratulated himself upon getting out of the scrape so easily. Wilton was very angry with Shuffles, who might have permitted him to land, if he had been so disposed; and he determined to take what he considered an ample vengeance upon the traitor. As soon as he had an opportunity to speak to Mr. Lowington, he intended to tell him all about the plan for a mutiny, and he was fully satisfied that Shuffles would be sent in disgrace from his pleasant position in the after cabin, to take up his abode in the steerage again.

On the morning of the ever-glorious Fourth, all hands were mustered on the deck of the Young America at four o'clock. Crackers were served out, and for two hours there was a tremendous racket from stem to stern, among the younger boys. At six o'clock, the port watch were piped to breakfast, and all the crackers having been burned, the decks were swept, and everything put in perfect order, by the starboard watch. A band of music, engaged for the day, came off, and the enlivening strains of the national airs sounded through the ship.

At seven o'clock, when all hands had breakfasted, an hour earlier than usual, the crew were piped to muster, wondering, as they always did, what was going to be done.

"All hands, up anchor ahoy!" shouted the boatswain, prompted by the first lieutenant; but this order was so common in the every-day practice of the crew, that no one supposed it had any unusual significance; and some of the boys even began to grumble at being compelled to go through the routine of ship's work on the Fourth of July.

"Bring to on the cable, and unbitt!" continued the officer in command. "Ship the capstan bars, and swifter them! Heave in the cable to a short stay!"

These orders were duly executed, under the direction of the various officers at their stations.

"Avast heaving!" called the first master. "Anchor apeak, sir," he reported to the first lieutenant.

"Pawl the capstan, stopper the cable, and unship the bars!" added the executive officers, all of which was done, and duly reported.

"Stations for loosing topsails!" which were shaken out by the ordinary routine, sheeted home, and hoisted up.

"Forecastlemen, loose the head sails! After-guard, clear away the spanker! Man the capstan bars, ship and swifter them! Heave around!"

This last was a manœuvre which the crew had never before been called upon to perform; and the order sent a thrill of delight to all hearts. The cable had often been heaved to a short stay, that is, so that it run nearly up and down; but that was as far as they had ever before been permitted to proceed. Now, with the anchor apeak, they were ordered to the capstan again, and they realized that the Young America was actually going to sea. The command kindled an enthusiasm which glowed on every face. The ship was going out of the harbor, and the evil doers in the mess rooms below were to be pitied.

"Anchor aweigh, sir," reported the excited boatswain, who, however, had to be prompted in this instance by Peaks, for it had never been in that position before since it first hooked the mud in Brockway harbor.

"Anchor aweigh, sir," repeated the second lieutenant.

"Man the jib and flying-jib halyards!" said the first lieutenant.

"Anchor's at the bow, sir," said the boatswain, which report went through the same channels as before, till it reached the executive officer.

"Hoist away on the jib and flying-jib halyards! Avast heaving! Pawl the capstan! Stopper the cable! Cat and fish the anchor!" shouted the first lieutenant. "Port the helm!"

The Young America was clear of the ground. The fore topsail, which had been trimmed to the fresh breeze, was full, and the ship began to gather headway. Two seamen had been placed at the wheel, under the charge of the quartermaster. The boys had often "made believe" do these things, but now they were real. The vessel was actually moving through the water, and they could hardly contain themselves, so exhilarating was the scene.

"Steady!" said the first lieutenant, when the ship had come up to her intended course.

"Steady, sir," repeated the quartermaster in charge of the helm.

"Stand by to set the spanker," added the first lieutenant. "Man the outhaul! Cast off the brails, and loose the vangs!"

The after-guard, which is the portion of the ship's company stationed on the quarter-deck, or abaft the mizzenmast, obeyed this order, and stood ready to set the spanker, which is the aftermost sail.

"Walk away with the outhaul!" and the after-guard ran off with the rope, which drew the sail out into its place on the gaff. "Stand by the spanker sheet — let it out!"

"You must attend to your main and mizzen topsails, Mr. Pelham," said the principal, in a low tone.

"Man the fore and main braces!" said the executive officer; and the young seamen sprang to their stations. "Let go and haul!"

The main and the mizzen topsails were thus trimmed, so that they took the wind.

"That was very well done, Captain Carnes, though your crew need more practice. They are very much excited," said Mr. Lowington.

"I don't wonder, sir; I think none of them knew we were going out of the harbor," replied the captain.

"I am glad they enjoy it," added the principal, "though I should not have left the anchorage, except as a substitute for the Fourth of July celebration."

"They will like this much better than going to the city."

"I have no doubt on that point; and last evening, when those students wished to run away, I was tempted to punish their disobedience by letting them go. The wind is pretty fresh, Captain Carnes, but I think you may set the top-gallant sails."

The captain gave the order to the first lieutenant.

"Aloft, sail-loosers of the top-gallant sails!" shouted Mr. Pelham; and the eager young salts dashed up the rigging. "Lay out! Loose! Let fall! Man your sheets and halyards! Sheets home, and hoist away!"

The addition of the top-gallant sails was sensibly felt by the Young America; and, "taking a bone in her teeth," she careened over, and dashed away merrily on her course.

The band played Hail, Columbia, and as the ship passed the fort, the crew mounted the rigging and gave three cheers. The excitement on board was immense, and never was Independence Day more thoroughly and enthusiastically enjoyed. The officers and crew were at the height of felicity, as the gallant little ship bowled over the waves, threading her way through the channels between the numerous islands of the bay.

"Can't we put on any more sail, Mr. Lowington?" asked Captain Carnes, as he met the principal on the quarter-deck.

"Not at present. We are making very good progress now."

"The boys want to see all sail on her."

"The wind is blowing half a gale now," added Mr. Lowington, with a smile. "I think we shall be able to give them quite enough of it when we get out into blue water. I'm afraid you will lose half your crew before noon!"

"Lose them?"

"By seasickness, I mean."

"Do you think they will be sick, sir?"

"I have no doubt of it. Many of them never saw the ocean before, and never looked upon a ship till they came on board of the Young America. I don't think it would be prudent to put on all sail, until we know what force we are to have to handle the ship."

"They don't look like being seasick at present."

"Wait till we get out into the heavy sea," laughed the principal, as he went forward.

At eight bells the ship was abreast of the last island, and she began to pitch and roll a little, though the motion was hardly perceptible, until she was well off from the land. Professor Paradyme was the first victim of seasickness, and the boys all laughed when they saw the woe-begone expression on the face of the learned man; but some of those who laughed the loudest were the first to be taken by the ridiculous malady.

The Young America pitched and rolled heavily as she receded from the land, and nothing more was said by the students about putting on more sail. The spray broke over the bow, and washed the decks; but most of the boys enjoyed the scene as they had never enjoyed anything before.

"What are you doing here, sir?" demanded Mr. Lowington, as he went forward, and discovered Wilton skulking under the lee of the foremast. "You were told to stay in your mess room, sir!"

"I couldn't, sir," whined the culprit.

"You could, and you will."

"I was seasick, sir."

"I can't help it; you must stay in your mess room," added the principal, sternly.

"If you please, sir, I will obey orders if you will let me stay on deck," said Wilton, humbly.

"No; return to your room;" and Wilton was compelled to obey.

It was a very severe punishment to him and Monroe to be obliged to stay in the steerage during the first trip of the Young America.

CHAPTER VII.

HEAVING THE LOG.

THE Young America, under topsails and topgallant sails, was making about ten knots an hour. After passing the last island in the bay, she was headed to the south-east, which brought the wind over the starboard quarter. The ship was of the clipper class, though not as sharp as many of this model. It was found that her sailing ability was excellent, and Mr. Lowington and Mr. Fluxion expressed much satisfaction at her performance, both in respect of speed and weatherly qualities.

When the ship left her moorings, the principal had not decided where to go, or how long to remain at sea, intending to be governed by the circumstances of the hour. It had never been his purpose to keep her at one anchorage, but to go from port to port, remaining a few days or a few weeks at each, as the discipline of the ship and the progress of the boys in their studies suggested. There were many elements of seamanship which could not be effectively practised while the ship lay at anchor, such as heaving the log, sounding and steering, though the boys had been carefully instructed in the theory of these operations.

The instructor in mathematics, the boatswain, the

carpenter, and the sailmaker, all of whom were good seamen, were in great demand as soon as the ship was under way; but when she had sea-room enough, the helm was handed over to the boys, under the charge of a juvenile quartermaster. Peaks stood by, and gave the necessary directions, till the students were able to do the work themselves.

"Now, my lads, we will heave the log," said the boatswain, when the ship was well out from the land.

"We know how to do that," replied Smith, one of the quartermasters.

"I dare say you do, young gentlemen; but in my opinion, you can't do it. You know how to write a psalm, but I don't believe you could write one," added Peaks. "You have to learn how to do these things by the feeling, so that they will do themselves, so to speak. After-guard, stand by to haul in the log-line. Here, quartermaster, you will hold the glass, and the officer of the deck will throw the chip."

"We know all about it, Mr. Peaks," repeated Smith.

"I know you do; but you can't tell within five knots how fast the ship is going," laughed the boatswain. "Let's do it right a few times, and then you can be trusted."

The quartermaster took the glass, and Gordon, then officer of the watch, the chip, which he cast into the water over the stern of the ship.

"Turn!" said he, when the stray line had run out.

Now, Smith, at this particular moment, was watching a vessel over the quarter, and he did not instantly turn the glass, as he should have done; but Peaks said nothing.

"Up!" cried the quartermaster, when the sand had all run through the glass.

Gordon stopped the reel from which the line was running out, and noted the mark.

"Seven knots," said he.

"Not right," replied the boatswain, sharply. "This ship is going nine or ten knots an hour, and any man who has snuffed salt water for six months could guess nearer than you make it. Now try it once again, and if you don't hit nearer than that next time, you may as well throw the reel overboard, and hire a Yankee to guess the rate of sailing."

"I thought we knew all about it," added Smith.

"I think you do, young gentlemen; but you were star-gazing when you ought to have been all attention. The line ran out two or three knots before you turned the glass."

Gordon took the chip again. It was a thin piece of board, in the form of a quarter circle. The round side was loaded with just lead enough to make it float upright in the water. The log-line was fastened to the chip, just as a boy loops a kite, two strings being attached at each end of the circular side, while the one at the angle is tied to a peg, which is inserted in a hole, just hard enough to keep it in place, while there is no extra strain on the board, but which can be drawn out with a smart pull. When the log-line has run out as far as desired, there would be some difficulty in hauling in the chip while it was upright in the water; but a sudden jerk draws the peg at the angle, and permits the board to lie flat, in which position the water offers the least resistance to its passage.

The half-minute glass used on board the Young America, held by the quartermaster, was like an hour glass, and contained just sand enough to pass through the hole in the neck in thirty seconds. The log-line was one hundred and fifty fathoms in length, and was wound on a reel, which turned very easily, so that the resistance of the chip to the water would unwind it. The log-line is divided into certain spaces called knots, the length of each of which is the same fractional part of a mile that a half minute is of an hour. If there be sixty-one hundred and twenty feet in a nautical mile, or the sixtieth part of a degree of a great circle, which is not far from accurate, and the ship be going ten knots an hour, she will run sixty-one thousand two hundred feet in an hour. If the chip were thrown overboard at eight o'clock, and the line were long enough, the ship would have run out sixty-one thousand two hundred feet, or ten miles, at nine o'clock, or in one hour. In one minute she would run one sixtieth of sixty-one thousand two hundred feet, which is ten hundred and twenty feet; in half a minute, five hundred and ten feet.

The half-minute glass is the measure of time generally used in heaving the log. While the sand is dropping through, the line runs out five hundred and ten feet, the ship going ten knots an hour being the basis of the calculation. One knot, therefore, will be fifty-one feet. If the line pays out five hundred and ten feet in thirty seconds, by the glass, the ship is going ten knots an hour. If it pays out four hundred and eight feet in half a minute, or eight hundred and sixteen feet in a minute, she will pay out a mile in as many minutes as eight hundred and sixteen feet is contained in sixty-one hundred and twenty feet, which is seven and a half minutes. Then the ship goes a mile in seven and a half minutes, or eight miles an hour.

A knot on the log-line is therefore invariably fifty-one feet; and the number of knots of the line run out in half a minute indicates also the ship's speed per hour, for fifty-one feet is the same part of a nautical mile that half a minute is of an hour. The calculations are given without allowances, merely to show the principle; and both the glass and the line are modified in practice.

On board the Young America, ten fathoms were allowed for "stray line;" this length of line being permitted to run out before the measuring commenced, in order to get the chip clear of the eddies in the wake of the ship. The ten fathoms were indicated by a white rag. drawn through the line; and when the officer paying out comes to this mark, he orders the quartermaster to turn the glass, and the operation actually begins. At every fifty-one feet (or forty-seven and six tenths, making the allowances) there is a mark — a bit of leather, or two or more knots. The instant the sands have all run through the glass, the quartermaster says, "Up,"and the officer notes the mark to which the line has run out. Half and quarter knots are indicated on the line.

"Now, quartermaster, mind your eye. When the officer of the deck says, 'Turn,' you repeat the word after him, to show that you are alive," continued Peaks.

"Ready!" said Gordon.

"Ready!" replied Smith.

The lieutenant threw the chip into the water, and when the stray line had run off, he gave the word to turn the glass.

"Turn!" repeated Smith.

Gordon eased off the log-line, so that nothing should prevent it from running easily.

"Up!" shouted Smith; and Gordon stopped the line.

"Very well," added Peaks. "What's the mark?"

"Ten and a quarter," replied the officer.

"That sounds more like it. I knew this ship was going more than seven knots. You see, young gentlemen, you can't catch flies and tend the log-line at the same time. Now, you may try it over again."

The experiment was repeated, with the same result. Other officers and seamen were called to the quarter-deck, and the training in heaving the log continued, until a reasonable degree of proficiency was attained.

"Land ho!" cried the lookout on the top-gallant forecastle, at about eleven o'clock in the forenoon.

"Where away?" called the officer of the deck.

"Dead ahead, sir."

"What is that land, Mr. Lowington?" asked Paul Kendall.

"Don't you know?"

"I'm sure I don't."

"Then you should study your map more. Look at the compass, and tell me how she heads."

"South-east, sir," replied Paul, after looking into the binnacle.

"Now, what land lies south-east of Brockway Harbor?" asked the principal.

"Cape Cod, I think."

"You are right; then that must be Cape Cod."

"Is it, really?"

"Certainly it is," laughed Mr. Lowington. "Have you no faith in your map?"

"I didn't think we could be anywhere near Cape Cod. I thought it was farther off," added Paul, who seemed to be amazed to think they had actually crossed Massachusetts Bay.

"The land you see is Race Point, which is about forty miles from the entrance to the bay, at the head of which Brockway is located. We have been making about ten knots an hour, and our calculations seem to be very accurate. By one o'clock we shall come to anchor in Provincetown Harbor."

This prediction was fully verified, and the Young America was moored off the town. Those who had been seasick recovered as soon as the motion of the ship ceased; and when everything aloft and on deck had been made snug, the crew were piped to dinner.

In the afternoon, part of the students were permitted to go on shore; the band played, and several boat-races took place, very much to the delight of the people on shore, as well as those on board. At six o'clock the ship was opened for the reception of visitors, who came off in large numbers to inspect the vessel. After dark there was a brilliant display of fireworks, and the Young America blazed with blue-lights and Roman candles, set off by boys on the cross-trees, and at the yard-arms. At ten the festivities closed, and all was still in the steerage and on deck.

The next morning, the ship got under way, and stood out of the harbor, bound for Brockway again. She had a light breeze, and a smooth time, and the boys had the satisfaction of seeing every rag of canvas spread, including studding-sails alow and aloft; but it was not till after dark that the ship came to anchor at her former moorings.

Wilton and Monroe were released from confinement in the morning, and permitted to go on deck. Whatever their shipmates might have said, they felt that they had been severely punished, especially as they had failed in their runaway expedition. Wilton did not feel any more kindly towards Shuffles when he was released than when he had been ordered to his room. He felt that his late crony had been a traitor, and he was unable to take any higher view of the circumstances.

"Wilton," said Mr. Lowington, when he met the runaway on deck, the day after the Fourth, "I told you that you had made a mistake. Do you believe it yet?"

"I suppose I do, sir."

"You suppose you do! Don't you know?"

"Yes, sir, I think I did make a mistake," replied Wilton, who found it very hard to acknowledge the fact.

"I do not refer to your punishment, when I allude to the consequences of your misdeed, for that was very light. You have fallen very low in the estimation of your superiors."

"Do you mean Mr. Shuffles, sir?"

"I did not mean the officers exclusively, though I believe they have a proper respect for the discipline of the ship."

"I don't think Shuffles need to say anything."

"He hasn't said anything."

"He is worse than I am."

"Shuffles has done very well, and merits the approbation of the principal and the instructors."

"They don't know him as well as I do," growled Wilton.

"They probably know him better. Your remarks do not exhibit a proper spirit towards an officer. He defeated your plan to escape, but he did no more than his duty. He would have been blamed, perhaps punished, if he had done any less."

"I don't find any fault with him for doing his duty, but I don't like to be snubbed by one who is worse than I am. If you knew what I know, sir, you would turn him out of the after cabin."

"Then it is fortunate for him that I don't know what you know," replied Mr. Lowington, sternly. "If you wish to injure him in my estimation, you will not succeed."

"He is going to get up a mutiny one of these days. He told me all about it," continued Wilton, desperately, when he found that the principal was in no mood to listen to his backbiting.

"That will do, Wilton; I don't wish to hear anything more about that matter. Your testimony against Shuffles, under present circumstances, is not worth the breath you use in uttering it."

"I thought it was my duty to tell you, if any one was trying to get up a mutiny."

"You did not think so; you are telling me this story to revenge yourself against the third lieutenant for his fidelity. Whether there is, or is not, any truth in what you say, I shall take no notice of it."

"It is all true, sir. He did speak to me about getting up a mutiny, locking up the professors, taking the ship, and going round Cape Horn; and he will not deny it."

"He will have no opportunity to deny it to me, for I shall not mention the subject to him. Go to your duty, and remember that you have injured yourself more than Shuffles by this course."

Wilton hung his head, and went forward, cheated of his revenge, and disconcerted by the rebuke he had received.

Mr. Lowington was quite willing to believe that Shuffles had talked about a mutiny, while he was in the steerage, but there was at least no present danger of such an extravagant scheme being put into operation. He understood Shuffles perfectly; he knew that his high office and his ambition were his only incentives to fidelity in the discharge of his duty; but he had fairly won his position, and he was willing to let him stand or fall by his own merits. He was not a young man of high moral principle, as Paul Kendall, and Gordon, and Carnes were; but the discipline of the ship was certainly doing wonders for him, though it might ultimately fail of its ends.

The ship came to anchor, the band was sent on shore, and the Fourth of July holidays were ended. On the following morning the studies were resumed, and everything on board went on as usual. A few days later, the ship went on a cruise to the eastward, spending a week in each of the principal ports on the coast. The students soon became so accustomed to the motion of the ship, that none of them were seasick, and the recitations were regularly heard, whether the Young America was in port or at sea.

When the cold weather came, stoves were put up in the cabins and in the steerage, and the routine of the ship was not disturbed; but Mr. Lowington dreaded the ice and snow, and the severe weather of midwinter, and in November, the Young America started on a cruise to the southward, and in the latter part of December she was in Chesapeake Bay. In March she returned to Brockway. By this time the crew were all thorough seamen, and had made excellent progress in their studies. Mr. Lowington was entirely satisfied with the success of his experiment, and was resolved to persevere in it.

The boys were in splendid discipline, and there had not been a case of serious illness on board during the year. Besides the six hours of study and recitation required of the pupils per day, they were all trained in gymnastics by Dr. Winstock, the surgeon, who had a system of his own, and was an enthusiast on the subject. This exercise, with the ordinary ship's duty, kept them in excellent physical condition; and while their brown faces and rosy cheeks indicated a healthy state of the body, their forms were finely developed, and their muscles scientifically trained.

Greek and Latin, German and French, with the ordinary English branches pursued in high schools and academies, were taught on board, and the instructors were satisfied that the boys accomplished twice as much as was ordinarily done in similar institutions on shore, and without injury to the students. Everything was done by rule, and nothing was left to the whims and caprices of teachers and scholars. Just so much study was done every day, and no more. There was no sitting up nights; there were no balls and parties, theatres and concerts, to interfere with the work; no late suppers of escalloped oysters and lobster salads to be eaten. Boys who had bad habits were watched, and injurious tendencies corrected.

But the students enjoyed their life on shipboard. As the vessel went from port to port, new scenes were opened to them. Those who could be trusted were allowed to go on shore in their off-time; and as all their privileges depended upon their good conduct, they were very careful to do their duty, both as students and as seamen, cheerfully and faithfully.

The Young America dropped her anchor in Brockway Harbor on the 5th of March, on her return from her southern cruise. The first term of the second year was to commence on the 1st of April, and it was understood that the ship would sail for Europe on the last day of March. The vessel needed some repairs, and all the students were allowed a furlough of twenty days to visit their homes.

Several of the larger boys, including Carnes, had obtained places in the navy, and were not to return. Two or three were to enter college in the summer, and a few were to go into mercantile houses; but these vacancies would be more than filled by the applicants who had been waiting months for an opportunity to join the ship.

After the departure of the students, the Young America was docked, and the necessary repairs made upon her. She was thoroughly cleansed and painted, and came out as good as new. Before the return of the boys, her provisions, water, and stores, were taken on board, and all the preparations made for a foreign voyage. On the 25th of the month she was anchored again at her old moorings, and in the course of the next two days all the instructors and pupils were in their places. There were eleven new boys.

"Young gentlemen," said Mr. Lowington, as he mounted his usual rostrum, "I am happy to see you again, and to welcome you on board. Our experience during the coming season will be much more interesting and exciting than that of the last year. We shall proceed immediately to Europe, and all who are worthy of the privilege will have an opportunity to visit the principal cities of Europe — London, Paris, Naples, St. Petersburg. We shall go up the Baltic and up the Mediterranean, in this or a subsequent cruise, and I can safely promise you, not only an interesting, but a profitable trip. In a circular I have informed your parents and guardians of my purposes, and you are shipped this time for a foreign voyage, with their consent and approval."

This speech caused no little excitement among the boys, who anticipated a great deal from the summer voyage. It was no small thing to visit London, Paris, and St. Petersburg, and not many boys obtain such an opportunity.

"But, young gentlemen, I believe in discipline and progress, as most of you know. I expect every student to do his whole duty; and I wish to tell you now, that misconduct, and failures at recitation, will bring heavy disappointments upon you. If you do nothing for yourselves, you need expect nothing from me. For example, when the ship is going up the Thames, if any one of you, or any number of you, should be guilty of flagrant misconduct, or gross neglect of your studies, you will see no more of the city of London than you can see from the cross-trees, for you shall not put a foot on shore."

"Rather steep," whispered one of the new comers.

"That's so, but he means it," replied an old student.

"We shall be at sea, out of sight of land, for twenty or thirty days," continued Mr. Lowington. "We shall encounter storms and bad weather, such as none of you have ever seen; for in going from port to port, last season, we were enabled to avoid all severe weather. We shall go to sea now with no harbor before us till we reach the other side of the Atlantic, and we must take whatever comes. But the ship is as strong as a ship can be built, and with good management she would stand any gale that ever blew. Good management includes good discipline, and every officer and seaman must be faithful in the discharge of his duty, for the safety of the ship and all on board of her will depend upon the fidelity of each individual.

"Young gentlemen, there are eleven new scholars: they must take the vacant berths after the ship's company is organized on the old plan. The offices will be given out and the berths drawn by the merit roll for January, February, and a portion of March — only about nine weeks of term time."

Shuffles, who stood near the principal, looked very much disconcerted when this announcement was made, and whispered to Paul Kendall that it was not fair to distribute the offices by last year's record. While the Young America was lying at anchor in Chesapeake Bay, in December, Shuffles, then second lieutenant, had received a letter from his mother, in which she had informed him that his family would visit Europe in the following spring, and that he would leave the ship, and form one of the party. This information had caused him to relax his efforts as a student, and he had fallen very low in rank. This was the reason why the proposed distribution of offices was not fair.

When Shuffles went home on his furlough of twenty days, he had behaved so badly that his father refused to have him form one of the party in the trip abroad, and compelled him to return to the ship for another year of wholesome discipline under Mr. Lowington. Angry and indignant, Shuffles did return, and the announcement that the offices were to be distributed by the merit roll did not add to his equanimity.

"I will now read the record of marks," said the principal, "and announce the officers for the next term."

The boys were silent and anxious; for places in the after cabin were more highly valued than ever, now that the Young America was going to Europe.

CHAPTER VIII.

OUTWARD BOUND.

MR. LOWINGTON read the merit roll, announcing the officers as he proceeded. The occupants of the after cabin, who were appointed for the succeeding three months, during which time the ship crossed the Atlantic, and visited various European ports, were as follows: —

CHARLES GORDON, *Captain.*

Joseph Haven, *First Lieutenant.*
Paul Kendall, *Second "*
Samuel Goodwin, *Third "*
Augustus Pelham, *Fourth "*

William Foster, *First Master.*
Henry Martyn, *Second "*
Thomas Ellis, *Third "*
Joseph Leavitt, *Fourth "*

Joseph O. Rogers, *First Purser.*
Edward Murray, *Second "*

George W. Terrill, *First Midshipman.*
John Humphreys, *Second "*
Mark Robinson, *Third "*
Andrew Groom, *Fourth "*

The students mentioned in the list made the required promise to behave themselves like gentlemen, and faithfully discharge the duties of their several offices, and were duly installed in their new positions in the after cabin. Most of them had been officers before, but all of them were higher in rank than at any former period. Richard Carnes had been captain four terms, for no one could get ahead of him.

The new captain had been first lieutenant, during the preceding year, three terms out of four, and was certainly the best qualified student on board for the command. He was a young man of high moral aims, with much dignity of character and energy of purpose.

The officers went to the after cabin, put on their uniforms, and assumed their proper places. The choice of berths in the steerage proceeded as usual, according to the merit roll, and the petty offices were given to the highest in rank. The new boys took the unoccupied berths by lot. The organization of the ship was now completed, and the students were directed to put their berths and lockers in order. The remainder of the day was fully occupied in preparing for the voyage. Great quantities of ice and fresh provisions were taken on board, and packed away in the store rooms of the hold, and all was bustle and confusion.

On Thursday morning the ship was put in order again. The vessel had been duly cleared at the custom house, and every article required for the voyage had been received. The boys were ordered to put on their best suits, and at nine o'clock a steamer came off, having on board a large number of the parents and friends of the students. The forenoon was given up to this interesting occasion. It was a beautiful day, with a gentle breeze from the westward, and at twelve o'clock, all hands were mustered on deck for religious services, to be performed by the chaplain, in the presence of the friends of the pupils.

Mr. Lowington was a religious man, and the position of the Rev. Mr. Agneau, as chaplain on board, was by no means a sinecure. Services had always been held twice a day on Sunday. At five minutes before eight in the morning, and at the same time in the evening, prayers were said on deck, or in the steerage, in the presence of the entire ship's company. On the point of leaving the shores of the United States, it seemed highly appropriate to invoke the blessing of God on the voyage and the voyagers, and the principal had directed that the service should be conducted in the presence of the parents and friends.

The prayer and the remarks of the chaplain were very solemn and impressive, and even the roughest of the students were moved by them. At the conclusion of the religious service, Mr. Lowington addressed the visitors, explaining the details of his plan more fully than he had done in his circulars, and saying what he could to inspire the parents with confidence in regard to the safety of their sons. It need not be said that there were many tears shed on this occasion.

At the close of the speech a collation was served to the visitors, in the cabins and steerage, after which another hour was allowed for social intercourse; and then the ship was cleared, the visitors going on board the steamer again, which was to accompany the Young America below the lighthouse. The boys were sent below to change their clothes again.

"All hands, up anchor, ahoy!" piped the boatswain; and the crew sprang to their stations with more than usual alacrity.

This was a greater event than they had ever known before. The anchor, which was now to be hauled up, was not to be dropped again for about a month, and then in foreign waters. They were going out upon the waste of the ocean, to be driven and tossed by the storms of the Atlantic. They were bidding farewell to their native land, not again to look upon its shores for many months. They were boys, and they were deeply impressed by the fact.

The capstan was manned, and the cable hove up to a short stay. The topsails and top-gallant sails were set; then the anchor was hauled up to the hawsehole, catted and fished. The Young America moved; she wore round, and her long voyage was commenced. The courses and the royals were set, and she moved majestically down the bay. The steamer kept close by her, and salutations by shouts, cheers, and the waving of handkerchiefs, were continually interchanged, till the ship was several miles outside of the lower light.

The steamer whistled several times, to indicate that she was about to return. All hands were then ordered into the rigging of the ship; and cheer after cheer was given by the boys, and acknowledged by cheers on the part of the gentlemen, and the waving of handkerchiefs by the ladies. The steamer came about; the moment of parting had come, and she was headed towards the city. Some of the students wept then; for, whatever charms there were in the voyage before them, the ties of home and friends were still strong. As long as the steamer could be seen, signals continued to pass between her and the ship.

"Captain Gordon, has the first master given the quartermaster the course yet?" asked Mr. Lowington, when the steamer had disappeared among the islands of the bay.

"No, sir; but Mr. Fluxion told him to make it east-north-east."

"Very well, but the masters should do this duty," added Mr. Lowington, as he directed the instructor in mathematics to require the masters, to whom belonged the navigation of the ship, to indicate the course.

William Foster was called, and sent into the after cabin with his associates, to obtain the necessary sailing directions. The masters had been furnished with a supply of charts, which they had studied daily, as they were instructed in the theory of laying down the ship's course. Foster unrolled the large chart of the North Atlantic Ocean upon the dinner table, and with parallel ruler, pencil, and compasses, proceeded to perform his duty.

"We want to go just south of Cape Sable," said he, placing his pencil point on that part of the chart.

"How far south of it?" asked Harry Martyn.

"Say twenty nautical miles."

The first master dotted the point twenty miles south of Cape Sable, which is the southern point of Nova Scotia, and also the ship's position, with his pencil.

He then placed one edge of the parallel ruler on both of these points, thus connecting them with a straight line.

A parallel ruler consists of two smaller rulers, each an inch in width and a foot in length, connected together by two flat pieces of brass, riveted into each ruler, acting as a kind of hinge. The parts, when separated, are always parallel to each other.

Foster placed the edge of the ruler on the two points made with the pencil, one indicating the ship's present position, the other the position she was to obtain after sailing two or three days. Putting the fingers of his left hand on the brass knob of the ruler, by which the parts are moved, he pressed down and held its upper half, joining the two points, firmly in its place. With the fingers of the right hand he moved the lower half down, which, in its turn, he kept firmly in place, while he slipped the upper half over the paper, thus preserving the direction between the points. By this process the parallel ruler could be moved all over the chart without losing the course from one point to the other.

On every chart there are one or more diagrams of the compass, with lines diverging from a centre, representing all the points. The parallel ruler is worked over the chart to one of these diagrams, where the direction to which it has been set nearly or exactly coincides with one of the lines representing a point of the compass.

The first master of the Young America worked the ruler down to a diagram, and found that it coincided with the line indicating east by north; or one point north of east.

"That's the course," said Thomas Ellis, the third master — "east by north."

"I think not," added Foster. "If we steer that course, we should go forty or fifty miles south of Cape Sable, and thus run much farther than we need. What is the variation?"

"About twelve degrees west," replied Martyn.

The compass does not indicate the true north in all parts of the earth, the needle varying in the North Atlantic Ocean from thirty degrees east to nearly thirty degrees west. There is an imaginary line, extending in a north-westerly direction, through a point in the vicinity of Cape Lookout, called the magnetic meridian, on which there is no variation. East of this line the needle varies to the westward; and west of the line, to the eastward. These variations of the compass are marked on the chart, in different latitudes and longitudes, though they need to be occasionally corrected by observations, for they change slightly from year to year.

"Variation of twelve degrees,"* repeated Foster, verifying the statement by an examination of the chart. That is equal to about one point, which, carried to the westward from east by north, will give the course east-north-east."

The process was repeated, and the same result being obtained, the first master reported the course to

* These calculations are merely approximate, being intended only to illustrate the principle.

Mr. Fluxion, who had made the calculation himself, in the professors' cabin.

"Quartermaster, make the course east-north-east," said the first master, when his work had been duly approved by the instructor.

"East-north-east, sir!" replied the quartermaster, who was conning the wheel — that is, he was watching the compass, and seeing that the two wheelmen kept the ship on her course.

There were two other compasses on deck, one on the quarter-deck, and another forward of the main-mast, which the officers on duty were required frequently to consult, in order that any negligence in one place might be discovered in another. The after cabin and the professors' cabin were also provided with "tell-tales," which are inverted compasses, suspended under the skylights, by which the officers and instructors below could observe the ship's course.

The log indicated that the ship was making six knots an hour, the rate being ascertained every two hours, and entered on the log-slate, to be used in making up the "dead reckoning." The Young America had taken her "departure," that is, left the last land to be seen, at half past three o'clock. At four, when the log was heaved, she had made three miles; at six, fifteen miles; at eight, the wind diminishing and the log indicating but four knots, only eight miles were to be added for the two hours' run, making twenty-three miles in all. The first sea day would end at twelve o'clock on the morrow, when the log-slate would indicate the total of nautical miles the ship had run after taking her departure. This is called her dead reckoning, which may be measured off on the chart, and should carry the vessel to the point indicated by the observations for latitude and longitude.

The wind was very light, and studding-sails were set alow and aloft. The ship only made her six knots as she pitched gently in the long swell of the ocean. The boys were still nominally under the order of "all hands on deck," but there was nothing for them to do, with the exception of the wheelmen, and they were gazing at the receding land behind them. They were taking their last view of the shores of their native land. Doubtless some of them were inclined to be sentimental, but most of them were thinking of the pleasant sights they were to see, and the exciting scenes in which they were to engage on the other side of the rolling ocean, and were as jolly as though earth had no sorrows for them.

The principal and the professors were pacing the quarter-deck, and doubtless some of them were wondering whether boys like the crew of the Young America could be induced to study and recite their lessons amid the excitement of crossing the Atlantic, and the din of the great commercial cities of the old world. The teachers were energetic men, and they were hopeful, at least, especially as study and discipline were the principal elements of the voyage, and each pupil's privileges were to depend upon his diligence and his good behavior. It would be almost impossible for a boy who wanted to go to Paris while the ship was lying at Havre, so far to neglect his duties as to forfeit the privilege of going. As these gentlemen have not been formally introduced, the "faculty" of the ship is here presented: —

Robert Lowington, *Principal.*
Rev. Thomas Agneau, *Chaplain.*
Dr. Edward B. Winstock, *Surgeon.*

INSTRUCTORS.

John Paradyme, A. M., *Greek and Latin.*
Richard Modelle, *Reading and Grammar.*
Charles C. Mapps, A. M., *Geography and History.*
James E. Fluxion, *Mathematics.*
Abraham Carboy, M. D., *Chemistry and Nat. Phil.*
Adolph Badois, *French and German.*

These gentlemen were all highly accomplished teachers in their several departments, as the progress of the students during the preceding year fully proved. They were interested in their work, and in sympathy with the boys, as well as with the principal.

It was a very quiet time on board, and the crew were collected in little groups, generally talking of the sights they were to see. In the waist were Shuffles, Monroe, and Wilton, all feuds among them having been healed. They appeared to be the best of friends, and it looked ominous for the discipline of the ship to see them reunited. Shuffles was powerful for good or evil, as he chose, and Mr. Lowington regretted that he had fallen from his high position, fearing that the self-respect which had sustained him as an officer would desert him as a seaman, and permit him to fall into excesses.

Shuffles was more dissatisfied and discontented than

he had ever been before. He had desired to make the tour of Europe with his father, and he was sorely disappointed when denied this privilege; for with the family he would be free from restraint, and free from hard study. When he lost his rank as an officer, he became desperate and reckless. To live in the steerage and do seaman's duty for three months, after he had enjoyed the luxuries of authority, and of a stateroom in the after cabin, were intolerable. After the cabin offices had been distributed, he told Monroe that he intended to run away that night; but he had found no opportunity to do so; and it was unfortunate for his shipmates that he did not.

"This isn't bad — is it, Shuffles?" said Wilton, as the ship slowly ploughed her way through the billows.

"I think it is. I had made up my mouth to cross the ocean in a steamer, and live high in London and Paris," replied Shuffles. "I don't relish this thing, now."

"Why not?" asked Wilton.

"I don't feel at home here."

"I do."

"Because you never were anywhere else. I ought to be captain of this ship."

"Well, you can be, if you have a mind to work for it," added Monroe.

"Work for it! That's played out. I must stay in the steerage three months, at any rate; and that while the burden of the fun is going on. If we were going to lie in harbor, or cruise along the coast, I would go in for my old place."

"But Carnes is out of the way now, and your

chance is better this year than it was last," suggested Monroe.

"I know that, but I can't think of straining every nerve for three months, two of them while we are going from port to port in Europe. When we go ashore at Queenstown, I shall have to wear a short jacket, instead of the frock coat of an officer; and I think the jacket would look better on some younger fellow."

"What are you going to do, Shuffles?" asked Wilton.

"I'd rather be a king among hogs, than a hog among kings."

"What do you mean by that?"

"No matter; there's time enough to talk over these things."

"Do you mean a mutiny?" laughed Wilton.

"Haven't you forgotten that?"

"No."

"I wonder what Lowington would say, if he knew I had proposed such a thing," added Shuffles, thoughtfully.

"He did know it, at the time you captured the runaways, for I told him."

"Did you?" demanded Shuffles, his brow contracting with anger.

"I told you I would tell him, and I did," answered Wilton. "You were a traitor to our fellows, and got us into a scrape."

"I was an officer then."

"No matter for that. Do you suppose, if I were an

officer, I would throw myself in your way when you were up to anything?"

"I don't know whether you would or not; but I wouldn't blow on you, if you had told me anything in confidence. What did Lowington say?"

"Nothing; he wouldn't take any notice of what I said."

"That was sensible on his part. One thing is certain, Wilton: you can't be trusted."

"You mustn't make me mad, then."

"I will keep things to myself hereafter," growled Shuffles.

"Don't be savage. You served me a mean trick, and I paid you off for it; so we are square."

"We will keep square then, and not open any new accounts."

"But you will want me when anything is up," laughed Wilton. "What would you do without me in getting up a mutiny?"

"Who said anything about a mutiny?"

"I know you are thinking over something, and you don't mean to submit to the discipline of the ship, if you can help it."

"Well, I can't help it."

"There goes the boatswain's whistle, piping to muster," said Monroe.

"Confound the boatswain's whistle!" growled Shuffles. "I don't like the idea of running every time he pipes."

Very much to the surprise of his companions, Shuffles, his irritation increased by the conduct of Wilton, took no notice of the call, and went forward, instead of aft. His companions, more wise and prudent, walked up to the hatch, which Mr. Lowington had just mounted.

"Groom, tell Shuffles to come aft," said the principal to one of the midshipmen.

The officer obeyed the order; Shuffles flatly refused to go aft. Mr. Lowington descended from his rostrum, and went forward to enforce obedience. This event created a profound sensation among the students.

"Shuffles," said Mr. Lowington, sternly.

"Sir," replied the malcontent, in a surly tone.

"The boatswain piped the crew to muster."

"I heard him."

"You did not obey the call. I sent for you, and you refused to come."

"I don't think I ought to obey the boatswain's call."

"May I ask why not?"

"I've been an officer three terms, and I should be now if we had had fair play," growled Shuffles.

"I am not disposed to argue this point in your present frame of mind. I order you to go aft."

"And I won't go!" replied Shuffles, impudently.

"Mr. Peaks," said the principal, calling the senior boatswain.

"Here, sir," replied Peaks, touching his hat to the principal.

"Mr. Leech," added Mr. Lowington.

"Here, sir."

"Walk this young gentleman aft."

"Let me alone!" cried Shuffles, as Peaks placed his hand upon him.

"Gently, my sweet lamb," said the boatswain, with affected tenderness.

"Take your hands off me!" roared the mutinous pupil, as he struggled to release himself from the grasp of the stalwart seaman.

Peaks took him by the collar with one hand, and held his wrist with the other, on one side, while Leech did the same on the other side.

"Walk him aft," repeated the principal.

"Mr. Fluxion, may I trouble you to bring up the irons?" continued Mr. Lowington, when the boatswain and carpenter had "walked" the rebel aft, in spite of his struggling and kicking.

"Irons!" gasped Shuffles, as he heard the request of the principal.

He trembled with rage as he uttered the word. The irons seemed to pierce his soul. Probably he did not think that the son of a wealthy gentleman would be compelled to submit to such an indignity as being put in irons.

Mr. Fluxion came on deck with a pair of handcuffs. It was the first time they had been seen, and no student even knew there were any on board. The discipline of the ship had been as gentle as it was firm, and this was the first time such instruments were necessary.

"Mr. Peaks, put the irons on him!" said Mr. Lowington, his usual dignity unruffled by angry emotions.

"Don't put them on me!" cried Shuffles, making an effort to disengage himself from the grasp of his captors.

"Put them on at once!" added the principal.

"You shall not put them on me! I will die first!" roared the rebel.

It was easier to talk than to do, in the hands of two sturdy sailors, one of whom had used the cat in the navy, when its use was tolerated. Shuffles did not die, and he was ironed, in spite of his struggles and his protest.

CHAPTER IX.

THE WATCH-BILL.

SHUFFLES struggled with the irons and with the stout men who held him until he had exhausted himself; and then, because his frame, rather than his spirit, was worn down, he was quiet. It was the first case of severe discipline that had occurred on board, and it created a tremendous sensation among the students.

Mr. Lowington stood with folded arms, watching the vain struggles of the culprit, until he was reduced to a state of comparative calmness. He looked sad, rather than angry, and his dignity was not impaired by the assault upon his authority.

"Shuffles, I am sorry to see one who has been an officer of the ship reduced to your condition; but discipline must and shall be maintained," said the principal. "We are on the high seas now, and disobedience is dangerous. You led me to believe that you had reformed your life and conduct."

"It isn't my fault," replied Shuffles, angrily.

"You had better not reply to me in that tone," added Mr. Lowington, mildly.

"Yes, I will!"

"Mr. Topliffe," continued the principal.

"Here, sir," replied the head steward

"You will have the brig cleared out for use."

"Yes, sir;" and the head steward went below to obey the order.

There was not a boy on board who knew what the "brig" was, though the establishment had existed in the steerage from the time when the boys first went on board the ship. It had never before been required for use, and Mr. Lowington had carefully veiled every disagreeable feature of discipline, until it was necessary to exhibit it. The brig was the prison of the ship — the lock-up. It was located under and abaft the main ladder, in the steerage, being an apartment five feet in length by three feet in width. The partitions which enclosed it were composed of upright planks, eight inches in width, with spaces between them for the admission of light and air.

The brig had been used as a store room for bedding by the stewards, and the students never suspected, till Shuffles' case came up, that it was not built for a closet. Mr. Topliffe and his assistants removed the blankets and comforters from this lock-up, and prepared it for the reception of the refractory pupil. When the room was ready he went on deck, and reported the fact to the principal.

"Shuffles, our discipline has always been of the mildest character," said Mr. Lowington, breaking the impressive silence which reigned on deck. "I regret to be compelled to resort to force in any form; even now I would avoid it."

"You needn't, on my account," replied Shuffles,

shaking his head. "You have done your worst already."

"Mr. Peaks, take him below, lock him up in the brig, and bring the key to me."

The manacled rebel made another effort to resist, but the stout sailors easily handled him, and bore him down into the steerage. He was thrust into the brig, ironed as he was, and the door locked upon him. Shuffles glanced at the interior of the prison, and broke out into a contemptuous laugh. He then commenced kicking the pales of the partition; but he might as well have attempted to break through the deck beneath.

"Shuffles," said Peaks, in a low tone, when he had locked the door, "be a man. You act like a spoiled child now."

"I have been insulted and abused," replied Shuffles, fiercely.

"No, you haven't. Aboard almost any ship, you would have got a knock on the head with a handspike before this time. Don't make a fool of yourself. You are only making yourself ridiculous now — 'pon my word as an old sailor, you are."

"I'll have satisfaction."

"No, you won't, unless you break your own head. I want to advise you, as a friend, not to make a fool of yourself. I'm sorry for you, my lad."

"Don't talk to me."

"I can forgive you for disobeying orders, but I can't forgive you for being a fool. Now, keep quiet, and be a man."

The well-meant effort of the boatswain to pacify the

culprit was a failure, and Peaks, going on deck, delivered the key of the brig to Mr. Lowington. Shuffles kicked against the partition till he was tired of the exercise.

"Young gentlemen, to-day we enter upon a new experience on shipboard," said the principal, without making any further allusion to Shuffles. "Our short trips last season were so timed that we kept no regular night watches, and, with two or three exceptions, the ship was at anchor when you slept. Of course that is not practicable on a long voyage, and you must all do duty by night as well as by day.

"This has been a difficult matter to arrange, for you are all too young to be deprived of your regular sleep, though in heavy weather I am afraid you will lose your rest to some extent. At eight o'clock this evening the starboard watch will be on duty. We have four times as many hands on board the Young America as are usually employed in merchant ships, so that a quarter watch will be able to handle the ship on all ordinary occasions. We shall, therefore, keep a quarter watch on ship's duty at all times through the twenty-four hours.

"During the night, including the time from eight in the evening until eight in the morning, each quarter watch will be on duty two hours, and then off six hours; and each hand will obtain six consecutive hours' sleep every night. At eight this evening, the first part of the starboard watch will have the ship in charge, and all others may turn in and sleep. At ten, the second part of the starboard watch will be called, without disturbing any others. At twelve, the first part of the port watch will be summoned; at two, the second part; and so on till eight in the morning.

"The first part of the starboard watch, which turned in at ten, will sleep till four, giving them six hours of rest all together, and they may turn in again at six o'clock, when relieved by the second part, and sleep till half past seven, which is breakfast time for those off duty.

"During the daytime, from eight in the morning till eight in the evening, the same routine will be observed. To-morrow, at eight in the morning, the first part of the port watch will take charge of the ship till ten; the second part will be off duty, and the time will be their own, to use as they think proper. At ten, the second part will be in charge, and the first will have their own time till twelve. All the starboard watch, during these four hours, will study and recite. In the afternoon the same course will be pursued with the other watch. Do you understand it?"

"Yes, sir," replied the boys.

"By this arrangement you will average three hours of duty every night. To-night the port watch will be on deck two hours, and the starboard watch, whose turn will come twice, four hours; but to-morrow night the operation will be reversed, and the port will have the deck four hours, and the starboard but two. Two copies of the watch bill will be posted in the steerage, and one in the after cabin. Young gentlemen, I recommend you to study it, until you are perfectly familiar with its requirements."

"How is it with the officers, Mr. Lowington?"

asked Paul Kendall, who was generally the spokesman for his companions.

"The officers are divided into watches in precisely the same manner as the crew. To the starboard watch belong the first and third lieutenant, the second and fourth master, and the first and third midshipman, which makes one officer of each grade for each quarter watch," replied Mr. Lowington. "Their off-time and study-time correspond with those of the crew."

It is quite possible that the officers and crew of the Young America understood the complicated arrangement of the principal. If they did not, they could refer to the posted document; and, as we cannot deprive our readers of this privilege, we insert in full,* the

WATCH BILL.

FIRST DAY.

First Watch, from 8 till 12 P. M.

From 8 till 10. 1st Lieut., 2d Master, 1st Mid. First Part of the Starboard Watch.

From 10 till 12. 3d Lieut., 4th Master, 3d Mid. Second Part of the Starboard Watch.

Mid Watch, from 12 till 4 A. M.

From 12 till 2. 2d Lieut., 1st Master, 2d Mid. First Part of the Port Watch.

From 2 till 4. 4th Lieut., 3d Master, 4th Mid. Second Part of the Port Watch.

Morning Watch, from 4 *till* 8 *A. M.*

From 4 till 6. 1st Lieut., 2d Master, 1st Mid. First Part of the Starboard Watch.

From 6 till 8. 3d Lieut., 4th Master, 3d Mid. Second Part of the Starboard Watch.

Forenoon Watch, from 8 *till* 12 *A. M.*

From 8 till 10. 2d Lieut., 1st Master, 2d Mid. First Part of the Port Watch. Second Part of Port Watch off Duty. All the Starboard Watch study and recite till 12.

From 10 till 12. 4th Lieut., 3d Master, 4th Mid. Second Part of Port Watch. First Part of Port Watch off Duty.

Afternoon Watch, from 12 *till* 4 *P. M.*

From 12 till 2. 1st Lieut., 2d Master, 1st Mid. First Part of Starboard Watch. Second Part of the Starboard Watch off Duty. All the Port Watch study and recite till 4.

From 2 till 4. 3d Lieut., 4th Master, 3d Mid. Second Part of the Starboard Watch. First Part of the Starboard Watch off Duty.

First Dog Watch, from 4 *till* 6 *P. M.*

From 4 till 5. 2d Lieut., 1st Master, 2d Mid. First Part of the Port Watch. Second Part of the Port Watch off Duty. All the Starboard Watch study and recite till 6.

From 5 till 6. 4th Lieut., 3d Master, 4th Mid. Second Part of the Port Watch. First Part of the Port Watch off Duty.

Second Dog Watch, from 6 till 8 P. M.

From 6 till 7. 1st Lieut., 2d Master, 1st Mid. First Part of the Starboard Watch. Second Part of the Starboard Watch off Duty. All the Port Watch study and recite till 8.

From 7 till 8. 3d Lieut., 4th Master, 3d Mid. Second Part of the Starboard Watch. First Part of the Starboard Watch off Duty.

Breakfast.

Port Watch,	$7\frac{1}{2}$ o'clock.
Starboard Watch,	8 o'clock.

Dinner.

Starboard Watch,	$11\frac{1}{2}$ o'clock.
Port Watch,	12 o'clock.

Supper.

Starboard Watch,	$5\frac{1}{2}$ o'clock.
Port Watch,	6 o'clock.

The watch bill for the second day was the same, with the exception of the names of the watches and quarter watches. The entire programme was reversed by the operation of the dog watches, which substituted "port" for "starboard," and "starboard" for "port," in the next day's routine.

When the boys were permitted to go below, they rushed to the watch bills, and studied them faithfully, till they fully understood the programme. Each student ascertained his duty for the night, and his off-time and study-hours for the next day, which were included in the first day's bill.

"I go on at twelve o'clock," said Paul Kendall, in the after cabin, when he had examined the bill.

"And I go on deck at eight o'clock," added Joseph Haven, the first lieutenant. "I shall have a chance to sleep from ten till four in the morning, and an hour and a half, from six till half past seven."

"I shall have my watch below from two till breakfast time. I don't think we need wear ourselves out under this arrangement."

"No; I thought we should be obliged to take four hours of duty at a time on deck."

"How will it be when we have rough weather?" asked Paul.

"I don't know; I suppose we must take our chances then."

"What do you think of Shuffles' case?" added Paul.

"He will get the worst of it."

"I'm sorry for him. He behaved first rate last year, though they say he used to be a hard fellow."

"What's the use of a fellow doing as he has done?" said Haven, with palpable disgust. "He can't make anything by it."

"Of course he can't."

"I would rather have him in the cabin than in the steerage, for he will not obey orders; and when he is ugly, he is a perfect tiger. I wonder what Mr. Lowington is going to do with him. There is no such thing as expelling a fellow in this institution now. If he means to be cross-grained, he can keep us in hot water all the time."

The officers were too much excited by the fact that the ship was outward bound to remain long in the cabin, and they returned to the deck to watch the progress of the vessel. At eight o'clock the Young America was out of sight of land, though it would have been too dark to see it ten miles distant. The quartermaster, at the helm, struck eight bells, which were repeated on the forecastle.

"All the first part of the starboard watch, ahoy!" shouted the boatswain, for it was now time to commence the programme of regular sea duty.

The first lieutenant took his place, as officer of the deck, near the helm; the second master on the forecastle, and the third midshipman in the waist. The first part of the starboard watch were stationed in various parts of the deck. Of the four quartermasters, one was attached to each quarter watch. The wheel was given to two hands for the first hour, and two were placed on the top-gallant forecastle, to act as the lookout men, to be relieved after one hour's service. The rest of the boys were required to keep awake, but no special duty was assigned to them. There were hands enough on deck to "tack ship," or to take in the sails, one or two at a time.

Though the ship was nominally in the hands and under the direction of her juvenile officers, who performed all the duties required in working her, yet they were closely watched by the principal, who, if there was anything wrong, informed the captain of the fact. The commander kept no watch, but he was responsible for every manœuvre, and for the regular routine of duty. Mr. Lowington seldom spoke to any other officer in regard to ship's duty or the navigation.

When the watch was set, at eight bells, most of the boys who were off duty went into the steerage. Some of them turned in; but the novelty of the occasion was too great to permit them to sleep. They collected in groups, to talk over the prospects of the voyage, and the duties required of them, as indicated by the watch bill.

Shuffles sat on a stool in the brig, still nursing his wrath. When his supper was carried to him by the steward, his irons had been taken off. He refused to eat, and the food was removed. As he was now quiet, the irons were not replaced. The prisoner was far from penitent for his offence.

Mr. Agneau, the chaplain, was very much concerned about the prisoner. He was shocked by his disobedience, and pained to find that one who had done so well could do so ill. The case had been fully considered in the professors' cabin; and Mr. Lowington declared that Shuffles should stay in the brig till he had repented of his folly, and promised obedience for the future. The chaplain was a tender-hearted man, and he thought that some gentle words might touch the feelings of the prisoner, and bring him to a sense of duty. With the principal's permission, therefore, he paid a visit to Shuffles in the evening.

"I am very sorry to find you here, Shuffles," said Mr. Agneau, when he had locked the door behind him.

"Has Lowington sent you to torment me?" demanded the prisoner.

"Mr. Lowington, you mean," added the chaplain, gently.

"No, I mean Lowington. When a man has abused and insulted me, I can't stop to put a handle to his name."

"I regret to find you in such an unhappy frame of mind, my young friend. I came here of my own accord, to do what I might to help you."

"Did you, indeed!" sneered Shuffles.

"That was my only object."

"Was it? Well, if you want to help me, you will induce Lowington to let me out of this crib, apologize for what he has done, and give me my place in the after cabin."

"That is plainly impossible," replied the astonished chaplain.

"Then you can't do anything for me; and I think I can take care of myself."

"I entreat you, my young friend, to consider the error of your ways."

"There is no error in my ways, Mr. Agneau."

"You are unreasonable."

"No, I'm not. I only want what is fair and right."

"Was it right for you, Shuffles, to refuse obedience to the principal, when he told you to go aft?"

"I have always obeyed all proper orders; and under the circumstances, I think it was right for me to refuse."

"You fill me with amazement!" exclaimed the chaplain.

"You know it was not fair to give out the offices by last year's marks," protested Shuffles.

"On the contrary, I think it was entirely fair."

"I haven't anything more to say if it was," replied Shuffles, in surly tones.

The chaplain, finding the prisoner was not in a proper frame of mind for edifying conversation, left him, and returned to the professors' cabin. The boys had been forbidden to go near the brig, or to speak to the prisoner; and thus far no one had exhibited any disposition to disregard the order. Many of them, as they passed near the brig, glanced curiously at him. After the departure of the chaplain, Wilton sat down on a stool near the lock-up.

"How are you, Shuffles?" said he, in a low tone.

"Come here, Wilton — will you?" replied the prisoner.

"I can't; we are not allowed to speak to you."

"What do you care for that? No one can see you."

"What do you want?"

"I want to talk with you."

"I shall be punished if I'm caught."

"You won't be caught. How are our fellows now?"

"First rate," replied Wilton, walking up and down the berth deck, rising and looking as though nothing was going on.

"You know what we were talking about just before the row," added Shuffles, drawing his stool up to the palings.

"You said you wouldn't trust me," answered Wilton, still pacing the deck in front of the brig.

"You told Lowington about something he had no business to know; but I forgive you, Wilton."

"You are very willing to forgive me, now you are in a tight place."

"It was mean of you to do it, Wilton; you can't deny that. Lowington was on the best of terms with me when I was in the after cabin, and I might have told him a hundred things about you."

"Didn't you tell him anything?"

"Not a word."

"Well, you are a good fellow, and I always thought you were. I couldn't see why you turned traitor to us when we intended to spend the Fourth of July on shore."

"I was obliged to do what I did. If I hadn't, I should have been turned out of my office."

"Perhaps you were right, Shuffles, and we won't say anything more about the past," replied Wilton, who was too willing to be on good terms with the powerful malcontent, even while he was a prisoner and in disgrace.

"Wilton, I am going to be captain of this ship within ten days," said Shuffles, in a whisper. "Now you may go and tell Lowington of that."

"Of course I shall not tell him," added Wilton, indignantly.

"I told you merely to show you that I had full confidence in you — that's all. You can betray me if you wish to do so."

"I don't wish to do anything of the kind. Of course we shall always go together, as we did before you were an officer."

"I shall be an officer again soon."

"What's the use of talking about such a thing?"

"I shall."

"Do you mean to get up the mutiny?"

"I do. I feel more like it now than I ever did before," replied Shuffles; and his low tones came from between his closed teeth.

"It's no use to think of such a thing. It's too wild."

"No matter if it is; it shall be carried out."

"The fellows won't go in for it; they won't dare to do it."

"Yes, they will. I know them better than you do, Wilton. It isn't quite time yet; but in three or four days they will be ready for anything."

"You can't bring them up to what you mean."

"Yes, I can."

"What do you expect to do, locked up in that place?" demanded Wilton, incredulously.

"When I get ready to go out of this place, I shall go. I needn't stay here any longer than I please."

"Do you really mean to get up a mutiny?"

"Hush! Don't call it by that name."

"What shall I call it?"

"Call it making a chain."

"I don't understand you," answered Wilton, puzzled by the expression.

"I know what I'm about, and I have got more friends in the ship than Lowington has. And I know exactly how to manage the whole thing," added Shuffles, confidently.

"But the fellows are all perfectly satisfied with their

condition. They wish to go to Europe, and are pleased with the prospect before them."

"Perhaps they are; and they shall all go to Europe, and travel about without being tied to Lowington's coat-tails. I shall come out of this place to-morrow, and we will work the thing up."

"I'm in for a time with any good fellow; but I don't think we can make this thing go," said Wilton. "Hush! Don't say another word. There comes an officer."

One bell, indicating half past eight in the evening, struck on deck. It was the duty of the master and midshipman on deck, alternately, to pass through the steerage every half hour during the watch, to see that there was no disorder, and that the lights were all secure, so as to avoid any danger from fire. Henry Martyn, the second master, performed this office on the present occasion. He descended the main ladder, and Wilton, who expected the visit when he heard the stroke of the bell, retreated to his mess room, and threw himself into his berth. Harry walked around the steerage, and glanced into the gangways, from which the rooms opened.

"Harry," said Shuffles, in a low tone, as the master was about to return to the deck.

"Did you speak to me?" asked Harry, stepping up to the bars of the cage.

"I did. Will you oblige me by telling the chaplain that I would like to see him?" added the prisoner.

"I will;" and Harry knocked at the door of the professors' cabin.

CHAPTER X.

MAKING A CHAIN.

THE chaplain was too glad of an opportunity to converse with the prisoner to refuse his request, and he hastened to the brig, hoping to find Shuffles in a better state of mind than when he had visited him before. Mr. Agneau entered the lock-up, and was securing the door behind him, when the prisoner spoke.

"You needn't lock it, sir; I will not attempt to escape," said he. "I sent for you to apologize for my rudeness."

"Indeed! Then I am very glad to see you," replied the delighted chaplain. "I have been sorely grieved at your misconduct, and I would fain have brought you to see the error of your ways."

"I see it now, sir," replied Shuffles, with apparent penitence. "I'm afraid I am a great deal worse than you think I am, sir."

"It is of no consequence what I think, Shuffles, if you are conscious of the wrong you have done," added the worthy chaplain. "You behaved exceedingly well last year, and it almost broke my heart to see you relapsing into your former evil habits."

"I am grateful to you for the interest you have

taken in me, and I assure you I have often been encouraged to do well by your kind words," continued the penitent, with due humility. "I have done wrong, and I don't deserve to be forgiven."

"'He that humbleth himself shall be exalted,'" said Mr. Agneau, gratified at the great change which had apparently been wrought in the prisoner. "If you are really sorry for your offence, Mr. Lowington, I doubt not, will pardon you, and restore you to favor again."

"I don't deserve it, sir. Since you left me, I have been thinking of my past life. I dare not tell you how bad I have been."

"You need not tell me. It is not necessary that you should confess your errors to me. There is One who knows them, and if you are sincerely repentant He will pity and forgive you."

"I think I should feel better if I told some one of my misdeeds."

"Perhaps you would; that is for you to judge. I will speak to Mr. Lowington about you to-night. What shall I say to him?"

"I hardly know. I deserve to be punished. I have done wrong, and am willing to suffer for it."

The tender-hearted chaplain thought that Shuffles was in a beautiful state of mind, and he desired to have him released at once, that he might converse with him on great themes under more favorable circumstances; but Shuffles still detained him.

"I'm afraid I have ruined myself on board this ship," continued Shuffles, persisting in his self-humiliation.

"If you manfully acknowledge your fault, you will be freely and generously forgiven."

"Mr. Lowington hates me now, after what I have done."

"O, far from it!" exclaimed the chaplain. "It will be a greater satisfaction to him than to you to forgive you. You are no longer of the opinion that you were unfairly used in the distribution of the offices, I suppose."

"Mr. Agneau, I was beside myself when I resisted the principal. I should not have done it if I had been in my right mind."

"You were very angry."

"I was — I was not myself."

"Anger often makes men crazy."

"You don't understand me, Mr. Agneau."

"Indeed, I do. You mean that you deluded yourself into the belief that you had been wronged, and that you ought not to obey the orders of your officers, and of the principal. The force that was used made you so angry that you did not know what you were about," added the sympathizing chaplain.

"In one word, Mr. Agneau, I had been drinking," said Shuffles, with something like desperation in his manner, as he bent his head, and covered his face with his hands.

"Drinking!" gasped the chaplain, filled with horror at the confession.

"I told you I was worse than you thought I was," moaned Shuffles.

"Is it possible!"

"It is true, sir; I say it with shame."

"Are you in the habit of taking intoxicating drinks?" asked the chaplain, confounded beyond measure at this complication of the difficulty.

"I am not in the habit of it, because I can't get liquor all the time. My father has wine on his table, and I always was allowed to drink one glass."

"Can it be!" ejaculated the chaplain. "A youth of seventeen —— "

"I'm eighteen now, sir."

"A youth of eighteen in the habit of taking wine!" groaned Mr. Agneau.

"I drank a great deal more than my father knew of while I was at home."

"I am amazed!"

"I knew you would be, sir; but I have told you the truth now."

"But where did you get your liquor to-day?"

"It was wine, sir."

"Where did you get it?"

"I brought two bottles on board with me when I reported for duty yesterday."

"This is terrible, Shuffles! Do you know what an awful habit you are contracting, my dear young friend?"

"I never thought much about it till to-night. It has got me into such a scrape this time, that I don't believe I shall ever drink any more."

"As you respect yourself, as you hope for peace in this world, and peace in the next, never put the cup to your lips again. 'Wine is a mocker; strong drink is raging; and whosoever is deceived thereby is not wise.' Did you drink the two bottles?"

"No, sir; only part of one bottle," replied Shuffles, with commendable promptness.

"Where is the rest of it?"

"Under my berth-sack."

"Are you willing I should take possession of it, and hand it to Mr. Lowington?"

"I will agree to anything which you think is right."

"Then I will take the wine and throw it overboard."

"Just as you think best, sir. You will find the two bottles in my berth, No. 43, Gangway D, — the forward one on the starboard side."

"I hope you will never touch the wine-cup again."

"I will not — till next time," added Shuffles, as the chaplain moved towards the door of the brig.

"'Look not thou upon the wine when it is red, when it giveth his color in the cup, at the last it biteth like a serpent, and stingeth like an adder,'" continued the chaplain, as he passed out of the lock-up.

Mr. Agneau went to the prisoner's berth, and found the two bottles of wine. They were a sufficient explanation of the remarkable conduct of Shuffles. The youth had "drank wine, and was drunken," otherwise he would not have been guilty of such flagrant disobedience. Though in his own estimation the excuse was worse than the original fault, yet it was an explanation; and if the root of the evil could be removed, the evil itself would cease to exist. The wine could be thrown overboard, and as no more could be obtained during the voyage, the good conduct of the young tippler would be insured, at least till the ship reached Queenstown, which was the port to which she was bound.

With the two bottles in his hands, the chaplain returned to the professors' cabin. Mr. Lowington was on deck. He did not deem it prudent to leave the ship in the hands of the students, at first, without any supervision, and it was arranged that the principal, Mr. Fluxion, and Mr. Peake, the boatswain, should take turns in observing the course and management of the vessel. Mr. Agneau carried the prize he had captured on deck, and informed Mr. Lowington what had just transpired in the brig.

"I knew the boy drank wine when he was at home," replied the principal; "and if he is ruined, his father must blame himself."

"But it is really shocking!" exclaimed the chaplain, as he tossed one of the bottles of wine over the rail. "How can a parent permit his son to drink wine, when he knows that more men are killed by intemperance than by war and pestilence? I am amazed!"

"So am I, Mr. Agneau."

"The boy is hardly to blame for his conduct, since he contracted this vicious habit under the eye of his father."

The discipline of the ship must be preserved."

"Certainly, Mr. Lowington."

"And the boy is just as much to blame for his act of disobedience as though it had been done in his sober senses."

"But you can afford to pardon him, under the circumstances."

"I will do that when he is willing to make a proper acknowledgment of his offence in the presence of the ship's company, before whom the act was committed."

"He is quite ready to do so now."

"If he will say as much as that to me, he shall be released at once."

"He will, sir."

"It is very strange to me that I noticed nothing peculiar in the boy's speech or manner at the time," added the principal. "He certainly did not seem to be intoxicated."

"Probably he had taken just enough to inflame his evil passions, without affecting his manner," suggested the chaplain.

"I did not even discover the odor of wine upon him."

"Perhaps you did not go near enough to him. If you please, Mr. Lowington, we will go down and see him; and you can judge for yourself whether or not it is prudent to release him."

"I will."

"Thank you, sir. I feel a deep interest in the young man, and I hope he may yet be saved."

When Mr. Agneau left the brig, after his second visit, Wilton, who was very anxious to know what Shuffles meant by "making a chain," came out of his mess room. He had been watching the chaplain, and wondering what the prisoner could have to say to him.

"What's up, Shuffles?" asked Wilton, when Mr. Agneau had left the steerage.

"I've been smoothing him down," laughed Shuffles,

with an audible chuckle. "I have concluded not to stay in here any longer."

"What do you mean?"

"I'm coming out pretty soon, though it has cost me a bottle and a half of old sherry to get out," laughed Shuffles.

"I don't know what you mean."

"I told the parson that I was drunk when I disobeyed orders, and that I was very sorry for it, and wouldn't get drunk any more."

"Did you tell him that?"

"I did; I assured him I was the worst fellow in the whole world, and ought to be hung, drawn, and quartered for my wickedness; and he swallowed it as a codfish does a clam."

"And you gave him all the wine?"

"No, I didn't; I gave him one full bottle, and what was left in the one from which we drank this afternoon. I have two more."

"We were going to have a good time with that wine."

"I have enough left."

"Where is it?"

"In my locker."

"They may find it."

"No, they won't; I will put it in some other place before inspection day. There is plenty of wine in the medical stores. It was a good joke for the parson to suppose I was drunk."

"Perhaps you were," suggested Wilton.

"I felt good; but I was as sober as I am now."

14*

"The drink I took went into my head, and I felt as though I was going up in a balloon."

"That was because you are not used to the article. It waked me up a little, but I knew what I was about."

"I think you were a confounded fool to do what you did."

"Wilton, I'm not going to live in the steerage — you may take my word for it. I've been an officer too long to come down to that. If we don't succeed in making a chain, I shall quit the concern the first time I put my foot on shore in Ireland."

"What do you mean by making a chain?" asked Wilton, eagerly.

"A chain is strong."

"Well; what of it?"

"It is composed of many links. Can't you understand that?"

"Hush up! Some one is coming," said Wilton, as he walked away from the brig.

"Here! who is that?" demanded Mr. Lowington, as he saw Wilton moving away from the lock-up.

"No. 59, sir — Wilton," replied he. "I was just going on deck to find you, sir."

"To find me?" asked the principal.

"Yes, sir. Shuffles called me when I was passing, and wished me to tell you he wanted to see you very much. I was just going after you, sir."

"If there is any blame, sir, it rests on me," interposed Shuffles, through the bars of his prison.

Mr. Lowington unlocked the door of the brig, and entered, followed by Mr. Agneau, leaving Wilton to congratulate himself on the result of the lies he had uttered.

"I am told you wish to see me, Shuffles," said the principal.

"Yes, sir; I wish to say that I am extremely sorry for what I have done."

"I thought you were crazy when you refused to obey; and now I find you were."

"I had been drinking, sir, I confess."

"Mr. Agneau has told me your story; it is not necessary to repeat it now. To-morrow I shall require you to acknowledge your error at muster, and promise obedience in the future. Are you willing to do so?"

"I am, sir."

"You are discharged from confinement then, and will at once return to your duty," replied Mr. Lowington, upon whom Shuffles did not venture to intrude his extremely penitential story. "To which watch do you belong?"

"To the port watch, first part, sir."

"It will be on deck during the first half of the mid watch, from twelve till two," added the principal, as he came out of the brig.

Mr. Lowington made no parade of what he had done. He never subjected any student to unnecessary humiliation. He indulged in no reproaches, and preached no sermons. He went on deck, intending to leave the culprit to the influence of the better thoughts which he hoped and believed had been kindled in his mind by the events of the day. Mr. Agneau remained a moment to give a final admonition to the penitent, as he regarded him, and then went to his cabin.

"Are you going to turn in, Shuffles?" asked Wilton.

"Not yet. Are there any of our fellows below?"

"Plenty of them."

"Our fellows" was a term applied to that portion of the crew who were understood to be ready for any scrape which might be suggested. Shuffles had coined the expression himself, while at the Brockway Academy, and introduced it on board the ship. Without concealment or palliation, they were bad boys. By the discipline of the ship they were kept in good order, and compelled to perform their duties.

As in every community of men or boys, where persons of kindred tastes find each other out, the bad boys in the Young America had discovered those of like tendencies, and a bond of sympathy and association had been established among them. They knew and were known of each other.

On the other hand, it is equally true, that there was a bond of sympathy and association among the good boys, as there is among good men. If a good man wishes to establish a daily prayer meeting, he does not apply to the intemperate, the profane swearers, and the Sabbath breakers of his neighborhood for help; there is a magnetism among men which leads him to the right persons. If a bad man intends to get up a mob, a raffle, or a carousal, he does not seek assistance among those who go to church every Sunday, and refrain from evil practices, either from principle or policy. He makes no mistakes of this kind.

In every community, perhaps one fourth of the whole number are positively good, and one fourth positively bad, while the remaining two fourths are more or less good or more or less bad, floating undecided between the two poles of the moral magnet, sometimes drawn one way, and sometimes the other.

The Young America was a world in herself, and the moral composition of her people was similar to that of communities on a larger scale. She had all the elements of good and evil on board. One fourth of the students were doubtless high-minded, moral young men, having fixed principles, and being willing to make great sacrifices rather than do wrong. As good behavior, as well as proficiency in the studies, was an element of success in the ship, a large proportion of the positively good boys were in the after cabin.

Another fourth of the students were reckless and unprincipled, with no respect for authority, except so far as it was purchased by fear of punishment or hope of reward. Occasionally one of this class worked his way into the cabin by superior natural ability, and a spasmodic attempt to better his condition on board.

The rest of the ship's company belonged to the indefinite, undecided class, floating more or less distant from the positive elements of good or evil. They were not bad boys, for, with proper influences, they could be, and were, kept from evil ways. They were not good boys on principle, for they could be led away in paths of error.

"Our fellows" were the positively bad boys of the floating academy; and they existed in no greater proportion in the ship's company than in the communities of the great world. To this class belonged Shuffles, Wilton, Monroe, and others. To the positively good boys belonged Gordon, Kendall, Martyn, and others — not all of them in the after cabin, by any means.

Shuffles and Wilton walked forward to find some of these kindred spirits. They seemed to know just where to look for them, for they turned in at Gangway D. Over each of the six passages from which the mess rooms opened, a lantern was suspended, besides four more in the middle of the steerage. It was light enough, therefore, in the rooms for their occupants to read coarse print.

In the lower berths of mess room No. 8 lay two students, while another sat on a stool between them. Their occupation was sufficient evidence that they belonged to "our fellows," for they were shaking props for money, on a stool between the bunks. As Shuffles and Wilton approached, they picked up the props and the stakes, and drew back into their beds.

"It's Shuffles," said Philip Sanborn. "How did you get out?"

"Worked out," replied Shuffles, gayly.

"You don't mean to say you broke jail?"

"No; that would have been too much trouble. There was an easier way, and I took that."

"How was it?"

"Why, I soft-sawdered the parson, and he soft-sawdered Lowington."

"It's all right; go ahead with the game," said Lynch, as he produced the props again.

Sanborn placed the money on the stool, consisting of two quarters in fractional currency. Lynch shook the props, and dropped them on the stool.

"A nick!" exclaimed he, snatching the money. "I'll go you a half now."

"Half it is," replied Sanborn, as he placed the requisite sum on the money the other laid down.

Lynch rattled the props, and threw them down again.

"A browner!" cried he, intensely excited, as he seized the money with eager hand.

"Don't talk so loud, you fool!" added Sanborn. "The fellows are asleep above us, and you will wake them up. I'll go you a half again."

"Half it is!" replied Lynch, in a whisper, as he shook again.

"An out!" said Sanborn, picking up the money.

"Three bells! Dry up!" interposed Wilton. "One of the officers of the deck will be down in a minute."

The young gamblers put away the implements, and drew back into their berths until the inspecting officer had looked into the room. When the master had gone on deck again, the play was resumed, and Shuffles and Wilton watched it with deep interest.

Gambling was a new thing on board the Young America. It had not been practised at all in the preceding year, having been introduced by Shuffles and Monroe, who had visited a prop saloon in the city where they resided, during their late furlough. Each of them had brought a set of props on board, with which they intended to amuse themselves during the voyage. As yet, the practice was confined to a few of " our fellows ; " but the crew in the steerage were certainly in very great danger of being carried away by the passion for gaming, for it was spreading rapidly.

The prop-shaking was carried on in the mess rooms, while the students were off duty. Shuffles had played with half a dozen boys the night before ; Sanborn and Lynch had been engaged in the game since the first watch was set, and another party had been employed in the same manner in another room. All of the boys were supplied with money in considerable sums, generally in sovereigns and half sovereigns, for use when they reached Europe. It was changing hands now, though no one had as yet been particularly lucky.

" Have a game, Shuffles ? " said Lynch, when Sanborn declared that he had no money left but gold.

" No," replied Shuffles, " I shall not play any more."

" Why not ? "

" I haven't time ; and I don't want to become too fond of it."

" Haven't time ! " exclaimed Lynch.

" No ; I've got a big job on my hands."

" What's that ? "

" Making a chain."

" Making a what ? "

" Making a chain."

" A watch chain ? "

" I think it will be a watch chain ; but I'll tell you about it when we are alone. Do you understand ? "

" No, I don't."

" Keep still then."

Shuffles turned in, and the others followed his example. He did not sleep, if they did, for his soul was full of rage and malice. He was studying up the means of revenge; and he had matured a project, so foolhardy that it was ridiculous, and his mind was fully occupied with it.

At twelve o'clock he was called to take his place with the first part of the port watch on deck. Belonging to each quarter watch, there were five petty officers, four of whom were to call the portion of the crew who were to relieve those on duty. Shuffles was called by one of these.

The wind was freshening when he went on deck, and the ship was going rapidly through the water. At the last heaving of the log she was making eleven knots, with her studding sails still set. Mr. Fluxion came on deck at eight bells.

Wilton, Sanborn, and Adler were in the watch with Shuffles, and the malcontent lost not a moment in pushing forward the scheme he had matured. Fortunately, or unfortunately, he was placed on the lookout with Wilton, and the solitude of the top-gallant forecastle afforded them a good opportunity for the conference.

CHAPTER XI.

THE GAMBLERS IN NO. 8.

"IT'S coming on to blow," said Wilton, as the lookouts took their stations on the top-gallant forecastle.

"I don't think it will blow much; it is only freshening a little," replied Shuffles.

"Now, what about the mutiny?" demanded Wilton, impatiently, after he had become more accustomed to the dash of the sea under the bows of the ship.

"Don't call it by that name," replied Shuffles, earnestly. "Never use that word again."

"That's what you mean — isn't it? You might as well call things by their right names."

"It's an ugly word, and if any one should happen to hear it, their attention would be attracted at once. We musn't get in the habit of using it."

"I don't know what you are going to do yet," added Wilton.

"It's a big job; but I mean to put it through, even if I am sure of failure."

"What's the use of doing that? Do you want to get the fellows into a scrape for nothing?"

"There will be no failure, Wilton; you may depend upon that. There will be a row on board within a day or two, and, if I mistake not, nearly all the fellows will be so mad that they will want to join us."

"What row?"

"Do you know the reason why I wouldn't shake props this evening?"

"I'm sure I don't."

"Lowington has found out what is going on in the rooms."

"He hasn't, though!"

"Yes, he has."

"How do you know?"

"What odds does it make how I know?" answered Shuffles, impatiently, for Wilton was much too inquisitive to suit his purposes. "I talked with the chaplain half an hour to-night. When he went to my berth after the wine, I rather think he heard the rattle of the props. At any rate the whole thing will be broken up to-morrow or next day."

"I don't see how that will make a row. Not more than a dozen fellows have played any; and they won't think of making a row about that."

"You see!" added Shuffles, confidently.

"Ugh!" exclaimed Wilton, as a cloud of spray dashed over the bow, and drenched the lookout; but they wore their pea-jackets, and such an occurrence was to be expected at sea.

"Stand by to take in studding sails!" shouted Paul Kendall, who was the officer of the deck; and the order was repeated by his subordinates in the waist and on the forecastle.

"We must go," said Wilton; and they descended from their position.

The wind had continued to freshen, until the ship labored somewhat under her heavy press of canvas. It was the policy of the principal to go as easily and comfortably as possible, and he had directed Mr. Fluxion, if the wind continued to increase, to have the sail reduced, though neither the safety of the ship nor of the spars absolutely required such a step. The quarter watch on deck was sufficient to perform this labor.

"Lay aloft, foretopmen!" said the second lieutenant; and those of the watch who had their stations in the fore rigging sprang up the shrouds. "Stand by the halyard of the top-gallant studding sails! Man the tacks and sheets!"

"All ready, sir," reported the second midshipman, who was in the foretop, superintending the operation.

"Lower on the halyards! Ease off the tacks, and haul on the sheet!"

The two top-gallant studding-sails were thus brought into the top, where they were made up. The foretopmast and the lower studding sails were taken in by a similar routine, and the Young America then moved along less furiously through the water.

"Now about the chain," said Wilton, when the the lookouts had returned to their stations.

"Let me see; where did I leave off?" replied Shuffles.

"You said there was to be a row; which I don't believe."

"I may be mistaken about that; if I am, the job will be all the more difficult. Lowington has got us out to sea now, and, in my opinion, he means to shake us up. He is a tyrant at heart, and he will carry it with a high hand. I hate the man!" added Shuffles, with savage earnestness.

"You, may, but the fellows don't generally."

"They will as soon as he begins to put the twisters on them. You won't hear him say, 'If you please, young gentlemen,' now that we are in blue water. You know how savage he was with me."

"Well, but you were disobedient. You told him, up and down, you wouldn't do what he ordered you to do."

"No matter for that. You had a chance to see the spirit of the man. He was a perfect demon. He put me in irons!" exclaimed Shuffles, still groaning under this indignity. "I have been insulted and outraged, and I will teach him that Bob Shuffles is not to be treated in that manner! I will be revenged upon him, if it costs me my life."

"The fellows won't go into any such desperate game as that," replied Wilton, cautiously.

"But there will be fun in the thing," added the malcontent, softening his tone. "We shall have the ship all to ourselves. We needn't trouble ourselves anything about Latin and Greek, and trigonometry and algebra. We shall go in for a good time generally."

"It is all moonshine; it can't be done. What's the use of talking about such a thing?" said Wilton.

"It can be done, and it shall be," replied Shuffles, stamping his foot on the deck.

"How?"

"I am not quite ready to tell you yet."

"Very well; I don't want to know anything more

about it," answered the timid conspirator, who was almost disgusted at the foolhardiness of the plan.

"I can get along without you," added Shuffles, with assumed indifference.

"I would rather have you do so."

"All right; but you will want to come in when we have got along a little farther."

"Perhaps I shall; if I do, I suppose the door will be open to me."

"It may be open; but perhaps you can't walk into the cabin then."

"Why not?"

"Do you suppose the fellows who do the burden of the work are going to be shut out of the cabin? If you join at the eleventh hour, you will have to be what you are now — a foremast hand."

"What can I be if I join now?"

"Second or third officer."

"Who will be first."

"I can't mention his name yet. He belongs in the cabin now."

"You don't mean so!" said Wilton, astonished to learn that his bold companion expected to find friends among the present officers of the ship.

"I know what I'm about," replied Shuffles, confidently.

With this information Wilton thought more favorably of the mad enterprise. If it was to be a winning game, he wished to have a part in it; if a losing one, he desired to avoid it. There was something in the decided manner of the chief conspirator which made an impression upon this doubting mind.

"I don't want to go in till I know more about it," said he, after walking two or three times across the top-gallant forecastle.

"You can't know anything more about it until you have been toggled," replied Shuffles.

"Toggled?" repeated the sceptic, curiously.

"This thing is to be well managed, Wilton. We shall not use any hard words, that outsiders can understand; and if any of them happen to hear anything that don't concern them, they will not know what it means. Will you join, or not?"

"I will," replied Wilton, desperately.

The strange words which Shuffles used, and the confidence he manifested in the success of his project, carried the hesitating lookout man. He was fascinated by the "clap-trap" which the leader of "our fellows" had adopted to help along his scheme, for it promised to afford no little excitement during the voyage.

"Now you talk like a man, Wilton," replied Shuffles. "You shall be a member of the league at once."

"What's the league?"

"The Chain League."

"Upon my word, Shuffles, you have been reading yellow-covered novels to some purpose."

"I didn't get this idea from a novel. I invented it myself."

"The Chain League!" repeated Wilton, who was pleased with the title of the conspirators.

"It will be called simply 'The Chain.' I am the

first member, and you are the second; or you will be when you have been toggled."

"Toggled again!" laughed Wilton. "What do you mean?"

"Initiated."

"Go ahead, then."

"Repeat after me."

"Go on," replied Wilton, deeply interested in the proceeding, even while he was amused at its formality.

"*I am a link of the chain.*"

"I am a link of the chain," repeated Wilton.

"*I will obey my superior officers.*"

"I will obey my superior officers."

"*And I will reveal none of its secrets.*"

"And I will reveal none of its secrets."

"*This I promise——*"

"This I promise——"

"*On penalty of falling overboard accidentally.*"

"On penalty of what?" demanded Wilton, both puzzled and terrified by the mysterious words.

"Repeat the words after me. On penalty," said Shuffles, sternly.

"I know what the words are, but I'll be hanged if I will repeat them. 'Falling overboard accidentally!' What does that mean?"

"It means that, if you betray the secrets of The Chain, you might fall overboard accidentally, some day."

"That is, you would push me over when no one was looking," added Wilton, involuntarily retreating from the conspirator, whom, for the moment, he regarded as a very dangerous companion.

"That's what the words mean," replied Shuffles, coolly.

"Have I been toggled?" demanded Wilton.

"No; you didn't repeat all the words."

"Then you needn't toggle me any more. I've got enough of this thing."

"All right; just as you say. But I can tell you this, my dear fellow; if you should whisper the first word of what has passed between us to-night, you might fall overboard," continued Shuffles, sharply, as he laid his hand on his companion's shoulder.

Wilton grasped the sheet of the fore-topmast staysail, which was the nearest rope to him, and held on as though he was then in imminent danger of "falling overboard accidentally."

"I won't say a word," protested he, vehemently; for he did not know but that Shuffles was wicked enough to push him into the sea.

"Wilton, you are a fool!" added the disappointed conspirator, with deep disgust. "Why didn't you say what I told you?"

"I don't want to be bound in any such way as that," replied the terrified student.

"Don't you see it is only a form?"

"No, I don't; or if it is, I don't want anything to do with such forms. You won't get any fellows to be toggled in that way."

"Yes, I shall; I shall get plenty of them. They are not babies, like you."

"I'm not a baby."

"Yes, you are — a great calf! What are you afraid of?"

"I'm not afraid; I didn't think you meant to have any murder in your Chain."

"I don't; no fellow will think of such a thing as betraying one of the secrets."

"Then what's the use of having such a penalty?"

"It will prevent any fellow from opening his mouth when he ought to keep it shut."

"I don't want anything to do with a concern that means murder. I'm not any better than I should be, but I'm too good for that."

"Suit yourself; but remember, if you should happen to say a word, you will fall overboard accidentally, some night when you are on the lookout, or out on the yard-arm."

"Two bells," said Wilton, greatly relieved to hear them, for he did not like to stand any longer on the top-gallant forecastle, where there was no railing, with such a dangerous fellow as Shuffles proved to be.

Two other members of the watch were sent forward to take their places. Wilton and Shuffles went down and mingled with their shipmates, who were talking about what they should do and what they should see in Ireland, where the ship would first make a harbor. Wilton breathed easier, and the topic was a more agreeable one than the dark and terrible matter which had been under discussion on the top-gallant forecastle.

Shuffles was disappointed by the scruples of his generally unscrupulous companion. He regarded the machinery of the plot, the clap-trap of the secret league, as decidedly attractive; and he depended largely upon it to influence his companions. Though he claimed that his plan was original, it was suggested by a secret political organization in Europe, of which he had read in a pamphlet; and the idea had doubtless been modified by his more extensive readings in the department of fiction, in which midnight juntos laid out robbery, treason, and murder; Venetian tales in which bravos, assassins, and decayed princes in disguise largely figured; in which mysterious pass-words opened mysterious dungeons beneath ruined castles; in which bravo met bravo, and knew him by some mysterious sign, or cabalistic word.

Shuffles had a taste for these things, and out of his lively imagination he had coined a similar association to be recruited from the crew of the Young America, which was to redress fancied wrongs, and even take the ship out of the hands of the principal. He could think of nothing but this brilliant enterprise; and while his shipmates were talking of the future, and indulging in the old salts' vocation of "spinning yarns," he was busy maturing the details of "The Chain League." He did not, for reasons best known to himself, attempt to make any more proselytes that night.

The ship continued to go along easily on her course till morning. It was a clear night, and though the wind was fresh, the sea was not rough, and the Young America behaved very handsomely. The programme for the watches was carried out to the letter, but on the first night out, the boys were too much excited by the novelty of the situation to be able to sleep much.

At eight bells in the morning, after the port watch had breakfasted, all the students off duty attended prayers. Then the starboard watch had their morning meal, after which all hands were piped to muster.

Mr. Lowington mounted the hatch, and it was understood that the case of discipline which had come up the day before was to be settled now.

"Shuffles!" called the principal.

The culprit came forward.

"Are you still of the same mind as when I saw you last evening?" continued Mr. Lowington.

"I am, sir," replied Shuffles, with a becoming exhibition of meekness.

"You will step upon the hatch, then."

Shuffles took position by the side of the principal.

"You will repeat after me," added Mr. Lowington.

The culprit was startled at these words, and began to suspect that Wilton had betrayed him in spite of his fear of falling overboard accidentally. It looked just then as though the principal intended to "toggle" him.

"I acknowledge that I have done wrong," Mr. Lowington continued.

Shuffles repeated the words, happy to find that he was not to take the obligation of "The Chain League."

"And I will hereafter endeavor to do my duty faithfully."

The promise was repeated with the lips, but of course it had no meaning, and did not reach the heart.

"That is all, Shuffles," added the principal.— "Young gentlemen, you are dismissed from muster."

This was certainly a very mild atonement for the grave offence which Shuffles had committed, and the lenity of the principal was generally commented upon by the boys. The starboard watch was piped below to study and recite, while the port watch were to be off and on during the forenoon. The first part now had the deck, while the second was off duty, and the boys belonging to it were permitted to remain on deck or to spend their time in the mess rooms. They were not allowed to linger in the steerage where the recitations were going on, but might pass directly through on their way to their apartments.

At ten o'clock the first part of the port watch was relieved, and the second part went on duty. Shuffles and Wilton were at liberty now, but there appeared to be a coldness between them, and Wilton sought another companion for his leisure hours. Sanborn and Adler belonged to his part of the watch, and he soon joined them.

"There isn't much difference between being off duty and being on," said Adler, as they seated themselves on the main hatch.

"There will be a difference when we have to make and take in sail every half hour. We had a big job taking in the studding sails last night."

"They don't drive the ship," added Sanborn. "I suppose if we were a merchantman, they would crack on all the sail she would carry."

"She goes along beautifully," said Wilton.

"She was only making five knots the last time the log was heaved."

"And the sea is as smooth as a mill-pond. We shall not get to Queenstown for two months at this rate."

"Stand by to set studding sails!" shouted Pelham, the officer of the deck.

"I wondered why they didn't do that before," said Sanborn.

The fore and main studding sails were set, two at a time, by the part of the watch on duty, the wind still being well aft.

"What shall we do?" asked Wilton, with a long yawn, after they had watched the operation of setting the studding sails for a time. "This is stupid business, and I'm getting sleepy."

"Let us go below," suggested Sanborn.

"What for? The professors won't let you speak out loud while the recitations are going on," added Adler.

"We don't want to speak out loud. What do you say to shaking a little?" continued Wilton.

"I'm with you," replied Wilton. "Can either of you change me a half sovereign?"

Neither of them could, but they were willing to take Wilton's due bills till his indebtedness amounted to ten shillings. The boys had already begun to talk the language of sterling currency, and many of them were supplied with English silver coins as well as gold. The three boys went down at the fore hatch, and removing their caps as they entered the steerage, walked silently to Gangway D, from which they went into mess room No. 8, which had thus far been the headquarters of the gamblers. Seating themselves on the stools, they used one of the beds as a table, and in a few moments were deeply absorbed in the exciting game. They spoke in whispers, and were careful not to rattle the props too loudly.

After they had played a few moments, Shuffles came in. They invited him to join them in the play, but he declined, and soon left the mess room, returning to the deck. In the waist he met Paul Kendall, who was the officer of his watch, and, like him, was off duty. They had generally been on good terms while in the after cabin together, for then Shuffles was on his best behavior.

"How do things go on in the after cabin now, Kendall — I beg your pardon — Mr. Kendall?" said Shuffles, in his most gentlemanly tones.

"About as usual, Mr. Shuffles," replied Paul.

"I am not a 'mister' now," laughed Shuffles.

"Well, it's all the same to me. I am sorry you are not with us now."

"So am I," added Shuffles. "I did not expect to be on board this year, or I should have been there now."

"You can be, next term, if you like."

"This thing yesterday has ruined all my prospects."

"That was rather bad. I never was so sorry for anything in my life before," answered Paul, warmly. "You and I were always good friends after we got well acquainted, though I did vote for another at the election a year ago."

"You did what you thought was right, and I don't blame you for that. I always did my duty when I was an officer."

"That you did, Shuffles; and we always agreed first rate. Isn't it a little strange that I have not lived in the steerage since the ship's company were organized?"

"That's because you were always a good boy, and a smart scholar. I think you would not like it."

"If it wasn't for losing my rank, I should like to try it," replied Paul. "I should like to get better acquainted with the fellows."

"You wouldn't like them in the steerage. You would see a great many things there which you never see in the cabin; a great many things which Mr. Lowington and the professors know nothing about."

"Why, what do you mean, Shuffles?" demanded Paul, astonished at this revelation.

"I ought not to say anything about it; but I believe these things will break up the Academy Ship one of these days, for the boys are growing worse instead of better in her, and their folks will find it out sooner or later."

"You surprise me!" exclaimed Paul, sadly, for he held the honor of the ship and her crew as the apple of his eye. "If there is anything wrong there, you ought to make it known."

"I suppose I ought; but you know I'm not a tell-tale."

"You have told me, and I'm an officer."

"Well, I blundered into saying what I have. What you said about going into the steerage made me let it out. I am sorry I said anything."

"You have raised my curiosity."

"I will tell you; or rather I will put you in the way of seeing for yourself, if you will not mention my name in connection with the matter, even to Mr. Lowington, and certainly not to any one else."

" I will not, Shuffles."

" The fellows are gambling in the steerage at this very moment," added Shuffles, in a low tone. "Don't betray me."

" I will not. Gambling!" exclaimed Paul, with natural horror.

" You will find them in No. 8," continued Shuffles, walking away, and leaving the astonished officer to wonder how boys could gamble.

CHAPTER XII.

THE ROOT OF ALL EVIL.

PAUL KENDALL, who had not occupied a berth in the steerage since the first organization of the ship, was greatly surprised and grieved to learn that some of the crew were addicted to vicious practices. Gambling was an enormous offence, and he was not quite willing to believe that such a terrible evil had obtained a foothold in the ship. He could hardly conceive of such a thing as boys engaging in games of chance; only the vilest of men, in his estimation, would do so. Shuffles had told him so, apparently without malice or design, and there was no reason to doubt the truth of his statement, especially as he had given the particulars by which it could be verified.

The second lieutenant went down into the steerage. Classes were reciting to the professors, and studying their lessons at the mess tables. There was certainly no appearance of evil, for the place was still, and no sound of angry altercation or ribald jest, which his fancy connected with the vice of gambling, saluted his ears. He cautiously entered Gangway D, and paused where he could hear what was said in mess room No. 8.

"I'm five shillings into your half sovereign," said

one of the gamblers; and then Paul distinctly heard the rattling of the props.

"There's the half sovereign," added another, whose voice the officer recognized as that of Wilton. "You own five shillings in it, and I own five shillings."

"That's so," replied Sanborn, who appeared to be the lucky one.

"Let us shake for the coin," added Wilton. "It's my throw."

"That's rather steep."

"We get along faster — that's all. If I throw a nick, or a browner, it's mine; if an out, it's yours."

"I am agreed — throw away," replied Sanborn, without perceiving that the one who held the props had two chances to his one.

The props rattled, and dropped on the bed.

"A browner!" exclaimed Wilton, thereby winning all he had lost at one throw.

"Hush! don't talk so loud," interposed Adler. "You'll have the profs down upon us."

"I'll go you another five shillings on one throw," said Sanborn, chagrined at his loss.

"Put down your money."

The reckless young gambler put two half crowns, or five shillings, upon the bed, and Wilton shook again.

"A nick!" said he, seizing the two half crowns.

"Try it again," demanded Sanborn.

Paul Kendall was filled with horror as he listened to this conversation. When he had heard enough to satisfy him that the speakers were actually gambling, he hastened to inform Mr. Lowington of the fact.

Paul was an officer of the ship, and this was so plainly his duty that he could not avoid it, disagreeable as it was to give testimony against his shipmates. It seemed to him that the ship could not float much longer if such iniquity were carried on within her walls of wood; she must be purged of such enormities, or some fearful retribution would overtake her. There was no malice or revenge in the bosom of the second lieutenant; he was acting solely and unselfishly for the good of the institution and the students.

He went on deck again. Shuffles was still there, and they met in the waist.

"You told me the truth," said Paul.

"You did not think I was joking about so serious a matter — did you?" replied Shuffles.

"No; but I hoped you might be mistaken."

"How could I be mistaken, when I have seen, at one time and another, a dozen fellows engaged in gambling? Of course such things as these will ruin the boys, and bring the ship into disrepute."

"You are right. My father, for one, wouldn't let me stay on board a single day, if he knew any of the boys were gamblers."

"It can be easily stopped, now you know about it," added Shuffles.

"Perhaps it can. I will inform Mr. Lowington at once."

"Remember, if you please, what I said, Mr. Kendall. I am willing to do a good thing for the ship; but you know how much I should have to suffer, if it were known that I gave the information. I didn't mean to blow on my shipmates; but you and I have been so intimate in the after cabin, that I spoke before I was aware what I was about," continued Shuffles.

"I shall not willingly betray you."

"Willingly! What do you mean by that?" demanded the conspirator, startled by the words of the officer.

"Suppose Mr. Lowington should ask me where I obtained my information," suggested Paul.

"Didn't you see for yourself in No. 8?"

"He might ask what led me to examine the matter so particularly. But, Shuffles, I will tell him honestly that I do not wish to inform him who gave me the hint; and I am quite sure he will not press the matter, when he finds that the facts are correct."

"Don't mention my name on any account," added Shuffles. "It was mean of me to say anything; but the ship was going to ruin, and I'm rather glad I spoke, though I didn't intend to do so."

"I will make it all right, Shuffles," replied Paul, as he descended the cabin steps.

Mr. Lowington was in the main cabin, and the second lieutenant knocked at the door. He was readily admitted, and invited to take a seat, for the principal was as polite to the young gentlemen as though they had been his equals in age and rank.

"I would like to speak with you alone, if you please, sir," Paul began, glancing at the cabin steward, who was at work in the pantry.

"Come into my state room," said the principal, leading the way.

"I hope your business does not relate to the discipline of the ship," continued Mr. Lowington, when they were seated, and the door of the room was closed. "If it does, you should have applied to the captain."

"This is a peculiar case, sir, and I obtained my information while off duty," replied Paul, with some embarrassment; for he had thought of communicating his startling discovery to Captain Gordon, and had only been deterred from doing so by the fear of betraying Shuffles.

"I will hear what you have to say."

"There is something very bad going on in the steerage," said Paul, seriously.

"Indeed! What is it?" asked the principal, full of interest and anxiety.

"Gambling, sir."

"Gambling!" repeated Mr. Lowington, his brow contracting.

Paul made no reply; and he expected to be asked how he had obtained the startling information.

"Are you quite sure of what you say, Mr. Kendall?"

"Yes, sir, I am. In mess room No. 8, there are three or four students now engaged in gambling. I stood at the door long enough to find out what they were doing."

"This is serious, Mr. Kendall."

"If you have any doubt about the fact, sir, I hope you will take measures to satisfy yourself at once, for I think the students are still there."

"I will, Mr. Kendall; remain in this cabin, if you please, until my return," added the principal, as he moved towards the door.

"You must be careful when you approach them, sir, for the gamblers are very sly."

Mr. Lowington passed from the professors' cabin into the steerage, and proceeding to the entrance of No. 8, he paused to listen. He heard the whispered conversation about the stakes, and "nicks," "browners" and "outs." The gamblers were by this time highly excited by the game, and had not only become imprudent, but absolutely reckless, so intense was the fascination of their employment. Suddenly, but with a light step, he entered the mess room. Wilton sat in the berth, while his companions occupied stools outside, and their heads were close together.

Mr. Lowington took Adler by the collar of his frock with one hand, and Sanborn with the other, just as Wilton had thrown the props upon the bed. With a vigorous jerk, he tossed them back upon the floor, so as to obtain a full view of the stakes and the gambling implements. The culprits were astounded at this sudden descent upon them; but before they could comprehend the situation fully, the principal turned upon his heel, and left the room without a word of astonishment or censure.

"We're in for it now," said Wilton, as his companions picked themselves up from the floor, and gazed at each other with a sheepish look.

"That's so," replied Sanborn.

"We shall catch it," added Adler.

"We shall find out how the inside of the brig looks, in my opinion," continued Wilton. "I was a fool to play here, right in the steerage. Shuffles told me that

Lowington smelt a mice, and would make a row about this thing."

"Shuffles told you so!" exclaimed Adler. "How did he know?"

"I don't know; I believe the parson told him last night, when he was in the brig."

"Why didn't you say so then?" demanded Sanborn. "You have got us into a pretty scrape! That is the reason why Shuffles wouldn't play himself."

"Yes, he said it was; but I didn't believe Lowington knew anything about it; I don't see how he could. He walked in here as straight as though he had been sent for, and knew just where to go," said Wilton.

"Of course he did: you say Shuffles told you Lowington knew all about it; and I suppose he has been on the watch to find some fellows at it so as to make an example of them."

"That's the whole of it. We might as well throw the props overboard now."

Mr. Lowington returned to the cabin, where he had left Paul Kendall. He was sadly disturbed by the discovery he had made, for he had no suspicion before that any of his pupils had made so much progress in vice. He knew what a terrible evil gambling was among men; that it was the forerunner of dissipation and crime; and he felt the responsibility which rested upon him as a guardian and instructor of youth.

"Mr. Kendall, your information was correct; and I commend the zeal you have displayed in bringing this fearful evil to light. How happened you to discover it?"

"I had a hint from a source which I would rather

not mention," replied the second lieutenant, with some embarrassment.

"Indeed!"

"Yes, sir; one of the students, who berths in the steerage, happened accidentally to let it out."

Paul said "accidentally," because he believed that Shuffles had been betrayed into the revelation by their former intimacy.

"And he does not wish to be regarded as an informer," added the principal.

"No, sir; after he had excited my curiosity, he told me where I could find the gamblers at play."

"I understand his position, precisely," said Mr. Lowington; "and I will not ask his name. The information proves to be painfully correct, and there appears to have been no malice in giving it."

"No, sir; I don't think there was: indeed, I know there was not," added Paul, when he considered that Wilton and the other gamblers were Shuffles' intimate companions.

"This is a very serious matter, Mr. Kendall," repeated the principal, thoughtfully.

"I think it is, sir; that is the reason why I came to you, instead of going to the captain."

"Perhaps it is better that you did so, on the whole," replied Mr. Lowington. "It has enabled me to see the evil for myself. Have you any views in regard to what should be done, Mr. Kendall?"

The principal often asked the opinion of the officers concerning similar matters under discussion, perhaps in order to teach them self-respect, rather than with the expectation of obtaining valuable suggestions from them.

"I think there should be stricter discipline in the mess rooms, sir," replied Paul, blushing to have his opinion asked. "The fellows——"

"The students, you mean," interposed the principal.

"Excuse me, sir," added Paul, blushing deeper than before at this gentle rebuke.

The boys had a language of their own, which was not tolerated by the faculty when it ran into coarseness and slang.

"What were you about to say, Mr. Kendall?" continued the principal, smiling at the confusion of the young officer.

"The students can now do anything they like in the mess rooms. They have plenty of money, and if they want to gamble, they can. They were playing last night when the first part of the starboard watch were on duty."

"You are right, Mr. Kendall," said Mr. Lowington. "The students must be looked after in their rooms. Has there ever been any gambling among the officers in the after cabin?"

"I never saw any, or heard of any. I don't think there has been."

"I hope not; but we must grapple with this question in earnest," added the principal, as he led the way out of the state room into the main cabin.

The chaplain and the doctor were there, and Mr. Lowington wished to take their advice upon the serious matter before him; and before he permitted the second lieutenant to retire, he stated the case to them.

"Gambling!" groaned the chaplain.

"I detected them in the act myself," added Mr. Lowington. "You may retire, Mr. Kendall."

"Why, this is awful!"

"Boys will do almost anything that men will," said Dr. Winstock, the surgeon.

"Drinking and gambling!" ejaculated the chaplain. "What are we coming to?"

"I fear there are other vices of which we know nothing yet," added the doctor.

"Why, I'm afraid the Academy Ship will prove to be a failure, after all," sighed Mr. Agneau.

"Not at all," argued Dr. Winstock. "We are in position here to treat these evils properly. There are no fond mothers and indulgent fathers to spoil the boys, when the discipline becomes sharp."

"What can we do?" demanded the chaplain. "Moral and religious influences seem to have no effect."

"Have faith in your own medicines, Mr. Agneau," said the doctor.

"I have full faith in the medicine, Dr. Winstock; but I fear I have not done my duty faithfully."

"You need not reproach yourself, Mr. Agneau. You have been earnest in your work," interposed the principal. "In a large community of young men, all these vices and evils will appear. It was to meet them that the keel of this ship was laid, and our institution organized. I expect to find vice, and even crime, among the boys. They that be sick need a physician, not they that be whole. These boys certainly behave better on board the ship than they did on shore at the various academies they attended. Pelham, who is now fourth lieutenant, and has been first, was one of the hardest boys in the school to which he belonged in New York. He has given us no trouble here, though he has been a little sulky since he fell from his former rank. Shuffles, who, in the Brockway Academy, was the worst boy I ever knew, without exception, behaved himself astonishingly well for a whole year. I am sorry to see that he has begun the second year badly."

"O, his is a very hopeful case!" said Mr. Agneau. "He is penitent for his folly, and I never saw so great a change in an individual as he exhibited on my second visit to him last evening."

"I hope he will not disappoint you. I only mentioned him to show what a benefit the ship had been to him; for if it keeps him out of trouble even a single year, it is so far a blessing to him, to say nothing of his intellectual progress, which has been more than satisfactory. The fact that there are gambling, and drinking, and other vices on board, does not diminish my faith in the institution."

"It certainly ought not to do so," added Dr. Winstock, who was not so sanguine a reformer as the chaplain, and was willing to wait till the medicine had time to produce an effect. "Here is an evil: we must meet it, and we needn't stop to groan over it. What's to be done? that's the question."

"The officer of the watch must be required to visit every room during the first watch at least," said the principal.

"But those who are disposed to gamble will find abundant opportunities to do so," suggested the doctor. "A couple of them up in the maintop, or even in the cross-trees, could shake props, 'odd or even,' and play other games of chance, without being seen. I don't think you have hit the nail on the head yet, Mr. Lowington."

"The utmost vigilance we can use will not entirely prevent evil. We depend upon moral influences, as well as discipline, for the prevention and cure of vice and error," added the principal.

"I'm afraid a lecture on gambling wouldn't do much good while the means of play were still in the hands of the students. It would influence some; but others are not to be influenced in any way: a strong arm alone will meet their case."

"We can take the props from them," said Mr. Lowington.

"You must go a step farther than that; you must search the berths and lockers for cards, dice, or other gambling implements. Even then you will not have struck at the root of the evil."

"What is the root of the evil?" asked the principal.

"Money, sir!" replied the doctor, with unusual energy.

"That is said to be the root of all evil," added Mr. Lowington, with a smile.

"Among boys, money does more injury than we can comprehend. A college friend of mine was wholly spoiled by his allowance of money. His purse was always full, which made him the prey of dissolute persons. He always had the means of gratifying his appetites, and is now a sot, if he is living. He began to drink, gamble, and dissipate generally, before he entered college: he was expelled in a year. Without money, as a boy, he would have been saved from a score of temptations. Every boy on board this ship has a pocket full of sovereigns for his European expenses. They are all young nabobs, and if you ever let them go ashore, you will have your hands full, Mr. Lowington. They will drink beer and wine, visit bad places, gamble and carouse. While they have plenty of money, you can hardly prevent them from being a nuisance to you and to themselves."

"There is a great deal of force in what you say, Dr. Winstock."

"Money will be the root of all evil to these boys, most emphatically. Those who are disposed to gamble will do so while they have money."

"The inference to be drawn from your remarks is, that the students should not have pocket money."

"Most decidedly that is my opinion. If I had a son, I wouldn't allow him a penny of pocket money."

"That would be rather hard," said the chaplain.

"I know it, but it would be the best thing in the world for the boy. I don't mean to say that I would never permit him to have money; but he should have no stated allowance; and when he had a dollar, I should want to know how it was to be expended."

"This question of money allowances has been under serious consideration with me."

"You can't handle the boys in Europe with money in their pockets. A regiment of soldiers could not keep them straight."

"I think you are right, doctor. I am tempted to take their money from them."

"Do it, by all means!" exclaimed Dr. Winstock.

The chaplain regarded the measure as rather high-handed. He thought it would belittle the boys, and deprive them of some portion of their self-respect. The instructors came into the cabin at seven bells, and their opinions were taken. Four of the six were in favor of taking all money from the boys. Mr. Lowington had already reached this view of the case, and it was resolved to take the important step at once, as the best means of effectually putting a stop to the practice of gambling.

Mr. Fluxion had been unable to attend this conference for more than a few moments, for he was the instructor in mathematics, which included navigation, and he was compelled to superintend the observations, which were made with separate instruments by himself and by the two masters of the forenoon watch. The position of the ship was found, and marked on the chart, and the "dead reckoning" compared with the result obtained by calculation.

At one bell in the afternoon watch, all hands were piped to muster, and the gamblers readily understood that this call was for their especial benefit.

"Wilton," said Mr. Lowington, from his usual position.

The culprit came forward.

"With whom were you gambling in mess room No. 8, this forenoon?" asked the principal.

Wilton looked up at the stern dispenser of discipline. If he did not know, it was not his business to tell.

"Answer me."

"I don't know."

"You are telling a falsehood."

"I don't remember their names now," said Wilton.

"You do remember them; and for each falsehood you utter you shall suffer an additional penalty."

"I'm not a telltale, sir," answered Wilton, doggedly. "I don't want to tell who they were."

"Very well; why didn't you say that at first? I have some respect for the student who dislikes to betray even his companions in error; none at all for a liar. Adler and Sanborn," added the principal; and the two gamblers stepped up to the hatch. "Young gentlemen, you are charged with gambling. Have you anything to say?"

"Nothing sir," they all replied.

"Wilton, how much money have you lost at play?"

"None, sir."

"How much have you made?"

"Ten shillings — half a sovereign."

"From whom did you win it?"

"From Sanborn."

"Return it to him."

Wilton obeyed. Adler had won about a dollar from Sanborn, which he was also compelled to restore. Mr. Lowington was satisfied that others had gained or lost by gambling, but as he did not know who the other gamblers were, he did not attempt to have the ill-gotten money restored; for he never made himself ridiculous to the students by endeavoring to do what could not be done.

Mr. Lowington then made a very judicious address

upon the evil of gambling, pointing out its dangerous fascination, and the terrible consequences which sooner or later overtook its victims. He illustrated his remarks by examples drawn from real life. The chaplain followed him, detailing the career of a young man whom he had attended in prison, and who had been utterly ruined by the habit of gaming, contracted before he was of age.

These addresses seemed to produce a deep impression on the boys, and one would have judged by their looks that they all regarded the dangerous practice with well-grounded horror. Mr. Lowington took the stand again, and followed with another address upon "the root of all evil;" adding that, having money in their possession, they would be tempted to gamble.

"Now, young gentlemen, I propose that you all deliver your funds to me, taking my receipt for whatever amount you deliver to me. When you have any real need of money, apply to me, and I will restore it," added Mr. Lowington.

"Take our money from us!" exclaimed several; and it was evident that the proposition was creating a tremendous sensation among the students.

CHAPTER XIII.

PIPING TO MISCHIEF.

AFTER the offensive announcement that the students were to deliver up their money to the principal, and take his receipt for it, the crew were dismissed from muster, after being informed that the business of receiving the funds would be immediately commenced in the steerage. The three gamblers were not punished, except by the mortification of the exposure, even by the loss of their marks, though Wilton was confined in the brig one hour for each falsehood he had uttered. Mr. Lowington knew that at least a dozen of the boys were guilty of gambling; and as the matter now came up for the first time, he did not deem it expedient to punish those who had been discovered, hoping that the preventive measures he had adopted would effectually suppress the evil.

Many of the students regarded the taking of their money as an indignity. Only a few of them, comparatively, had engaged in gambling, though many of the occupants of the steerage knew of the existence of the practice on board the ship. They were willing to believe, and did believe, after the impressive addresses to which they had listened, that games of chance were a perilous amusement, but they were not quite willing to acknowledge the justice of Mr. Lowington's measures.

Most of the officers, and many of the crew, cheerfully complied with the new regulation. They handed their money to the pursers, and received a receipt for the amount, signed by the principal. Others emptied the contents of their exchequer sullenly, and under protest; while not a few openly grumbled in the presence of Mr. Lowington. Some of "our fellows" attempted to keep back a portion of their funds, and perhaps a few succeeded, though the tact of the principal exposed the deceit in several instances. Whatever may be thought of the justice or the expediency of depriving the students of their money, it was evidently an exceedingly unpopular step.

In the second dog watch, when Shuffles and Paul Kendall were off duty, they happened to meet in the waist; and the exciting topic of the day came up for discussion, as it had in every little group that collected that afternoon. Shuffles had accomplished his purpose; he had accomplished far more than he intended. He had expected nothing more than a general onslaught upon gambling, followed by increased stringency in the regulations, and a closer watch over the students in their rooms, which would produce sufficient irritation among the boys to suit his purposes. Now the crew, and even some of the officers, were in a ferment of indignation, and ripe for a demonstration of any kind.

"The business is done," said Paul Kendall, as he met the conspirator.

"I'm afraid it's overdone," answered Shuffles, seriously, though he was actually in a state of exultation over the effect which had been produced by the new regulation.

"I hope not. I did not mention your name to the principal in connection with the matter," added Paul.

"Didn't he ask you?"

"He did; but when I stated the case to him, and told him the person who had given me the information had let it out accidentally, and did not wish to be known, he asked no more questions."

"Thank you, Mr. Kendall. This last measure is so unpopular that I should have been cast out like an unclean bird, if it were known that I gave the hint."

"No one shall know anything about it from me, Shuffles. You did a good thing for the ship, and for every fellow in it."

"They wouldn't be willing to believe that just now," said Shuffles, laughing.

"Perhaps not; but it is a fact, none the less."

"I didn't think Mr. Lowington would go it quite so strong. If I had, I shouldn't have told you what I did."

"Why, are you not satisfied with what has been done?" asked Kendall, with some astonishment.

"No, I am not. I am glad enough to see the gambling stopped, but I don't think the principal had any more right to take my money away from me than he had to take my head off," replied Shuffles, earnestly.

"Don't you think it will be better for the fellows to be without money than with it?"

"Perhaps it will; I don't know about that. Your neighbor might be a better man if he were poor than if he were rich: does that make it that you have any right to take his property from him?"

"I don't think it does," replied Paul.

"The State of Massachusetts, for instance, or the State of Ohio, makes laws against games of chance. Why not make a law, if a man gambles, that all his money shall be taken from him?"

"The state has no right to make such a law, I suppose."

"But the principal goes a long reach beyond that. He takes every man's money away from him, whether he is accused of gambling or not. Do you think he had any right to do that?"

"He hasn't made any law; but if you want law, I'll give you some!" laughed Paul, who was disposed to treat the subject very good-naturedly, especially as there was so much loose indignation floating about the decks.

"I don't mean law alone, but justice," added Shuffles. "I call it high-handed injustice to take the fellows' money away from them."

"Let me give you a little law, then," persisted Paul. "How old are you, Shuffles?"

"Eighteen."

"Good! You are an infant."

"In law, I am."

"Suppose your uncle, or somebody else, should die to-day, and leave you fifty thousand dollars: wouldn't you have a good time with it?"

"I should, as soon as I got hold of it, you had better believe," replied Shuffles.

"As soon as you got hold of it!" exclaimed Paul.

"I suppose I should have a guardian till I became of age."

"Who would appoint your guardian?"

"The court, I believe."

"Exactly so! The law! What, take your money away from you, or not let you touch it!"

"That's law, certainly."

"Well, wouldn't the law have just as much right to take off a fellow's head, as to take his money?" demanded Paul, triumphantly.

"Mr. Lowington is not our guardian."

"Yes, he is, for the time being; and I hold that he has just as much right to take your money from you as your father would have."

"I don't see it; I don't believe it. The money was given us by our fathers to spend in Europe when we get there."

"Mr. Lowington is to pay all our expenses on shore, by the terms of the contract. Besides, the regulations of the Academy Ship, to which all the parents assented, require that the control of the boys shall be wholly given up to the principal. It's a plain case, Shuffles."

Mr. Lowington and his policy had an able and zealous defender in the person of Paul Kendall, who, by his arguments, as well as his influence, had already reconciled several of the students to the new regulation.

"If I were willing to grant the right of the principal to take the fellows' money from them — which I am not — I think it is treating them like babies to do so. It is punishing the innocent with the guilty."

"Mr. Lowington said, in so many words, that the

measure was not intended as a punishment; that it was purely a matter of discipline, intended to meet certain evils which must appear when we landed in Europe, as well as to prevent gambling."

Paul certainly had the best of the argument; but Shuffles was not convinced, because he did not wish to be convinced.

At eight bells, when the first part of the port watch went on duty, the wind had shifted from west to north; the studding-sails had been taken in, the spanker, main spencer, and all the stay-sails had been set, and the ship, close-hauled, was barely laying her course. The wind was fresh, and she was heeled over on the starboard side, so that her decks formed a pretty steep inclined plane. Under these circumstances, it required a great deal of skill and watchfulness on the part of the wheelmen to keep the sails full, and at the same time to lay the course. As the ship's head met the heavy seas, a great deal of spray was dashed on deck, and the position of the lookout-men on the top-gallant forecastle was not as comfortable as if the weather had been warmer. There was no dodging; every student was obliged to stand at his post, wet or dry, blow high or blow low.

Wilton had been discharged from confinement in the brig, where Mr. Agneau had visited him, giving him good advice and religious instruction, as he did to all who were punished in any manner, and was now with his watch on deck. The new regulation was particularly odious to "our fellows," and Wilton regarded himself as a martyr to the popular cause, forgetting that he had been punished for the lies he had told. He and twenty others were forward to say they "wouldn't stand it;" and the indignation seemed to be increasing rather than subsiding.

"Well, Wilton, how do you like the inside of the brig?" asked Shuffles, when they met in the main-top, having been sent aloft to clear away the bowline bridle on the main-topsail.

"I like it well enough," replied Wilton. "I wasn't going to blow on the fellows; I would stay in there a month first."

"Did you give up your money?"

"Of course I did; I couldn't help myself."

"How do you like the new regulation?"

"I don't like it any better than the rest of the fellows do," answered Wilton, in surly tones. "I won't stand it, either."

"O, I guess you will," laughed Shuffles. "I told you Lowington was a tyrant, but you wouldn't believe me."

"Yes, I would; and I did."

"The fellows will find out what he is before they are many days older."

"I think they have found out now. I say, Shuffles, was this the row you spoke about last night?"

"Yes; only there's more of it than I expected."

"How did you know anything about it beforehand?"

"I have a way of finding out these things," replied the artful conspirator, mysteriously. "I have one or two friends at court."

"Is Paul Kendall one of them?"

"No; he is a simpleton. He don't know which

side his bread is buttered. If Lowington takes snuff, Kendall sneezes."

"I have seen you talking with him two or three times to-day."

"I was only pumping him."

"Well, there is a jolly row on board now, anyhow," added Wilton, as he prepared to descend over the cat-harpings.

"Hold on; don't let's go on deck yet," interposed Shuffles. "I want to know what our fellows are going to do."

"They will call us down, if we stop here."

"When they do, we will go down, then," replied Shuffles, as he seated himself in the top, with his legs through the lubber's-hole. "What are our fellows going to do? Do they mean to stand this thing?"

"They can't help themselves; they are mad enough to do anything; but what's the use?" added Wilton, as he seated himself by the side of his companion.

"Don't you think they will join the League now?"

"They would join anything that would give them their rights. I'll join now; but I don't want to be toggled in such a way as you said last night."

"Then you can't be toggled at all."

"I haven't any idea of falling overboard accidentally. I'd rather lose my money than do that."

"It's nothing but a form, Wilton. Between you and me, it's only a bugbear, intended to work upon the nerves and the imagination. Of course we shouldn't help any fellow overboard; no one would dare to do any such thing."

"I don't like the sound of the thing."

"If you really mean to expose the secrets which are intrusted to you, I advise you not to join."

"I don't mean any such thing," added Wilton, indignantly.

"If you didn't, you wouldn't be afraid of the penalty."

"Toggle me, then; and see what I mean."

"I don't want you to go in if you don't believe in it."

"But I do believe in it; so go ahead."

Shuffles pronounced the ridiculous obligation again, and Wilton repeated it after him.

"Now you are toggled," said the leader.

"What are we going to do?"

"Bring in the rest of our fellows; that is the first job. In my opinion we can get over fifty of them now."

"I don't know about that," answered Wilton, doubtfully.

"I'm very sure we can. If we get enough to take the ship, we can have all the rest as soon as we have done the job."

"Take the ship!" exclaimed Wilton, appalled at the idea.

"That's what we mean."

"I don't believe you can do it," replied the doubtful "link in the Chain."

"It's the easiest thing in the world. The affair will come off at supper time, when the professors are all in their cabin. All we have to do is to clap the hatch on the after companion-way, and secure the doors leading from the main cabin into the steerage. Then we have them, and they can't help themselves."

"But the boatswain, carpenter, and sailmaker will be loose."

"No, they won't. At the right time, we will pass the word for them, and say that Lowington wants to see them in the main cabin. As soon as they go below we will put the hatch on."

"The cooks and stewards will still be at large."

"We can lock them up in the kitchen. If they make trouble, I have a revolver," whispered Shuffles.

"A revolver! I won't have anything to do with it if you are going to use pistols," said the alarmed confederate.

"It's only to look at; there will be no occasion to use it," answered Shuffles, soothingly.

"There will be twelve men, besides the stewards, locked up in the main cabin."

"That's so."

"How long do you suppose it would take them to break down the bulkhead between the cabin and the steerage, or to climb up through the skylight?"

"If they attempt anything of that kind, we can show them the revolver; that will quiet them."

"You might frighten the parson in that way; but do you suppose men like Mr. Lowington, Mr. Fluxion, and Peaks, who have been in the navy so long, will be afraid of a pistol?"

"They won't want to be shot, if they have been in the navy all their lives."

"Then you mean to shoot them?"

"They will think we do, and it will be all the same."

"I don't know about this business. I'm afraid the pistol might go off, and hurt somebody."

"I suppose you could raise objections all night," added Shuffles, contemptuously. "I'm not going to have any man tyrannize over me, Wilton. I suppose if Lowington wants to pull every fellow's teeth out, you won't object."

"I'm as much opposed to his tyranny as you are, and I will do anything that is reasonable; but I want to know whether the water is hot or cold before I put my fingers into it. What's the use of blundering into an enterprise, and making a failure of it?"

"I have no idea of making a failure of it. Did you ever know me to make a failure of anything that I attempted?"

"Yes. I have."

"What?"

"You failed to get elected captain when we first came aboard of the ship."

"That was only because we had just come on board; the fellows didn't know me, and I didn't know them. We are better acquainted now, and I am just as sure of success as though we had already won it," added Shuffles, confidently. "I don't believe in making failures."

"I don't believe there is more than one chance in ten for you to succeed," continued the sceptic.

"There isn't more than one chance in ten for us to fail. You are a bird of evil omen. You have no faith in anything; and if you are going to croak like this, I don't want you in the Chain," added Shuffles, petulantly.

"I'm in for it, already; and when I can see my way clearly, I shall be as strong as you are."

"Then don't croak any more. We must go to work while the fever is on the fellows, and make up —— "

"In the main-top, ahoy!" shouted the master, from the waist.

"On deck!" replied Shuffles.

"Lay down from aloft!"

"Yes, sir."

The conspirators descended, after Shuffles had admonished his shaky companion to be discreet.

"What are you doing in the top so long?" demanded Foster, the first master, as the truants reached the sheer-pole.

"Watching the sea, sir," replied Shuffles. "It looks fine from the top."

"When you have done what you are sent aloft for, it is your duty to come down and report it," added the officer.

Shuffles made no reply, as he probably would have done if he had not had a heavy operation on his hands, which prevented him from indulging in any side quarrels.

Except the wheelmen and the lookout, the watch on deck was divided into little groups, who were quartered in the most comfortable places they could find, telling stories, or discussing the exciting topic of the day.

"Shuffles, some of our fellows want to see you

and Wilton," said Adler, as the first master went below, to inspect the steerage, at two bells.

"What's up?" demanded the conspirator.

"Don't say anything," added the messenger, as he led the way to the steerage skylight, under the lee of which Sanborn and Grimme had stowed themselves away, out of the reach of the stream that was flowing along the water-ways, and of the spray which was dashing over the weather bows.

The party from aloft, with the messenger, increased the group to five, which was the total number of " our fellows" that could be mustered in the first part of the port watch.

"What's up?" demanded Shuffles, when he had seated himself by the skylight.

"We intend to pipe to mischief, to-night. Shuffles, and we want some help from you," said Sanborn, in reply.

"We have been robbed of our money, and we are going to have satisfaction, somehow or other," added Grimme, in explanation. "We are not going to stand this sort of thing. We must teach Lowington and the professors that they can't put our noses to the grindstone."

"Exactly so!" exclaimed Shuffles. "And you intend to put them there yourselves. In other words, you mean to get into some scrape, and be punished for it, as I was."

"No, we don't. We are going to work man-of-war style. Old Peaks told us how to do it, when we were on watch last night," replied Grimme.

"Peaks?"

"Yes, he spun us a yarn about man-of-war life, and told us how the men serve out the officers when they don't behave themselves."

"Peaks told you this — did he?" demanded Shuffles.

"Of course he didn't mean to have us do anything of the kind."

"Well, how did he tell you to serve out the officers?"

"Make them uncomfortable; keep them in a hornet's nest all the time."

"How? How?" asked Shuffles, impatiently.

"Why, if the unpopular officer went forward, a belaying pin was sure to drop on his head or his feet; a tar can or a paint pot would be upset on his back; or, if he went below, a cannon ball was liable to roll out of a shot case upon him. Of course no one ever knew the author of this mischief."

"Do you propose to play off any of these tricks on Lowington?" demanded Shuffles.

"We have got a rod in pickle for him," replied Grimme, chuckling.

"What is it?"

"We intend to give him a dose of kerosene oil, to begin with," laughed Sanborn.

"One of the stewards left his oil can on the fore-scuttle ladder, after the hatch was put on to keep the spray out, and I took possession of it," added Grimme, hardly able to keep his mirth within the limits of prudence.

"What are you going to do with it?" asked Shuffles.

"We are going to give Lowington the contents of the can, and then throw it overboard."

"Indeed! Who is the fellow that has boldness enough to do this thing?"

"I have; and I have volunteered to do the job," answered Grimme, with a degree of assurance which astonished even Shuffles.

"You dare not do it!"

"I dare, and I will, if the fellows will stand by me. Lowington is sitting at the table in the professors' cabin, right under the skylight, reading. One section of the skylight is open, and you can see him, as plain as day. It's as dark as a pocket on deck, and the officers can't see you twenty feet off. All I have to do is to pop the oil through the opening, and get out of the way."

"What then?"

"Why, he will come on deck, and try to find out who did it; but he can't."

"Perhaps he can."

"No, he can't; only half a dozen of the fellows will know anything about it, and of course they won't let on."

"Suppose he don't find out. What good will this trick do?"

"The second part of the port watch must follow up the game. Lowington will come on deck at eight bells, and Monroe, in the starboard watch, will give him another dose."

"What will that be?"

"Slush the first step of the ladder at the after companion-way, and let him tumble down stairs," chuckled Grimme.

"Then Lynch will give him some more," said Adler.

"Well, you may break his neck when he tumbles down the ladder. I'll have nothing to do with any of those tricks," added Shuffles, decidedly. "If you want to pipe to mischief, I'm with you, but in no such way as that. Those are little, mean, dirty tricks."

"But they will keep him in hot water all the time, and he will get sick of being a tyrant over the fellows in less than a week. There are twenty things we might do to annoy him, which would help to bring him to his senses. For instance, when the steward carries the coffee into the professors' cabin, one fellow might engage his attention, while another drops a lump of salt, a handful of pepper, or a piece of tobacco into the urn."

"I don't want to hear any more of such low-lived tricks," interposed the magnificent conspirator. "If you want to pipe to mischief, let us do it like men."

"What would you do? Fifty of the fellows, at least, will go into anything to punish Lowington for his tyranny."

"Join the Chain, then," said Shuffles, in a whisper, and with a suitable parade of mystery.

"The what?"

"The Chain."

The object of the League was duly explained; and before the second part of the port watch came on deck, three new members had been "toggled." Greatly to the satisfaction of Shuffles, and to the astonishment of Wilton, they did not hesitate at the penalty of the obligation, and seemed to be entirely willing to "fall overboard accidentally" if they failed to make strong and faithful "links in the Chain."

CHAPTER XIV.

ALL HANDS, REEF TOPSAILS!

AUGUSTUS PELHAM, the fourth lieutenant of the Young America, was almost the only malcontent among the officers; the only one who persistently declined to be reconciled to the new regulation. Others objected to it; others criticised it, and even regarded the act as tyrannical; but the good offices of Paul Kendall, who argued the question with them, as he did with Shuffles, had in a measure conciliated them, and they were at least disposed to submit gracefully to the order. But Pelham was not of this number. He was above the average age, and, like the chief conspirator on board, expecting to leave the ship at the end of the first year, had not exerted himself to the extent of his ability. He had been first lieutenant, and had now fallen to fourth. He was older than the captain, and it galled him to be subject to one younger than himself.

He was dissatisfied with his rank, and this had a tendency to make him a grumbler. It needed only an appearance of tyranny or injustice to array him in spirit against the authorities of the ship. Shuffles knew his state of mind, and was prepared to take advantage of it, hoping through him to gain other discontented spirits in the cabin.

When the first part of the port watch was relieved, the "Chain" consisted of five links, and the conspirators were well satisfied with the present success of the enterprise. Each of the new members of the League was commissioned to obtain a recruit, whose name was given to him, and he was required to report upon the case, to Shuffles, before eight bells in the afternoon watch. As a measure of precaution, it was required that no meetings should be held; that not more than three members should assemble for business at any one time. The utmost care and circumspection were urged, and it was agreed that not a word should be said in the steerage, where it was possible for any of the professors to overhear it.

The second part of the port watch, with Pelham as officer of the deck, went on duty at ten o'clock. The wind had been freshening for the last two hours, and it was now necessary to reduce sail. The royals were first taken in, and then the top-gallant sails.

"We can't lay this course, sir," said Burchmore, the quartermaster, who was conning the helm. "The wind is hauling to the eastward."

"Make the course east by north then," replied Pelham, without taking the trouble to consult the captain or Mr. Fluxion, both of whom were on deck.

"The wind is north-north-east, sir," reported the quartermaster, a short time afterwards.

"Keep her east then."

At six bells the wind was north-east, and coming heavier and heavier every moment. The ship was headed east-south-east, and it was evident that she still had on more sail than she could easily carry.

"What's the course, Mr. Pelham?" asked Captain Gordon.

"East-south-east, sir," replied Pelham.

"The course given out was east-north-east."

"I have changed it three times within the last hour," answered the fourth lieutenant, in rather surly tones.

"By whose order?" demanded the captain.

"By no one's order, sir."

"You know the regulation for the officer of the deck. He is not permitted to alter the course of the ship, unless to avoid some sudden danger, without informing the captain."

"I had to alter the course, or have the topsails thrown aback," replied Pelham.

"Very likely it was proper to alter the course; but it was also proper to inform me, especially when I was on deck."

"Very well, Captain Gordon. I will not alter the course again without your order," added the fourth lieutenant, stiffly.

"The regulation is not mine, Mr. Pelham," continued the captain, sternly.

As the wind increased, sail was reduced to topsails and courses, jib and spanker; but at seven bells even these were found to be too much for her.

"Captain Gordon, it is coming heavier," said Mr. Fluxion. "I think it will be necessary to reef."

"I was thinking of that, sir. The wind is north-east, and blowing a gale."

"You had better call all hands, and do it at once."

"Mr. Pelham, you will call all hands to reef topsails!"

"All hands, sir?"

"Certainly, Mr. Pelham; that was my order," replied the captain, more sharply than usual, for there was something in the manner of the officer of the deck which he did not like, and he found it necessary to maintain the dignity of his position.

Pelham touched his cap; he felt the weight of authority upon him heavier than ever before. Until recently he had always performed his duty cheerfully, and was considered a first-rate officer. Since the new regulation had been put in force, and he had been compelled to deliver up ten sovereigns in his possession, he had been rather disagreeable. In the cabin he had used some language reflecting upon the principal, and he was now regarded as a malcontent by the captain, and by those who still sustained the discipline of the ship.

"Morrison," called he, as he went forward to the waist.

"Here, sir," replied the boatswain, who belonged in this quarter watch; and there was a boatswain's mate in each of the others.

"Call all hands to reef topsails."

The shrill pipe of the boatswain's whistle soon rang above the howling winds, which now sounded gloomily through the rigging. The call was repeated in the steerage, and at the door of the after cabin, where it could be heard by the officers, for no one on board is exempted when all hands are called. This was the first taste of the hardships of a seaman's life to which the students had been invited. It is not pleasant, to say the least, to be turned out of a warm bed in a gale, when the wind comes cold and furious, laden with the spray of the ocean, and be sent aloft in the rigging of the ship, when she is rolling and pitching, jumping and jerking, in the mad waves. But there is no excuse at such a time, and nothing but positive physical disability can exempt officer or seaman from duty.

It was the first time the boys had seen a gale at sea, and though it was not yet what would be called a strong gale, it was sufficiently terrific to produce a deep impression upon them. The ship was still close-hauled, under topsails and courses, with jib and spanker. The wind came in heavy blasts, and when they struck the sails, the Young America heeled over, until her lee yard-arm seemed to be dipping the waves. Huge billows came roaring down from the windward, crowned with white foam, and presenting an awful aspect in the night, striking the ship, lifting her bow high in the air, and breaking over the rail, pouring tons of water on the deck.

Before the whole crew had been called, every opening in the deck had been secured, and the plank guards placed over the glass in the skylights. Life lines had been stretched along the decks, and the swinging ports, through which the water that came over the rail escaped, were crossed with whale line by Peaks, to prevent any unlucky boy from being washed through, if he happened to be thrown off his feet by a rush of water to the scuppers.

The scene was wild and startling; it was even terrible to those who had never seen anything of the kind before, though the old sailors regarded it quite as a matter of course. Peaks had never been known to be so jolly and excited since he came on board. He was full of jokes and witty sayings; he seemed to be in his element now, and all his powers of body and mind were in the keenest state of excitement.

The students were disposed to look upon it as a rough time, and doubtless some of them thought the ship was in great peril. Not a few of them pretended to enjoy the scene, and talked amazingly salt, as though they had been used to this kind of thing all their lives. Mr. Lowington came on deck, when all hands were called; and though, to his experienced eye, there was no danger while the ship was well managed, he was exceedingly anxious, for it was a time when accidents were prone to happen, and the loss of a boy at such an hour, would endanger the success of his great experiment. On deck, the students could not get overboard without the grossest carelessness; but it was perilous to send them aloft in the gloom of the howling tempest. He had hoped that he might be permitted to meet the onslaught of the first gale the ship encountered in the daytime; but as the " clerk of the weather" otherwise ordained it, he was compelled to make the best of the circumstances.

Before the manœuvre of reefing, in the gale, was begun, Mr. Fluxion was sent forward. Bitts was placed in the fore rigging, Peaks in the main, and Leach in the mizzen, to see that the young tars did not needlessly expose themselves, and that they used all proper precautions to avoid an accident. All the officers were at their stations.

"Man the topsail clewlines, and buntlines, and the weather topsail braces," shouted Haven, the first lieutenant, who always handled the ship when all hands were called. "Stand by the lee braces, bowlines, and halyards."

The clewlines are ropes fastened to the corners of the topsail, passing through blocks on the topsail yard, and leading down to the deck through the lubber's hole. They are used in hauling the corners of the sail up when they are to be reefed or furled.

The buntlines are two ropes attached to cringles, or eyes, in the bottom of the sail, which are used for hauling up the middle, or bunt, of the topsail.

The braces are the ropes secured to the ends of the yards, leading down to the deck directly, or to a mast first, and thence below, by which the yards and the sails attached to them are hauled round so as to take the wind. They are distinguished by the terms "weather" and "lee," the former being those on the side from which the wind comes, the latter on the opposite side. They also have their specific names, as the "weather fore-top-gallant brace," the "lee main brace."

The bowlines are ropes attached to the leeches of square sails to draw the edge forward, so that they may take the wind better. They are fastened to the bridles, which are loops like those of a kite, two or three of them extending from the side of the sail.

The halyards are the ropes by which any sail is hoisted. For square sails they are secured to the yards, which, with the exception of the lower one on each mast slide up and down.

"Clear away the bowlines," said the first lieutenant, when all hands were reported ready for the manœuvre which had been ordered.

At this command the bowlines on the topsails and courses were unfastened.

"All clear, sir," reported the officers from their stations.

"Round in the weather braces, ease off the lee braces!" was the next order. "Settle away the topsail halyards! Clew down!"

To round in the weather braces was simply to haul them up as the lee braces were slacked, so that the yard was squared. As the command was executed, the sail was "spilled," or the wind thrown out of it.

"Haul out the reef tackles! Haul up the buntlines!" continued the executive officer.

To reef a sail is to tie up a portion of it, so as to present less surface of canvas to the force of the wind. Topsails are reefed in the upper part; a portion of the sail nearest to the yard from which it is suspended being rolled up and secured by strings to the yard. Fore and aft sails, like the spanker, the fore and main spencers, or the mainsail of a schooner, are reefed at the foot, the lower part being tied down to the boom.

The topsails of the Young America had three reef bands, or strips of canvas sewed crosswise over them, in which were the reef points, or strings by which the sail is tied up when reefed. When the first or highest row of reef points was used, the sail was single reefed; when the second was used, it was double reefed; and when the third row was used, it was close reefed. On each side of the sail, at the end of each reef band, was a cringle, or eye, in which the reef pendent was fastened. The reef tackle consists of a rope passing from the eye, at the end of the reef band, through a block at the extremity of the yard, thence to the mast, and down to the deck. Hauling on this rope draws the required portion of the sail up to the yard in readiness to be reefed.

The reef tackles were hauled out, and the buntlines hauled up to bring the sail where it could be easily handled. When the sail is to be reefed, the seamen have to "lay out" on the yards, and tie up the sail. To enable them to do this with safety, there are horses, or foot-ropes, extending from the slings, or middle of the spar, to the yard-arms. This rope hangs below the yard, the middle parts being supported by stirrups. When a man is to "lay out," he throws his breast across the yard with his feet on the horse. The man at the "weather earing," or eye for the reef pendent, has to sit astride the yard, and pull the sail towards him.

The foot-rope sometimes slips through the eyes in the stirrups when only one hand goes out upon it, which does, or may, place him in a dangerous position. During the preceding day, when the barometer indicated a change of weather, Mr. Lowington had sent the old boatswain aloft to "mouse the horses," in anticipation of the manœuvre which the boys were now compelled to perform at midnight, in a gale of wind. Mousing the horses was merely fastening the foot-ropes to the eyes of the stirrups, so that they could not slip through, and thus throw the entire slack of the horse under one boy, by which he sank down so low that his neck was even with the spar.

At the foot of each mast there is a contrivance for securing ropes, called the fife-rail. It is full of belaying pins, to which are secured the sheets, halyards, buntlines, clewlines, lifts, braces, reef tackle, and other ropes leading down from aloft. Looking at the mast, it seems to be surrounded by a perfect wilderness of ropes, without order or arrangement, whose uses no ordinary mortal could comprehend. There were other ropes leading down from aloft, which were fastened at the sheer-poles and under the rail. Now, it is necessary that every sailor should be able to put his hand on the right rope in the darkest night; and when the order to haul out the buntlines was given in the gloom and the gale, those to whom this duty was assigned could have closed their eyes and found the right lines.

"Aloft, topman!" continued the first lieutenant, when the topsails were in readiness for reefing.

At this order thirty of the young tars ran up the shrouds, over the cat-harpings, and up the rigging, till they reached the fore, main, and mizzen topsail yards. Twelve of them were stationed on the main, ten on the fore, and eight on the mizzen topsail yard. The first, second, and third midshipmen were aloft to superintend the work, and when the studding-sail booms had been triced up, they gave the order to lay out, and take two reefs.

When the hands were at their stations on the yard, the first lieutenant ordered the quartermaster to "luff up;" that is, to put the helm down so as to throw the ship up into the wind and spill the sail, or get the wind out of it, that the young tars might handle it with the more ease.

The boys had been frequently trained in the manœuvre which they were now executing under trying circumstances, and all of them knew their duty. If any one trembled as the mast swayed over when the ship rolled, he was afraid to mention the fact, or to exhibit any signs of alarm. Perhaps most of them would have been willing to acknowledge that it was rather "ticklish" business to lay out on a topsail yard at midnight in a gale of wind; and if their anxious mothers could have seen the boys at that moment, some of them might have fainted, and all wished them in a safer place.

The boom tricing-lines were manned again, and the studding-sail booms restored to their places.

"Lay down from aloft!" shouted Haven, when the midshipman in charge aloft had reported the work done; and he was obliged to roar at the top of his lungs through the speaking trumpet, in order to be heard above the piping of the gale and the dashing of the sea. "Man the topsail halyards! stand by the braces."

"All ready, sir," reported the fourth lieutenant, after the others.

"Hoist away the topsails!"

The hands on deck walked away with the halyards, until the topsails were hauled up to a taut leech.

The same operation was repeated on the fore and main course; the yards were trimmed; the bowlines attached and hauled out, and then the ship was under double-reefed topsails and courses.

"Boatswain, pipe down!" said the executive officer, when the work was done.

But the crew did not care to pipe down, just then. This was the first time they had ever seen a gale at sea, and there was something grand and sublime in the heaving ocean, and the wild winds that danced madly over the white-crested waves. It was now after midnight, eight bells having struck before the courses were reefed, and the first part of the starboard watch were to have the deck. Mr. Lowington insisted that all others should go below and turn in, assuring them that they would see enough of the gale in the morning, or as soon as their quarter watches were called.

The principal and Mr. Fluxion were earnest in their commendation of the behavior of the Young America. She was not only a stiff and weatherly ship, but she behaved most admirably, keeping well up to the wind, and minding her helm. The four boys at the wheel handled it with perfect ease.

The ship did not labor in the gale as she had before the sails were reefed; and though she jumped, plunged, and rolled, making a terrific roar as she went along, everything was ship-shape about her, and the boys soon became accustomed to the exciting scene. She was making but little headway, but she still kept within three points of her general course. Mr. Lowington remained on deck the rest of the night, anxiously watching the ship and her crew in the trying experience of the hour.

Augustus Pelham, the discontented lieutenant, went below when his quarter watch was relieved. The little incident, before all hands were called, between himself and the captain, had disturbed him more than he would have been willing to acknowledge. He thought it was harsh of the captain to say anything to him, though he had broken one of the rules of the ship; and he regarded the gentle reproof he had received as a very great indignity.

He went to his state room. The ship was rolling fearfully, and he could not stand up without holding on at the front of his berth. Goodwin, the third lieutenant, who was his room-mate, had already turned in; but it was impossible for him to sleep. Pelham took a match from his pocket and lighted the lamp, which swung on gimbals in the room.

"What are you doing, Pelham?" demanded Goodwin. "It is against the rule to light a lamp after ten o'clock."

"I know it; but I'm not going to blunder round here, and have my brains knocked out in the dark," growled Pelham.

"Put the light out; you will get into trouble," remonstrated his room-mate.

"I won't do it."

"What are you going to do?"

"Go to sleep, Goodwin, and don't bother me."

"What's the matter, Pelham? What ails you? I never knew you to think of breaking one of the rules before."

"I should like to break them all, as Moses did the ten commandments. I have been insulted."

"Who insulted you?"

"The captain."

"Gordon?" asked Goodwin, in astonishment.

"Yes."

"I never knew him to do such a thing as that. I think you didn't understand him; or he must have been excited by the gale."

"It was before it came on to blow very hard," replied Pelham, seating himself on a stool, and bracing his feet against the front of the berth to prevent being thrown down.

"What did he do?"

"He snubbed me, told me I knew the rule, and was as overbearing as though I had been his servant, instead of an officer of the ship."

"But what did you do? He wouldn't have done anything of the kind if you hadn't given him some provocation."

"I told the quartermaster, when the wind was heading off the ship, to alter the course."

"Didn't you tell the captain beforehand?"

"Not I."

"Then I don't blame him for snubbing you. What's the use of being captain if the officers don't obey you?"

"If he had anything to say to me, he might have been a little more gentle about it."

Pelham neglected to say that he was not particularly gentle himself.

"Put that light out, Pelham, for my sake, if not for your own," said Goodwin, when he found that his companion was too much out of sorts to be reasonable.

"Neither for yours nor my own will I put it out,"

replied Pelham, as he took a cigar from its hiding-place, under the lower berth.

"What are you going to do, Pelham?" demanded Goodwin, filled with astonishment, as he observed the conduct of his fellow-officer.

"I'm going to have a smoke."

"But you know that smoking is positively prohibited either on ship or shore."

"I haven't had a smoke since vacation," replied Pelham, as he lighted the cigar.

"See here, Pelham; I won't stand this!" exclaimed the third lieutenant, rising up in his bed, in which act he was nearly pitched out of his berth by a heavy roll of the ship. "The companion-way is closed."

"That's the very reason why I'm going to smoke," replied the malcontent, coolly.

"But I shall be stifled here."

"Can't help it."

"I can," retorted Goodwin, as he leaped out on the floor.

"What are you going to do?"

"I am going to inform Mr. Lowington what you are doing."

"Are you such a fellow as that?" asked Pelham, indignantly.

"I am, if you are such a fellow as to attempt to stifle me with cigar smoke in my own room. It would make me as sick as a horse in five minutes."

"Seasick, you mean," sneered Pelham. "I'm going to have my smoke, if there is a row about it."

Goodwin put on his pea-jacket, and left the room.

CHAPTER XV.

AFTER THE GALE.

ONE of the most singular traits observable in the character of some boys is the willingness, and even the desire, under certain circumstances, to get into trouble. A young gentleman, feeling that he has been slighted, or his merit overlooked, permits himself to fall into a mental condition in which he feels no responsibility for his conduct: in which he recklessly breaks through all regulations, places himself in an attitude of opposition to constituted authority, and seems to court the heaviest penalty which can be inflicted upon him for disobedience, impudence, and rebellion.

The fourth lieutenant of the Young America had worked himself up to this disagreeable pitch. He was not only disposed to assume an attitude of opposition to the principal, who had made the obnoxious regulation which was the immediate cause of his rebellious condition, but to all who supported his authority, or willingly submitted to it.

Smoking was a high crime on board the Young America — not in the relation of the practice to the ship, but to the student. It was condemned, not simply because it would be offensive in the cabins and steerage, and on deck, but because it was a bad habit for a boy to acquire. The adult forward officers, the cooks and the stewards, were allowed to smoke on the forecastle at certain prescribed hours; but it was a punishable offence for a student to smoke at any time or in any place, whether on board or on shore.

Goodwin was indignant at the conduct of his roommate, for the third lieutenant was not only opposed to smoking on principle, but the fumes of tobacco were intensely offensive to him; and there was no doubt that, in the confined space of the state room, insufficiently ventilated, while all the openings in the deck were closed during the gale, the smoke would make him " as sick as a horse." He was a noble-minded, manly youth, and had all a boy's detestation for tattling and tale-bearing. He did not like to go on deck and inform the principal of the conduct of Pelham, but he could not submit to the indignity cast upon him. He went out into the cabin, and threw himself upon the cushioned divan, under the stern ports of the ship.

This would have been a very satisfactory place to sleep under ordinary circumstances; but Goodwin had hardly secured a comfortable position, before the heavy rolling and pitching of the vessel tumbled him off, and he measured his length on the cabin floor — a very undignified situation for a third lieutenant. He picked himself up in the darkness, and tried it again, but with no better success than before. He had fully intended to go on deck and inform the principal of the misconduct of Pelham, which had driven him from his room; but he shrank from the task.

What Goodwin was attempting to do on the divan many of the officers were striving to do in their berths, though with better success than attended his efforts. It was not an easy matter to stay in the berths; and this done, the situation was far from comfortable. Avoiding the rude fall on the one side, the occupant was rolled over against the partition on the other side. Sleep, in anything more than " cat naps," was utterly impracticable, for as soon as the tired officer began to lose himself in slumber, he was thumped violently against the pine boards, or was roused by the fear of being tumbled out of his berth.

Mr. Lowington comprehended the situation of the students, and when the topsails and courses had been reefed, he called up all the stewards, and sent them through the after cabin and steerage, to ascertain the condition of the boys, and to give them the benefit of certain expedients known to old voyagers for such occasions. Jacobs, the steward of the after cabin, entered to perform his duty. He had no light, not even a lantern; for fire is so terrible a calamity at sea, that every lamp was extinguished by the stewards at ten o'clock, and no light was allowed, except in the binnacle, without the special permission of the principal. Even the captain could not allow a lamp to be lighted after hours.

Jacobs went to all the state rooms on the port side first, and pulled up the berth sacks above the front of the bunks, so as to form a kind of wall, to keep the occupant from rolling out. A bundle of clothing was placed on the inside of the berth, and the body was thus wedged in, so as to afford some relief to the unstable form. Pelham's room was the second one on the starboard side, and Jacobs came to it at last, in his humane mission. He opened the door, and started back with unfeigned astonishment to see the lamp lighted, and the fourth lieutenant puffing his cigar as leisurely as the violent motion of the ship would permit.

"Contrary to regulation, sir," said Jacobs, respectfully, as he touched his cap to the reckless officer.

"Take yourself off, Jacobs," replied Pelham, coarsely and rudely.

"Yes, sir."

Jacobs did take himself off, and hastened on deck to inform Mr. Lowington of the conduct of the infatuated officer.

The principal immediately presented himself. Pelham had fully believed, in his self-willed obstinacy, that he could look Mr. Lowington full in the face, and impudently defy him. He found that he was mistaken. The experience of Shuffles in the hands of the boatswain and carpenter would intrude itself upon him, and he quailed when the principal opened the door and gazed sternly into his face.

"Smoking, Mr. Pelham?"

"Yes, sir," replied the rebel, with an attempt to be cool and impudent, which, however, was a signal failure.

"You will put out that cigar, and throw it away."

"I will: I've smoked enough," answered Pelham.

"Your light is burning, contrary to regulation."

"The ship rolls so, I should break my neck without one," replied Pelham, sourly.

"That is a weak plea for a sailor to make. Mr. Pelham, I confess my surprise to find one who has done so well engaged in acts of disobedience."

The reckless officer could make no reply; if the reproof had been given in presence of others, he would probably have retorted, prompted by a false, foolish pride to "keep even" with the principal.

"For smoking, you will lose ten marks; for lighting your lamp, ten more," added the principal.

"You might as well send me into the steerage at once," answered Pelham.

"If either offence is repeated, that will be done. You will put out your light at once."

The fourth lieutenant obeyed the order because he did not dare to disobey it; the fear of the muscular boatswain, the irons, and the brig, rather than that of immediate degradation to the steerage, operating upon his mind. The principal went on deck; Pelham turned in, and was soon followed, without a word of comment on the events which had just transpired, by Goodwin.

The night wore away, the gale increasing in fury, and the rain pouring in torrents. It was a true taste of a seaman's life to those who were on deck. At daybreak all hands were called again, to put the third reef in the topsails. At eight bells the courses were furled. The gale continued to increase in power during the forenoon, and by noon a tremendous sea had been stirred up. The ship rolled almost down to her beam ends, and the crests of the waves seemed to be above the level of the main yard.

In the popular exaggerated language, "the waves

ran mountain high," which means from twenty to forty feet; perhaps, on this occasion, twenty-five feet from the trough of the sea to the crest of the billow. Even this is a great height to be tossed up and down on the water; and to the boys of the Young America the effect was grand, if not terrific. The deck was constantly flooded with water; additional life-lines had been stretched across from rail to rail, and every precaution taken to insure the safety of the crew.

Study and recitation were impossible, and nothing was attempted of this kind. The storm was now what could justly be called a heavy gale, and it was no longer practicable to lay a course. Before eight bells in the forenoon watch, the royal and top-gallant yards had been sent down, and the ship was laid to under a close-reefed main-topsail, which the nautical gentlemen on board regarded as the best for the peculiar conditions which the Young America presented.

When a ship is laying to, no attention is paid to anything but the safety of the vessel, the only object being to keep her head up to the sea. In the gale, the Young America lay with her port bow to the wind, her hull being at an angle of forty-five degrees, with a line indicating the direction of the wind. Her topsail yard was braced so that it pointed directly to the north-east — the quarter from which the gale blew. The helm was put a-lee just enough to keep her in the position indicated. She made little or no headway, but rather drifted with the waves.

. The young tars had a hard forenoon's work; and what was done was accomplished with triple the labor required in an ordinary sea. All hands were on duty during the first part of the day, though there were intervals of rest, such as they were, while the boys had to hold on with both hands, and there was no stable abiding-place for the body. The ship rolled so fiercely that no cooking could be done, and the only refreshments were coffee and " hard tack."

"This is a regular muzzler, Pelham," said Shuffles, in the afternoon, as they were holding on at the life-lines in the waist.

"That's a fact; and I've got about enough of this thing."

"There isn't much fun in it," replied Shuffles, who had been watching for this opportunity to advance the interests of the "Chain."

"No, not a bit."

"It's better for you officers, who don't have to lay out on the yards when they jump under you like a mad horse, than for us."

"I suppose I shall have a chance to try it next term."

"Why so?"

"I lost twenty marks last night. I got mad, lighted the lamp, and smoked a cigar in my state room."

"Will the loss of the twenty marks throw you over?"

"Yes; I'm a goner!" added Pelham, with a smile.

"What made you mad?"

"The captain snubbed me; then Lowington came the magnificent over me. A single slip throws a fellow here."

A single slip in the great world throws a man or woman; and young men and young women should be taught that "single slips" are not to be tolerated. More children are spoiled by weak indulgence than by over-severe discipline. But a boy had a better chance to recover from the effects of his errors in the Young America, than men and women have in the community.

By gradual approaches, Shuffles informed the fourth lieutenant of the object of the "Chain," which Pelham promptly agreed to join, declaring that it was just the thing to suit his case. He was in a rebellious frame of mind; and though he could not feel that the enterprise would be a complete success, it would afford him an opportunity to annoy and punish the principal for his degrading and tyrannical regulation, as the recreant officer chose to regard it.

By the exercise of some tact, the conspirators found a convenient place under the top-gallant forecastle to consider the project. Pelham was duly "toggled," and offered no objection to the penalty; indeed, he only laughed at it.

"Suppose we get possession of the ship — what then?" asked Pelham.

"We will go on a cruise. I understand that she has provisions for a six months' voyage on board. I'm in favor of going round Cape Horn, and having a good time among the islands of the South Sea."

Pelham laughed outright at this splendid scheme.

"Round Cape Horn!" exclaimed he.

"Yes; why not? We should be up with the cape by the first of June; rather a bad time, I know, but this ship would make good weather of it, and I don't believe we should see anything worse than this."

"What will you do with the principal and the professors?" asked Pelham, lightly.

"We can run up within ten or fifteen miles of Cape Sable, give them one of the boats, and let them go on shore."

"Perhaps they won't go."

"We have ten fellows already in the Chain, who are seventeen years old. If we get half the crew, we can handle the other half, and the professors with them."

"All right! I'm with you, whether you succeed or not. I'm not going to be ground under Lowington's feet, and be snubbed by such fellows as Gordon. If I want to smoke a cigar, I'm going to do it."

"Or take a glass of wine," suggested Shuffles.

"If there is any on board."

"There is, plenty of it. I'll make you a present of a bottle, if you wish it."

"Thank you. Suppose we get the ship, Shuffles, who are to be the officers?" asked Pelham.

"We shall have good fellows for officers. You will be one, of course."

"I suppose I am higher in rank now than any fellow who has joined the Chain."

"Yes, that's a fact; but we are not going to mind who are officers now, or who have been before. We intend to take the best fellows — those who have done the most work in making the Chain."

"Whether they are competent or not," added Pelham.

"All the fellows know how to work a ship now, except the green hands that came aboard this year."

"This is rather an important matter, Shuffles, for

everything depends upon the officers. For instance, who will be captain?" asked Pelham, with assumed indifference.

"I shall, of course," replied Shuffles, with becoming modesty.

"That's a settled matter, I suppose."

"Yes; without a doubt it is."

"I may not agree to that," suggested the new convert.

"You have already agreed to it. You have promised to obey your superiors."

"But who are my superiors?"

"I am one of them."

"Who appointed you?"

"I appointed myself. I got up the Chain."

"I think I have just as much right to that place as you have, Shuffles."

"I don't see it! Do you expect me to get up this thing, and then take a subordinate position?" demanded Shuffles, indignantly.

"Let the members choose the captain; that's the proper way."

"Perhaps they will choose neither one of us."

"Very well; I will agree to serve under any fellow who is fairly elected."

"When shall he be chosen?" asked Shuffles, who was so sure of a majority that he was disposed to adopt the suggestion.

"When we have thirty links, say."

"I will agree to it."

The conspirators separated, each to obtain recruits as fast as he could. During the latter part of the day, the gale began to subside, and at sunset its force was broken, but the sea still ran fearfully high. The fore course was shaken out, and the ship filled away again, plunging madly into the savage waves.

On Sunday morning, the gale had entirely subsided; but the wind still came from the same quarter, and the weather was cloudy. The sea had abated its fury, though the billows still rolled high, and the ship had an ugly motion. During the night, the reefs had been turned out of the topsails; the jib, flying-jib, and spanker had been set, and the Young America was making a course east-south-east.

"Sail ho!" shouted one of the crew on the top-gallant forecastle, after the forenoon watch was set.

"Where away?" demanded the officer of the deck.

"Over the lee bow, sir," was the report which came through the officers on duty.

The report created a sensation, as it always does when a sail is seen; for one who has not spent days and weeks on the broad expanse of waters, can form only an inadequate idea of the companionship which those in one ship feel for those in another, even while they are miles apart. Though the crew of the Young America had been shut out from society only about three days, they had already begun to realize this craving for association — this desire to see other people, and be conscious of their existence.

After the severe gale through which they had just passed, this sentiment was stronger than it would have been under other circumstances. The ocean had been lashed into unwonted fury by the mad winds. A fierce gale had been raging for full twenty-four hours, and the tempest was suggestive of what the sailor dreads most — shipwreck, with its long train of disaster — suffering, privation, and death. It was hardly possible that such a terrible storm had swept the sea without carrying down some vessels with precious freights of human life.

The Young America had safely ridden out the gale, for all that human art could do to make her safe and strong had been done without regard to expense. No niggardly owners had built her of poor and insufficient material, or sent her to sea weakly manned and with incompetent officers. The ship was heavily manned; eighteen or twenty men would have been deemed a sufficient crew to work her; and though her force consisted of boys, they would average more than two thirds of the muscle and skill of able-bodied seamen.

There were other ships abroad on the vast ocean, which could not compare with her in strength and appointments, and which had not one third of her working power on board. No ship can absolutely defy the elements, and there is no such thing as absolute safety in a voyage across the ocean; but there is far less peril than people who have had no experience generally suppose. The Cunard steamers have been running more than a quarter of a century, with the loss of only one ship, and no lives in that one — a triumphant result achieved by strong ships, with competent men to manage them. Poorly built ships, short manned, with officers unfit for their positions, constitute the harvest of destruction on the ocean.

Mr. Lowington believed that the students of the Academy Ship would be as safe on board the Young

America as they would on shore. He had taken a great deal of pains to demonstrate his theory to parents, and though he often failed, he often succeeded. The Young America had just passed through one of the severest gales of the year, and in cruising for the next three years, she would hardly encounter a more terrific storm. She had safely weathered it; the boys had behaved splendidly, and not one of them had been lost, or even injured, by the trying exposure. The principal's theory was thus far vindicated.

The starboard watch piped to breakfast, when the sail was discovered, too far off to make her out. The boys all manifested a deep interest in the distant wanderer on the tempestuous sea, mingled with a desire to know how the stranger had weathered the gale. Many of them went up the shrouds into the tops, and the spy-glasses were in great demand.

"Do you make her out, Captain Gordon?" asked Mr. Fluxion, as he came up from his breakfast, and discovered the commander watching the stranger through the glass.

"Yes, sir; I can just make her out now. Her foremast and mainmast have gone by the board, and she has the ensign, union down, hoisted at her mizzen," replied the captain, with no little excitement in his manner.

"Indeed!" exclaimed the teacher of mathematics, as he took the glass. "You are right, Captain Gordon, and you had better keep her away."

"Shall I speak to Mr. Lowington first, sir?" asked the captain.

"I think there is no need of it in the present

instance. There can be no doubt what he will do when a ship is in distress."

"Mr. Kendall, keep her away two points," said the captain to the officer of the deck. "What is the ship's course now?"

"East-south-east, sir," replied the second lieutenant, who had the deck.

"Make it south-east."

"South-east, sir," repeated Kendall. "Quartermaster, keep her away two points," he added to the petty officer conning the wheel.

"Two points, sir," said Bennington, the quartermaster.

"Make the course south-east."

"South-east, sir."

After all these repetitions it was not likely that any mistake would occur; and the discipline of the ship required every officer and seaman who received a material order, especially in regard to the helm or the course, to repeat it, and thus make sure that it was not misunderstood.

It was Sunday; and no study was required, or work performed, except the necessary ship's duty. Morning prayers had been said, as usual, and there was to be divine service in the steerage, forenoon and afternoon, for all who could possibly attend; and this rule excepted none but the watch on deck. By this system, the quarter watch on duty in the forenoon, attended in the afternoon; those who were absent at morning prayers were always present at the evening devotions; and blow high or blow low, the brief matin and vesper service were never omitted, for young men in the midst of the sublimity and the terrors of the ocean could least afford to be without the daily thought of God, "who plants his footsteps in the sea, and rides upon the storm."

Every man and boy in the ship was watching the speck on the watery waste, which the glass had revealed to be a dismasted, and perhaps sinking ship. The incident created an intense interest, and was calculated to bring out the finer feelings of the students. They were full of sympathy for her people, and the cultivation of noble and unselfish sentiments, which the occasion had already called forth, and was likely to call forth in a still greater degree, was worth the voyage over the ocean; for there are impressions to be awakened by such a scene which can be garnered in no other field.

CHAPTER XVI.

THE WRECK OF THE SYLVIA.

THE people in the dismasted ship had discovered the Young America, as it appeared from the efforts they were using to attract her attention. The booming of a gun was occasionally heard from her, but she was yet too far off to be distinctly seen.

On the forecastle of the Academy Ship were two brass guns, four-pounders, intended solely for use in making signals. They had never been fired, even on the Fourth of July, for Mr. Lowington would not encourage their use among the boys. On the present occasion he ordered Peaks, the boatswain, to fire twice, to assure the ship in distress that her signals were heard.

The top-gallant sails were set, and the speed of the ship increased as much as possible; but the heavy sea was not favorable to rapid progress through the water. At four bells, when all hands but the second part of the port watch were piped to attend divine service in the steerage, the Young America was about four miles distant from the dismasted vessel. She was rolling and pitching heavily, and not making more than two or three knots an hour.

Notwithstanding the impatience of the crew, and

their desire to be on deck, where they could see the wreck, the service on that Sunday forenoon was especially impressive. Mr. Agneau prayed earnestly for those who were suffering by the perils of the sea, and that those who should draw near unto them in the hour of their danger, might be filled with the love of God and of man, which would inspire them to be faithful to the duties of the occasion.

When the service was ended the students went on deck again. The wreck could now be distinctly seen. It was a ship of five or six hundred tons, rolling helplessly in the trough of the sea. She was apparently water-logged, if not just ready to go down. As the Young America approached her, her people were seen to be laboring at the pumps, and to be baling her out with buckets. It was evident from the appearance of the wreck, that it had been kept afloat only by the severest exertion on the part of the crew.

"Mr. Peaks, you will see that the boats are in order for use," said Mr. Lowington. "We shall lower the barge and the gig."

"The barge and the gig, sir," replied the boatswain.

"Captain Gordon," continued the principal, "two of your best officers must be detailed for the boats."

"I will send Mr. Kendall in the barge, sir."

"Very well; he is entirely reliable. Whom will you send in the gig?"

"I am sorry Shuffles is not an officer now, for he was one of the best we had for such service," added the captain.

"Shuffles is out of the question," replied Mr. Lowington.

"Mr. Haven, then, in the gig."

"The sea is very heavy, and the boats must be handled with skill and prudence."

"The crews have been practised in heavy seas, though in nothing like this."

The barge and the gig — called so by courtesy — were the two largest boats belonging to the ship, and pulled eight oars each. They were light and strong, and had been built with especial reference to the use for which they were intended. They were life-boats, and before the ship sailed, they had been rigged with life-lines and floats. If they were upset in a heavy sea, the crews could save themselves by clinging to the rope, buoyed up by the floats.

The Young America stood up towards the wreck, intending to pass under her stern as near as it was prudent to lay, the head of the dismasted ship being to the north-west.

"Boatswain, pipe all hands to muster," said the captain, prompted by Mr. Lowington, as the ship approached the wreck.

"All hands on deck, ahoy!" shouted the boatswain, piping the call.

The first lieutenant took the trumpet from the officer of the deck, and the crew, all of whom were on deck when the call was sounded, sprang to their muster stations.

"All hands, take in courses," said the executive officer; and those who were stationed at the tacks and sheets, clew-garnets and buntlines, prepared to do their duty when the boatswain piped the call.

"Man the fore and main clew-garnets and buntlines!" shouted the first lieutenant. "Stand by tacks and sheets!"

The fore and main sail, being the lowest square sails, are called the courses. There is no corresponding sail on the mizzenmast. The ropes by which the lower corners of these sails are hauled up for furling, are the clew-garnets — the same that are designated clewlines on the topsails.

The tacks and sheets are the ropes by which the courses are hauled down, and kept in place, the tack being on the windward side, and the sheet on the leeward.

"All ready, sir," reported the lieutenants forward.

"Haul taut! Let go tacks and sheets! Haul up!"

These orders being promptly obeyed, the courses were hauled up, and the ship was under topsails and top-gallant sails, jib, flying-jib, and spanker.

"Ship, ahoy!" shouted the first lieutenant through his trumpet, as the Young America rolled slowly along under the stern of the wreck.

"Ship, ahoy!" replied a voice from the deck of the wreck. "We are in a sinking condition! Will you take us off?"

"Ay, ay!" cried Haven, with right good will.

"You will heave to the ship, Mr. Haven," said the captain, when she had passed a short distance beyond the wreck.

"Man the jib and flying-jib halyards and downhauls," said the first lieutenant.

"All ready forward, sir," replied the second lieutenant, on the forecastle.

"Stand by the main-top bowline! Cast off! Man the main braces!"

"Let go the jib and flying-jib halyards! Haul down!" And the jibs were taken in.

"Slack off the lee braces! Haul on the weather braces!"

The main-topsail and top-gallant were thus thrown aback, and the Young America was hove to, in order to enable her people to perform their humane mission.

"Stand by to lower the barge and gig!" continued Haven.

"Mr. Haven, you will board the wreck in the gig," said Captain Gordon.

"Yes, sir," replied he, touching his cap, and handing the trumpet to the second lieutenant.

"Mr. Kendall, you will take charge of the barge," added the captain.

"The barge, sir," answered Kendall, passing the trumpet to Goodwin, the third lieutenant, who, during the absence of his superiors, was to discharge the duty of the executive officer.

The boats were cleared away, and every preparation made for lowering them into the water. This was a difficult and dangerous manœuvre in the heavy sea which was running at the time. The professors' barge, which was secured at the davits on the weather side of the ship, was to be lowered with her crew on board, and they took their places on the thwarts, with their hands to the oars in readiness for action. The principal had requested Mr. Fluxion to go in the barge and Mr. Peaks in the gig, not to command the

THE NEW YORK
PUBLIC LIBRARY

ASTOR, LENOX AND
TILDEN FOUNDATIONS
R   L

THE WRECK OF THE SYLVIA.
Page 253.

boats, but to give the officers such suggestions as the emergency of the occasion might require.

"All ready, sir," reported Ward, the coxswain of the barge, when the oarsmen were in their places.

"Stand by the after tackle, Ward," said Haven. "Bowman, attend to the fore tackle."

At a favorable moment, when a great wave was sinking down by the ship's side, the order was given to lower away, and in an instant the barge struck the water. Ward cast off the after tackle, and the bowman did the same with the forward tackle. At the moment the order to lower was given, as the wave sank down, the ship rolled to windward, and the boat struck the water some eight feet from the vessel's side.

"Up oars!" said the coxswain, with energy.

"Lively, Ward," added the first lieutenant.

"Let fall!" continued the coxswain, as a billow lifted the boat, so that those on board could see the ship's deck. "Give way together!"

The barge, tossed like a feather on the high seas, gathered headway, and moved off towards the wreck.

The lowering of the barge had been so successful that the same method was adopted with the gig; but as she was under the lee of the ship, there was less difficulty in getting her off. She pulled round the ship's bow, and having made less stern way in starting, both boats came up under the counter of the wreck at about the same time. When the barge and gig reached the ship, a line was thrown to each of them over the quarter, which the bowman caught, and made fast to the ring.

"Where is the captain of the ship?" demanded Mr. Haven.

"Here," shouted that officer.

"How many have you aboard?"

"Eighteen!"

"You must slide down on a rope over the stern; we can't go alongside," continued the first lieutenant.

"Ay, ay, sir!" responded the captain of the ship. "I have two women and two children on board."

"You must lower them in slings," added Haven, prompted by Mr. Fluxion.

The people on board the wreck went to work, and one of the women was lowered into each boat at the same time. A long loop was made in the end of the rope, and the woman sat down in the bight of it, holding on to the line with her hands. At a moment when the sea favored the movement, the boats were hauled up close to the ship's stern, the passenger caught by two of the crew, and hauled on board. A boy and a girl were let down in the same manner. The captain, mates, and seamen came down the rope hand over hand.

Each boat now had nine passengers, who were stowed in the stern sheets and on the bottom. The ropes from the ship were cast off, and the oarsmen were ordered to give way. The barge and the gig rose and fell, now leaping up on the huge billows, and then plunging down deep into the trough of the sea; but they had been well trimmed, and though the comb of the sea occasionally broke into them, drenching the boys with spray, the return to the Young America was safely effected.

"How happens it that you are all boys?" asked the captain of the wrecked ship, who was in Paul Kendall's boat.

"That's the Academy Ship," replied the second lieutenant.

"The what?" exclaimed the captain.

"It is the Young America. She is a school ship."

"O, ay!"

There was no disposition to talk much in the boats. The officers and crews were fully employed in keeping the barge and gig right side up in the tremendous sea, and though all hands were filled with curiosity to know the particulars of the wreck, all questions were wisely deferred until they were on the deck of the ship.

When the gig came up under the counter of the Young America, a line was thrown down to the bowman, who made it fast to the ring. The passengers were then taken aboard in slings rigged on the spanker-boom, which was swung over the lee quarter for the purpose. Part of the boat's crew were taken on board in the same way, and then the gig was hoisted up to the davits with the rest in her.

Before the barge was allowed to come up under the counter, the officer of the deck wore ship, so as to bring the port quarter, on which the boat was to be suspended, on the lee side. Her passengers were taken on deck as those from the gig had been, and she was hoisted up.

"Mr. Kendall, I congratulate you upon the success of your labors," said Mr. Lowington, when the second lieutenant reached the deck. "You have handled your boat exceedingly well, and you deserve a great deal of credit."

"That's a fact, sir," added Boatswain Peaks, touching his cap. "I hardly spoke a word to him, and I've seen many a boat worse handled in a sea."

Paul blushed at the praise bestowed upon him, but he was proud and happy to have done his duty faithfully on this important occasion. The same commendation was given to the first lieutenant, after the barge had been hauled up to the davits, and the order given for the ship to fill away again.

The women and children were conducted to the professors' cabin as soon as they came on board, and the seamen were taken into the steerage. All of them were exhausted by the anxiety and the hardships they had endured, and as soon as their safety was insured, they sank almost helpless under the pressure of their physical weakness.

"This is a school ship, I'm told," said Captain Greely, the master of the shipwrecked vessel, who had also been invited to the main cabin.

"Yes, sir; we call it the Academy Ship, and we have eighty-seven young gentlemen on board," replied Mr. Lowington.

"They are smart boys, sir. I never saw boats better handled than those which brought us off from the ship," added Captain Greely, warmly.

"Your voyage has come to an unfortunate conclusion," said Mr. Lowington.

"Yes, sir; I have lost my ship, but I thank God my wife and children are safe," answered the weather-beaten seaman, as he glanced at one of the women, while the great tears flowed down his sun-browned cheeks.

"Poor children!" sighed Mr. Agneau, as he patted the little girl on the head; and his own eyes were dim with the tears he shed for others' woes.

Captain Greely told his story very briefly. His ship was the Sylvia, thirty days out of Liverpool, bound to New York. She had encountered a heavy gale a week before, in which she had badly sprung her mainmast. Finding it impossible to lay her to under the foresail, they had been compelled to set the main-topsail, reefed; but even this was too much for the weak mast, and it had gone by the board, carrying the second mate and five men with it. The Sylvia was old, and the captain acknowledged that she was hardly sea-worthy. She became unmanageable, and the foremast had been cut away to ease off the strain upon her. Her seams opened, and she was making more water than could be controlled with the pumps. For eighteen hours, all hands, even including the two women, had labored incessantly at the pumps and the buckets, to keep the ship afloat. They were utterly worn out when they discovered the Young America, were on the point of abandoning their efforts in despair, and taking to the boats, in which most of them would probably have perished.

After the boats started from the Young America, Mr. Lowington had ordered the cooks to prepare a meal for the people from the wreck; and as soon as they came on board, coffee and tea, beefsteaks, fried potatoes, and hot biscuit were in readiness for them. Tables were spread in the main cabin and in the steerage, and the exhausted guests, providentially sent to this bountiful board, were cordially invited to partake. They had eaten nothing but hard bread since the gale came on, and they were in condition to appreciate the substantial fare set before them.

By the forethought of Captain Greely, the clothing of the women and children had been thrown into one of the boats. The bundle was opened, and its contents dried at the galley fire. The doctor and the chaplain gave up their state room to the captain, his wife and children, while Mr. Lowington extended a similar courtesy to the other woman, who was Mrs. Greely's sister. Mr. Fluxion was the first to offer his berth to the mate of the Sylvia, which was reluctantly accepted; and all the professors were zealous to sacrifice their own comfort to the wants of the wrecked visitors.

In the steerage, every boy, without an exception, wanted to give up his berth to one of the seamen from the Sylvia; but the privilege was claimed by the adult forward officers, the cooks, and stewards. The principal was finally obliged to decide between them; and for obvious reasons, he directed that the guests should occupy the quarters of the men, rather than of the boys. The people from the Sylvia needed rest and nourishment more than anything else. They were warmed, and fed, and dried, and then permitted to sleep off the fatigues of their severe exertion.

At three o'clock, though they had slept but an hour or two, most of the shipwrecked people appeared at divine service, for this was a privilege which they had long been denied, and it would be strange, at such a time, if the hearts of those who had been saved from the angry flood were not overflowing with gratitude to God for his mercy to them. Mr. Agneau, whose sensitive nature had been keenly touched by the events of the day, made a proper use of the occasion, delivering a very effective address to the students and to the shipwrecked voyagers, who formed his little congregation.

The next morning the wind came up fresh and warm from the southward, knocking down the heavy sea, and giving a delightful day to those on board the ship. The passengers appeared on deck, and were greatly interested in the Young America and her juvenile crew. Captain Greely's son and daughter were little lions, of the first class, among the boys. All hands vied with each other in their efforts to do something for the guests of the ship, and it really seemed as though the era of good feeling had dawned upon them. Even Shuffles and Pelham forgot, for a time, the interests of the Chain League, and joined with others in petting the children of the wreck, and in laboring for the happiness of the involuntary guests.

On this day, observations for latitude and longitude were obtained, and at noon the ship was found to be in latitude 42°, 37', 5" N.; longitude 64°, 39', 52" W. The position of the ship was marked on the chart by the masters, in council assembled, and the calculations made for the course. Bowditch's Navigator, an indispensable work to the seaman, was consulted frequently, both for the rules and the nautical tables it contains. The course, after allowing for the variation of the compass, was found to be north-east by east, which, agreeing with the calculations of Mr. Fluxion, was given out to the quartermaster conning the wheel.

The wind continued to blow fresh from the south and south-west during the rest of the day and the succeeding night; and the log-slate showed ten and eleven knots until midnight, when the wind hauled round to the westward, and soon came strong from that quarter. At noon on Tuesday, April 5, the Young America had made two hundred and forty-four miles during the preceding twenty-four hours, which was the best run she had had during the voyage.

On the afternoon of this day, a ship, bound to the westward, was seen, and Captain Greely expressed a desire to be put on board of her, with his family, as he did not wish to return to the point from which he had just come. The Young America bore down upon the sail, and spoke her at sundown. Her captain was willing to take the shipwrecked voyagers on board his ship, which was bound to New York, and they were transferred in the barge and gig. Captain Greely and his party were very grateful for the attentions they had received; and the little boy and girl almost rebelled at the idea of leaving their new and partial friends.

As the two ships were filling away, after the transfer of the passengers, the seamen of the New York ship, having learned what the Young America was, gave three cheers, and dipped her ensign in compliment to her. All the young tars were immediately ordered into the rigging by Captain Gordon, and "three times three" were most lustily given. The

American flag at her peak was lowered three times, in reply to the salute of the stranger. As the Academy Ship stood off on her course, the two children of Captain Greely were seen, on the poop-deck of the other vessel, waving their handkerchiefs; and they continued to do so as long as they could be seen.

The departure of the guests had a saddening effect upon the crew of the Young America, as they missed the children and the ladies very much; for, during their presence on board, the ship had assumed quite a domestic aspect, and all the idlers on deck found pleasing companions in the little boy and girl.

The limits of this volume do not permit a full detail of the entire voyage across the ocean. Enough has been given to show the discipline of the ship, and the daily life of the boys on board of her. For the next ten days the weather was generally favorable, and she laid her course all the time. Some days she made two hundred miles, and others less than one hundred.

On the sixteenth day from her departure, she was in latitude 51°, 4', 28" N.; longitude 31°, 10', 2" W.; course, E. by N. In going from Cape Race, the southern point of Newfoundland, to Cape Clear, the southern point of Ireland, the Young America did not lay a straight course, as it would appear when drawn on a map or chart. La Rochelle, on the western coast of France, and Cape Race are nearly on the same parallel of latitude, and the former is exactly east of the latter. But the parallel on which both points lie would not be the shortest line between them. A great circle, extending entirely around the earth in the broadest part, going through both, would not coincide with the parallel, but would run to the north of it a considerable distance at a point half way between the two places, the separation diminishing each way till the great circle crosses the parallel at Cape Race and La Rochelle. The shortest course between the two points, therefore, would be the arc of the great circle lying between them. A skilful navigator would find and follow this track. This is called great circle sailing.

The Young America followed a great circle from Cape Race to Cape Clear. Off the former point, her course was two points north of east; off the latter, it was half a point south of east. On her twentieth day out she sailed due east.

After the excitement of the wreck and the departure of the passengers, Shuffles and his confederates resumed their operations in the Chain League, assisted somewhat by a case of discipline which occurred at this time. When the ship was sixteen days out the Chain consisted of thirty-one links, in the cabalistic language of the conspirators, and Shuffles was in favor of striking the blow.

CHAPTER XVII.

PEAS AND BEANS.

THE business of the Chain had been managed with extreme caution by the conspirators, and more than one third of the crew had been initiated without the knowledge of the principal and professors, or of the officers and seamen who were not members. Pelham and Shuffles ordered the affairs of the League, and no " link " was allowed to approach an outsider for the purpose of inducing him to join without the consent of one of these worthies.

As the scheme progressed, various modifications had been made in the plan to adapt it to circumstances, the principal of which was the choice of two " shackles," who should be deemed the officers of the League until a regular election had taken place. By this invention, Shuffles and Pelham had been enabled to compromise their differences, for they assumed the newly-created offices, and labored as equals in the bad cause. Each endeavored to make as many new " links " as possible, for already the conspirators consisted of two factions, one of which favored the election of Shuffles, and the other that of Pelham, to the captaincy. Each, in a measure, controlled his own recruits, and was reasonably sure of their votes when the election should be ordered.

These young gentlemen were not only plotting to take the ship, but to "take in" each other. While both worked for the League as a whole, each worked for himself as an individual. Shuffles was much more thorough than his rival in the making of his converts. He told them the whole story, and taught them to look full in the face the extreme peril of the undertaking. He did not conceal anything from them. On the other hand, Pelham merely represented the project as a means of redressing the grievances of the officers and crew; of having their money restored to them, and abolishing certain portions of the regulations which pressed hard upon those who were disposed to be unruly.

Though the number of "links" in the "Chain" has been mentioned, it was not known to either of the rivals. Each knew his own peculiar followers, but he did not know how many the other could muster. Though there were signs and passwords by which the members could know each other, there were no means by which any one could precisely sum up the whole number of "links." Shuffles could count thirteen including his rival, while Pelham could number nineteen without his coequal in authority. The former believed the list to consist of about twenty four, while the latter estimated it above thirty. With them it was a struggle for an office, as well as to redress their fancied wrongs, and they mutually deceived each other in order to obtain the advantage.

"How many do you suppose we can muster now?"

asked Shuffles, on the evening of the eighteenth day out, as they met in the waist, when both were off duty.

"About twenty," replied Pelham.

"There are more than that."

"Perhaps there are."

"But it is time to stretch the Chain," added Shuffles, in a whisper.

"Not yet."

"If we are ever going to do anything, we must begin soon. We have so many members now that the danger of exposure increases every day."

"We can't do anything here. Besides, I am not in favor of having the time or the manner of accomplishing the work talked about among the members. I believe in one-man power in an affair of this sort. There should be one head, who should plan and command; all the rest should obey. If every step in the thing must be discussed and agreed upon, we shall never do anything. One fellow will want it done in one way, and another in some other way."

"I think you are more than half right," replied Shuffles, who was confident that he should be the person chosen to arrange the plans and issue the commands.

"I know I am wholly right," added Pelham, who was equally confident that he should enjoy the undivided sway of the League. "If you are chosen captain, I will cheerfully obey your orders. I go a step farther: whoever is elected captain should appoint his own officers."

"I will agree to that also," replied the complaisant Shuffles.

"Very well, then; the understanding is, that when one of us is elected captain, he shall appoint his own officers, and do all the planning and all the commanding," answered Pelham.

"Exactly so; we are now in about longitude thirty-one, and Cork Harbor is in longitude eight, according to Bowditch, for I was looking the matter up in the steerage to-day. We have to make about twenty-three degrees more. A degree of longitude, in latitude fifty-one, is thirty-seven and three quarters miles, which would make it eight hundred and sixty-eight miles more to run in order to reach Queenstown. You see I am posted," said Shuffles.

"I see you are. By the way, had you noticed that Queenstown is not in the Navigator, or on the older maps?" added Pelham.

"Yes; the place was called the Cove of Cork until 1849, when, in honor of her majesty's visit to the town, the name was changed to Queenstown."

"All right," said Pelham.

It need not be supposed that the distance to Queenstown and the change in the name of that place had anything to do with the League. The fact was, that Mr. Fluxion had passed near the conspirators, and had paused a moment in the waist to glance up at the fore-top-gallant sail, which was not in good trim; and the conversation had been changed to suit the occasion. In talking of the affairs of the "Chain," it was required that one of the party should look forward, and the other aft, if there were two of them; and that the third, if there were three, should stand back to the nearest rail. It was further required that the conversation should not take place in a situation where it would be possible for any one to overhear them. The lee side of the waist, — the midshipman of the watch always being on the weather side, — the top-gallant forecastle, and the tops were the favorite resorts of the conspirators. If any one approached, the parties in conversation were instantly to change the topic, as Shuffles had done.

"I think it is about time for the election to take place," continued Shuffles, when Mr. Fluxion had gone aft.

"Whenever you are ready, I am," replied Pelham.

"I am ready now."

"So am I."

"Very well; it shall come off to-morrow, say."

"To-morrow it is, then."

"But how shall it be conducted?" asked Shuffles.

"That will not be an easy matter. I think, however, we can hit upon some plan for having it fairly done."

"Of course the matter lies between you and me," added Shuffles.

"To be sure."

"I suppose both of us are ready to abide the issue, whatever it may be," said Shuffles, who was not a little fearful that his powerful rival would refuse to acknowledge him when he was chosen, as he confidently expected to be.

"I pledge you my word and honor, that I will obey you in all things if you are fairly elected captain," replied Pelham, who was equally sure of being chosen himself.

"Fairly? Who is to decide whether it is fairly done or not?" demanded Shuffles, unwilling to leave a loophole through which his companion could crawl out of the bargain.

"When we have agreed upon the means of electing the captain, the choice shall be final."

"Good! You and I shall have no difficulty!" exclaimed Shuffles, rather astonished to find his rival so easily managed, as he regarded it.

"We will make it a little more binding, if you choose," suggested Pelham, who, the reader has already been assured by the figures given, was completely outwitting the author and inventor of the Chain League.

"With all my heart!"

"We will toggle each other on this special question, if you like."

"The stronger we make the bond the better," said Shuffles. "Repeat after me."

"Not here, Shuffles. There is a steamer on our weather bow. Let's go up into the mizzen-top, and have a look at her with a night glass."

Mr. Haven, the first lieutenant, who was in charge of the deck, permitted them to go aloft with the glass, for the officers were empowered to grant small favors. On reaching the top, they glanced at the steamer, and then resumed the conversation which had been suspended on deck, it being too dark for the officers below to see what they were doing

"Now go ahead," said Pelham.

"Repeat after me."

"All right."

"I promise, without any reservation, to acknowledge Shuffles as captain, if he is chosen, and faithfully to obey his orders, on penalty of falling overboard accidentally."

Pelham repeated these words, and then "toggled" his rival in the same manner.

"Now we understand each other perfectly, and there will be no chance of dragging the anchor," said Shuffles, satisfied that his sway would be undisputed. "Let me say, in addition to this, that if I should happen to be chosen, I shall make you my first officer, Pelham."

"And I will make you my first officer, if I should happen to be chosen," replied the obliging Pelham. "Of course I don't expect to be chosen; you have had the swing of this affair, and you will have all the advantage."

"No, I think not; you are an officer now, and you have more influence than I have," added the modest Shuffles.

If both had been laboring for the organization of the League on the same terms, Shuffles would certainly have the better chance of an election; but Pelham had been taking in members on false pretences, merely representing to those whom he approached that the League was an association having for its object the redress of their grievances. To only a few had he mentioned the fact that a regular mutiny was contemplated; that the ship was to be taken out of the hands of the principal, and an independent cruise commenced. He was afraid the whole truth would be more than some of them could bear; and perhaps he had so little faith in the extreme measures to be carried out by the League, that he was unwilling even to mention them.

Those who serve the evil one can neither trust each other nor trust their master.

The only real confidence in each other which can exist among men or boys must be based on moral and religious principle.

The man who pays his debts, or who performs his obligations to his fellow-men, for his reputation's sake, rather than from devotion to pure principle, will fail of his duty when he can conceal his infidelity, or when his reputation will not suffer from his acts.

A man or a boy without principle is not to be trusted out of the line of his own interest.

While Shuffles and Pelham were pledging themselves to a kind of romantic fidelity, they were plotting each against the other, each being satisfied that he had the advantage of the other.

"Now, I'm afraid the election will give us some trouble," continued Shuffles. "It will not be an easy matter to conduct it fairly — not that any fellow means to cheat, but it must be conducted with so much secrecy that we can't superintend the ballot properly."

"I know there is all that difficulty, but I have thought of a method which I believe will give us a fair election," replied Pelham.

"Have you? So have I."

"Well, what is your plan? If it is better than mine, I am willing to adopt it."

"I was thinking, as you and I are the only candidates, that each of us might be represented by one side of the ship. You shall be port, and I will be starboard. Then every link in the Chain shall hand his vote, on which shall be written the single word port or starboard either to you or me; and if there are more port than starboard, you will be captain; if more starboard than port, I shall be captain. How does that idea strike you?"

"Pretty well; but the fellows have all got to write their votes, and others will want to know what it means. It will set outsiders to thinking, and I don't believe the plan is quite safe."

"Well, what is your method?" asked Shuffles, who was willing to acknowledge the force of his rival's objections.

"Perhaps my plan is as open to objection as yours," answered Pelham; "but it will require no writing. Each of us shall get a handful of beans and a handful of peas. We can easily obtain them when the store rooms are opened. You shall be beans, and I will be peas."

"How are you, Peas?" said Shuffles, laughing at the idea.

"How are you, Beans?" added Pelham.

"Go on with your soup."

"We will give to every fellow belonging to the Chain one pea and one bean."

"I understand the plan now; but where are the fellows to deposit their vegetable ballots?"

"We can have a receiver; appoint some good fellow for the purpose — say, Greenway, the captain of the forecastle; or Tom Ellis, the third master."

"Tom Ellis! Does he belong?"

"Of course he does," laughed Pelham, who realized that he had been a little too fast in betraying the strength of his faction.

"I wouldn't appoint an officer."

"Well, you mention some fellow," said the politic Pelham.

"Say Wilton."

"Mention another."

"Lynch."

"No; try again."

"Grossbeck."

"Very well; I will agree to him."

"But he might make some mistake."

"If he does, it will be in your favor, I suppose; for you nominated him, and, of course, he will give you the benefit of any doubt," replied Pelham.

"I want a fellow who will do it fairly. I don't wish to get in by any mistake," said Shuffles, magnanimously.

"Neither do I; and I don't think there will be any mistakes."

"There is a chance for a great many. The fellows may get mixed between beans and peas. When they come to vote, there will be some who don't know beans," laughed Shuffles.

"Well, if they don't, they will know peas, which will do just as well," replied Pelham.

"It would not be pleasant for me to have them know peas, when they ought to know beans."

"We will give them P. P. as a clew to the whole thing."

"P. P.? That means P's, I suppose."

"It means that, and more. P. for Pelham, and P. for peas. If they get one right, they can't very well get the other wrong."

"That's true," answered Shuffles, silenced, rather than convinced, by the tactics of his fellow-conspirator.

It was settled that he who knew peas must certainly "know beans."

"When shall the fellows vote?" asked Shuffles.

"After dinner to-morrow afternoon. Every fellow will be off duty an hour in the first or second dog watch," replied Pelham, who seemed to have an answer ready for every question. "The polls shall be kept open till eight o'clock. The peas and beans shall be distributed before eight bells in the forenoon watch, so that every fellow will be ready to vote."

"Where will Grossbeck stand when he receives the ballots?"

"He won't stand anywhere in particular. We will see him together, and give him his instructions. I think it will be better for him to walk about the ship, and let the fellows hand him the votes on the sly, which he must put in his pocket. He shall count them in the presence of both of us."

"Suppose he should lose some of them?" suggested Shuffles.

"If he does, he is as likely to lose peas as beans."

"I don't want to be chosen in any such manner as by the loss of the votes."

"I can't see that there is any more danger of his losing them than there is of his losing his head. I see you are not entirely satisfied with the plan."

"To tell you the truth, Pelham, I am not. There is, at least, a chance for mistakes."

"I'm willing to do anything you like, that will make the election a fairer one."

"I have it!" exclaimed Shuffles. "We can give each fellow two peas and two beans, and let him vote twice."

"What good will that do?"

"I'll tell you. We want another receiver; then let each fellow vote twice, giving a pea or a bean to both of the receivers. If the two results don't agree, it shall not be an election."

"That's a first-rate idea, Shuffles, and I go in for it with all my might," replied Pelham, with so much warmth that his companion was put in the best of humor. "Who shall be the other receiver?"

"Name some one," said Shuffles, generously conceding the nomination to his confederate.

"Perth."

"No."

Shuffles objected because Pelham had done so when he had mentioned two names.

"Richton."

"Once more."

"McKeon."

"Right. McKeon is an honest, careful fellow," added Shuffles. "Now I think there can be no mistake."

The minor details of the election were carefully arranged, and the boys went below again. They gave satisfactory replies to the first lieutenant, who questioned them in regard to the steamer they had gone aloft to examine. Pelham thought she was a "Cunarder," but Shuffles was confident she belonged to the Inman line; and it is quite certain neither of them had any opinion whatever in regard to her, except that she was going west; for the red light on her port side was visible.

On the following day, Grossbeck and McKeon, the receivers who had been appointed, were waited upon, separately, by the two "Shackles." They accepted the important trust which was confided to them, and each was duly and solemnly admonished of the necessity of entire fairness. They were informed that any discrepancy in the number of ballots in the hands of the two receivers would cause the vote to be rejected; and they individually promised to be both faithful and careful.

The beans and the peas were readily obtained, and were distributed among the members of the League, with the necessary secrecy. Some of the independent voters needed a little persuasion to induce them to vote, when informed that the choice was between the "Shackles" only; but they yielded the point, and entered heartily into the excitement of the event; for, secret as were the proceedings, they were attended with no little exhilaration of feeling.

The voting commenced in the afternoon watch. The second part of the starboard watch, being off duty, gave in their peas and beans first. The receivers, without even knowing all the members of the League, took whatever was handed to them "on the sly," and looked as careless and indifferent as though nothing was going on. The only responsibility that rested upon them, besides the general duty of carefulness and fidelity, was to see that no one voted twice. "Vote early and vote often" was not countenanced; and one receiver acted as a check upon the other.

The election progressed so secretly that no occasion for suspicion was given; and though the ballots were deposited under the eyes of the principal and the professors, they saw nothing, and had not the remotest idea that anything wrong was in progress.

In the last half of the first dog watch, Shuffles began to be excited. He was too much of a politician to be idle while any voting was going on; and so far as his duty would permit, he had watched the receivers since the balloting commenced. He had seen seven or eight vote of whose membership in the Chain he had no previous knowledge. He saw that Pelham had made more initiates than he had been willing to acknowledge, apparently concealing the facts for the purpose of favoring his own election. He observed that all the officers of his rival's quarter watch voted, and he was almost certain that he had been defeated.

Shuffles was angry and indignant when he discovered the treacherous shrewdness of his fellow-conspirator; but he had solemnly promised to abide the result of the election, and he could not recede from his position without a violation of the "honor among thieves" which is said to exist. The poll would not be closed for half an hour; and as he had been cheated, he deemed it quite right to restore the equilibrium by a resort to the same policy.

"Wilton, I have been cheated," said he, angrily, as he met his old crony in the waist.

"How do you know you have?"

"I know it. I will explain by and by. Something must be done. I am beaten as sure as you live."

"Well, I can't help it if you are. You and Pelham have fixed things to suit yourselves, and now you must fight it out between you." replied Wilton, as he turned on his heel, and left the mighty mischief-maker alone and disconcerted.

"Where do all these beans come from?" said Paul Kendall, as he noticed the rejected ballots of the Pelhamites, which they had not even taken the trouble to throw over the rail.

"It's a new game the fellows are playing," replied Shuffles, with apparent indifference, as he walked aft with the second lieutenant.

"What's that?" asked Paul, curiously.

"It's called 'Don't know Beans,'" answered Shuffles, in deep thought. "The fellows have a good deal of sport out of it in the off-time."

"'Don't know Beans!' I never heard of such a game before. Tell me about it."

"You see Grossbeck and McKeon?"

"Yes."

"Well, they are the *butts*, as we call them. All the fellows in our watch have some beans," added Shuffles, taking a handful of them from his pocket.

"What do they do with them?"

"You try it yourself. Take two of these beans." Paul took them.

"Now you must give one to Grossbeck, and the other to McKeon, without letting any fellow see you do it. If any fellow does see you give it to either of them, he will say, in a low tone, 'Don't know Beans,' and then the butt must drop it on deck. When the even bell strikes, Grossbeck and McKeon must count their beans. The one who has the most must appoint the next two bean-pots, or butts; and the one who has the smaller number must pick up all the beans that have been dropped on the deck. There is fun in it; though, perhaps, you wouldn't think so."

"I will try it, at any rate."

Paul did try it, and succeeded, as all others did, in giving the beans to the receivers without any one uttering the warning words. He was rather pleased with the game, so suddenly invented, and the two officers of his watch were induced to try the experiment. Then Blackburn, Endicott, and Bennington were supplied with beans by Shuffles, who instructed his auditors that not a word must be said about the matter to the "butts," or to any one in the waist. The last three were as successful as the first three. Then Thompson and Cartwright were equally fortunate. Finally, Captain Gordon's attention was attracted, and he descended so far from his dignity as to deposit the beans.

Shuffles was satisfied. He had procured nine votes, and he was confident that he had thus defeated his rival. As a matter of precaution, he directed McKeon to pick up the beans scattered in the waist; and the "outsiders" who had cast the nine votes believed that he was the unlucky butt, who had been beaten in the game.

"The captain and half the officers voted," whispered Grossbeck at four bells.

"Certainly; that's all right. You and McKeon will meet Pelham and me in the waist at eight bells," replied Shuffles, as he went below.

CHAPTER XVIII.

THE RESULT OF THE BALLOT.

THE first part of the port watch went on duty at eight o'clock, when the secret poll for the choice of a captain, under the new order of events, was closed. Shuffles was in this watch, but as neither his "trick at the wheel" nor his turn on the lookout came within the first hour, he had an opportunity to attend to the important business of the League. Pelham and the two receivers of votes belonged in the second part of the port watch, and there was nothing to prevent them from attending the conference which Shuffles had appointed.

While Shuffles had been teaching the "outsiders" the game of "Don't know Beans," Pelham, as officer of the deck, remained abaft the mizzenmast, and had failed to notice what was taking place in the waist. The officers who were off duty, and who had unconsciously voted for Shuffles, said nothing to those in charge of the ship. In accordance with the requirements of man-of-war discipline, the weather side of the deck was given up to the captain and the officers on duty, while all the idlers were required to keep on the lee side. Captain Gordon was a privileged person. On the weather side, even the denizens of the after cabin did not presume to address him on any question not connected with the discipline of the ship. When he went over to the lee side, it was understood that he was simply a student, and even an ordinary seaman might speak to him when he walked forward.

Shuffles had explained the game to the outsiders on the lee side, out of the hearing of the officer of the deck; and Pelham, entirely satisfied that he was already elected, did not trouble himself about the matter.

If "Don't know Beans" was not much of a game, it was better than nothing, and Shuffles soon found that there was danger of his little scheme being exposed. During the second dog watch, at supper time, and as other opportunities were presented, he told Wilton, Monroe, Adler, and others, that the second lieutenant, seeing so many beans on the deck, wished to know where they came from, and that, to deceive him and the rest of the officers, he had invented the game which he described, and wished them to play while off duty on deck. "Our fellows" thought this was a good joke, and the new pastime was soon understood throughout the ship, and "butts" were appointed in each quarter watch to play it the next day.

"The fellows have all voted, I suppose," said Pelham, when the party had obtained a good position for the conference.

"The time is out, whether they have or not," replied Grossbeck.

"All we have to do now is to count the votes," added Shuffles, impatiently, for he was afraid his little trick would be exposed before the result of the ballot was obtained.

"Well, let us have it counted at once," said Pelham, who, having no doubt of the result, had no thought of offering any objection to the fairness of the election.

"We can't count the votes here," suggested McKeon. "Some one would see us, and want to know what we were doing."

"I can't leave the deck; I'm on duty," replied Shuffles.

"Let the receivers count it themselves."

"We ought to see them do it."

"That is not necessary. They don't know how many votes they have."

"I'm sure I don't," said Grossbeck.

"Neither do I," added McKeon.

"I'll tell you how we can manage it, without exciting the attention of any one."

"I will agree to anything that is fair," replied Shuffles.

"Grossbeck shall go forward, and McKeon aft as far as the mainmast, so that each cannot know what the other is about. They can count the votes separately, without being seen."

"I don't see how we can," said McKeon.

"Can you tell a pea from a bean by the feeling?"

"Of course we can."

"Where did you put the votes, Grossbeck?" asked Pelham.

"In my trousers' pocket."

"So did I," added McKeon.

"Both of you have on your pea-jackets now, and

there is a pocket on each side of them. Take out all the peas first, and put them in the right-hand pocket of your pea-jacket; then all the beans, and put them in the left-hand pocket; then count each."

"Some fellow may see us counting them," said Grossbeck.

"You must take care of that," answered Pelham.

"If they do, it will not make much difference. Some of the fellows were careless, and threw their beans on the deck."

"Did they?" laughed Pelham; "I suppose they had no use for them."

"The second lieutenant saw them, and wanted to know what they meant," added Shuffles.

"Whew!" exclaimed Pelham.

"I made it all right, though I was obliged to invent a new game to throw him off the track."

"Good!" said Pelham. "But we must go on with the counting. When you have found the number of peas and of beans, you will write the result on a piece of paper, each of you. McKeon, you will hand your paper to Shuffles, and, Grossbeck, you will hand yours to me. That's fair — isn't it?"

"Certainly," replied Shuffles.

"Then we will put the two papers together; if they agree, the election is made; if they do not agree, we must do it all over again," continued Pelham.

"All right," added Shuffles.

The two receivers were sent away to count the votes. As one went forward, and the other aft, and the two "Shackles" stood between, no communication whatever could pass from one to the other. It was now quite dark, and most of those off duty had turned in, for the students had become so well accustomed to sea life that they could sleep whenever their presence was not required on deck.

"I hope this thing will be settled now once for all," said Pelham, who feared that some mistake might defeat his hopes.

"So do I," replied Shuffles, who was disturbed by the same dread.

"Have you any idea what the result will be?" asked Pelham, who, in spite of the mutual "toggling," and the mutual assurances of good faith, had some doubts whether his rival would be willing to accept the result.

"Well, I don't know," replied Shuffles, cautiously, and with the same want of confidence which disturbed his companion. "There is no knowing who will be governor till after election."

"Of course not, but you might have some idea of the way the thing is going?"

"I might, but what's the use of talking when we shall know all about it in ten or fifteen minutes?"

"Of course you have some hopes."

"To be sure I have; and I suppose you have, too."

"Certainly I have; if I hadn't, I should have given the thing up without the trouble and risk of a ballot," replied Pelham.

"We both expect it, and it follows that one of us must be disappointed."

"You know the bond."

"I do."

"Here is my hand, Shuffles. I pledge myself over

again to abide the result of the vote, whether it is for me or against me," continued Pelham, extending his hand.

"And here is my hand, Pelham, with the same pledge, honor bright," replied Shuffles, as he took the offered hand.

"I am tolerably confident of the result," added Pelham.

"I am quite confident that I shall be chosen," replied Shuffles.

"Don't be too certain, my dear fellow," laughed the fourth lieutenant. "I have taken in a great many recruits."

"I'm glad you have — the more the better. I have also taken in a good many. Pelham, do you know this is very shaky business?"

"Shaky?"

"Yes — between you and me, I mean. If either of us should back down, the whole thing would fall to the ground."

"Back down!" exclaimed Pelham. "Why, after what has passed between us, I consider it impossible that either of us should back down. I am pledged; so are you; and if either of us should back down, I hope he will — fall overboard accidentally."

"So do I," replied Shuffles, heartily.

"My dear fellow, if you should back out, I should be mad enough to help you over the rail, some dark evening, if I had a good chance."

"I don't believe I should feel any better-natured if you should break your agreement. One of us is doomed to disappointment. We have tried to make this thing as fair as possible."

"Certainly we have, and it will be as fair as anything can be. I am entirely satisfied with the voting."

"Are you?"

"Of course I am."

Shuffles was very glad of this acknowledgment in advance of the reception of the result.

"But, after all, Pelham," said he, "there may be an appearance of unfairness in the voting, after the result is declared."

"There may be; but each of us is pledged not to claim anything on account of such an appearance. If the figures of the two receivers agree, that is the end of the whole thing, and you or I will be the captain."

"That's so; but here comes McKeon," replied Shuffles, as the receiver gave him the paper on which the result of the votes he had received was written.

It was too dark to see it, and the rivals waited, in great excitement of mind, for the appearance of Grossbeck. He came, and his paper was handed to Pelham. The conditions of the agreement had now all been complied with, and the two papers were to be placed side by side, where both of the candidates could see them at the same instant. It was necessary, in the darkness, to obtain the use of a light for a moment, and they decided to wait till the midshipman on duty in the waist went into the steerage to make the half-hourly inspection.

"When one bell struck, the officer left his post, and the conspirators walked up to the binnacle in the waist. By raising one of the slides in the side of the machine, the lamp which threw its light on the face of the compass would enable them to examine the papers.

"Hold your paper by the side of mine," said Pelham, as he placed the important document in a position to receive the light from the binnacle when the slide should be moved.

"Open it," replied Shuffles, nervously, as he complied with the direction of his rival.

Pelham raised the slide, and the contents of the papers were read by both.

>   Peas, ... 19
>   Beans, ... 22

The results given in by the two receivers were the same, and by the terms of the bond, it was an election.

"Shut the slide," said Shuffles.

"Who opened that binnacle?" demanded the first master, walking aft from his station on the forecastle.

"I did, sir," replied Shuffles, unwilling to permit the fourth lieutenant to answer the question. "We were looking at some figures I had made."

The master, finding that the fourth lieutenant was one of the party gathered around the binnacle, said no more, and returned to his place.

"Are you satisfied, Pelham?" asked Shuffles, in the softest of tones.

"I don't understand it," answered the disappointed candidate.

"Don't you? Well, you will remember that neither of us was to raise any question about the fairness of the ballot."

"I don't say a word about its fairness; I only said

I did not understand it," answered Pelham, in surly tones.

"I don't understand it any better than you do; but the point just now is, whether you acknowledge me as captain, or not."

"Of course I do. When I pledge myself to do a thing, I always do it. I hail you as captain."

"All right," added Shuffles. "Then nothing more need be said. You have kept your bond like a gentleman, and I now appoint you my first officer, as I promised to do."

"Thank you," replied Pelham, in a sneering tone.

"What's the matter, my dear fellow? Are you not satisfied?" demanded Shuffles.

"Entirely satisfied with the result;" but he talked like one who was anything but satisfied.

"It was a fair thing — wasn't it?"

"I suppose it was; I don't know."

"You speak as though you were not satisfied, Pelham."

"I am not disposed to grumble. I only say that I don't understand it."

"What don't you understand?" asked Shuffles, sharply. "The election was conducted on a plan furnished by yourself; the receivers were of your own choice; the results agree; and I can't see, for the life of me, that there is any chance to find fault."

"I don't find fault. The result perplexes me, because I can't see through it."

"What do you mean by that?"

"I don't see where your twenty-two votes came from."

"And I don't see where your nineteen came from," retorted the successful candidate.

"The whole number of votes was forty-one," added Pelham, who was quite sure there was something wrong.

"The long and short of it is, that there are more fellows on board that 'know beans,' than you thought there were," laughed Shuffles.

"Can you tell me where the forty-one votes came from, Shuffles?" demanded Pelham.

"Came from the fellows, of course."

"It's no use to snuff at it, my dear fellow. I do not purpose to set aside the election. I acknowledge you as captain. Can I do any more?"

"You can't; but you seem disposed to do something more."

"I merely wish to inquire into this thing, and find out how we stand. Had you any idea that forty-one fellows belonged to the Chain?"

"I had not," replied Shuffles, honestly. "I was never more surprised in my life, than when I saw Tom Ellis and Andy Groom vote."

"That was all right. Both of them joined."

"I can tell you what took me all aback," interposed McKeon, who, with Grossbeck, had been walking back and forth in the waist.

"No matter what took you all aback," added Shuffles, sharply. "The question is settled; what's the use of raking up every thing that may seem to be strange?"

"What was it that took you aback, McKeon?" demanded Pelham.

"It was when the captain voted," replied the receiver.

"The captain!" exclaimed Pelham.

"Yes."

"Do you mean Captain Gordon, McKeon?" asked Pelham, with intense surprise.

"Of course I do."

"All the officers of the first part of the port watch voted," added Grossbeck.

"They did!" exclaimed Pelham.

"Well, was it any stranger that the officers of the first part of the port watch voted, than it was that those of the second part did so?" inquired Shuffles, with earnestness.

"I think it was," replied Pelham, decidedly.

"Paul Kendall was one of them," said McKeon.

"Paul Kendall! Does any fellow suppose he has joined the Chain?" demanded the defeated candidate.

"Why not?"

"And Captain Gordon?"

"Why not?"

"How did the captain vote?" asked Pelham.

"No matter how he voted," said Shuffles, indignantly. "I protest against this raking up of matters which are already settled."

"He voted beans," replied McKeon, who, it is hardly necessary to add, was a Pelham man.

"Then he is one of your friends, Shuffles," continued Pelham, who was beginning to understand how his rival had been elected.

"I don't claim him."

"Did you take the captain into the Chain, Shuffles?"

"I won't answer," replied the captain elect.

"If Captain Gordon and Paul Kendall are members, I would like to know it. I am first officer of the ship under the new order of things, and if I command Gordon to do anything, I mean that he shall obey me."

"Of course you will give him no orders till we are in possession of the ship," added Shuffles, not a little alarmed.

"Well, as Gordon and Kendall are members of the Chain — of course they are, or they wouldn't have voted — we can talk over the matter freely with them," said Pelham, chuckling.

"If you make the signs, and they make them, of course you can," replied Shuffles. "No member can speak to another about the business of the Chain until both of them have proved that they belong, by giving the required signals."

"Shuffles, do you suppose Captain Gordon knows the signs?"

"How should I know? I never tried him. I don't know why he shouldn't make them as well as Tom Ellis."

"Tom Ellis is all right. I vouch for him, for I admitted him myself. Who will vouch for the captain? Who took him in?"

"I don't know."

"I don't; but if anybody has admitted him, and not given him the signs, he ought to be instructed in them. Of course he must have been admitted, or he would not have voted," added Pelham, sarcastically.

"I have nothing more to say about this matter,"

replied Shuffles, disgusted with the cavils of his first officer.

"Nor I; but I shall satisfy myself whether the captain is a member or not," said Pelham, decidedly.

"Well, you must be very cautious what you do."

"Certainly I shall. I will give him the first sign; if he don't answer it, I shall conclude he is not a member; or, if he is, that he has not been properly instructed."

"Better not say anything to him," said Shuffles.

"Why not? He voted, and it must be all right."

"Don't you say a word to him, unless he proves that he is a member."

"I think he has proved that already by voting."

"You know our rule."

"I do; it requires me to satisfy myself that the person to whom I speak is a member. I am entirely satisfied now that the captain and Paul Kendall belong; they would not have voted if they had not belonged."

This was a "clincher," and even Shuffles had not wit enough to escape the conclusion of the dogmatic reasoner. The captain elect of the League knew very well that nine persons who were not members had voted — that he had secured his election by a gross fraud. He was afraid that Pelham, disappointed by his defeat, would do something to compromise the enterprise; but his own treachery had placed him in such a position that he could say nothing without exposing himself.

"Of course it's all right," added Pelham. "I find we have plenty of friends in the after cabin. As soon as you have any orders to give, Captain Shuffles, I am in a position to execute them to the best advantage."

"When I am ready, I will give them to you."

"It will be an easy matter now to obtain possession of the ship; in fact, all you have to do is to order Captain Gordon to turn the command over to you. He has been 'toggled,' and must obey his superiors — of course he has been toggled; he couldn't have voted if he hadn't been."

Shuffles was terribly exercised by the repeated flings of his disconcerted rival. He was already satisfied that the enterprise had come to an end, unless Pelham could be quieted; and he was about to propose a new ballot, when he was ordered by the quartermaster on duty to take his trick at the wheel.

"What does all this mean?" demanded Pelham of the receivers, when the captain-elect had gone to his duty.

"I only know that the captain and all the officers of the first part of the port watch voted, and other fellows who would no more join this thing than they would jump overboard," replied McKeon.

"How could they vote — how could the captain vote — without understanding the whole thing?" demanded Pelham, perplexed at the inconsistency of the facts.

"I think I know something about it," added Grossbeck.

"What do you know?"

"Haven't you heard of the new game?"

"What new game?"

"'Don't know Beans.'"

"Shuffles said something about it, but I did not comprehend his meaning."

Grossbeck explained the game, whose history had been circulated among " our fellows."

"And this game was played while the voting was going on?" said Pelham, who began to see the trick which his rival had put upon him.

"I didn't know anything about it till supper time," answered Grossbeck.

"I see it all," continued Pelham. "The receivers were the 'butts,' and about a dozen fellows voted for Shuffles, including Gordon and Kendall, supposing they were simply playing 'Don't know Beans.'"

It did not require a great deal of penetration on the part of the fourth lieutenant to comprehend the trick of his rival. He was indignant and angry, and all the more so because he had been outwitted, even while he was attempting to outwit his unscrupulous competitor.

The next day, the quarter watches off duty played "Don't know Beans" to their satisfaction. It was found, when everybody was watching the "butts," that very few could deposit their beans without detection. A few hours' trial of the new pastime convinced all except "our fellows" that it was a senseless game, and it was speedily abandoned.

On the nineteenth day of the voyage, the Young America encountered another gale, but it was not nearly so severe as the one through which she had passed when off Cape Sable. The ship ran for twelve hours under close-reefed topsails; but as the gale came from the south-west, she laid her course during the whole of it, and behaved herself to the entire satisfaction of all on board. On the following day, the wind had hauled round to the north-west, and the sea subsided, so that the ship went along very comfortably.

Notwithstanding his doubts of the good faith of Pelham, who, however, nominally adhered to the terms of the compact, Shuffles arranged his plans for the capture of the ship. He had decided to defer the grand strike until the ship had come up with Cape Clear, so that the faculty, and all the students who would not take a part in the enterprise, might be put on shore immediately. In the course of three days, the land would probably be sighted. The rising was to take place in Pelham's watch, the officers of which were members of the League. All the details had been carefully arranged, and trusty "links" appointed to perform the heavy work. As soon as the "old folks" had been locked up in the cabin, and the new captain had taken the command, the ship was to be headed for the shore. The great event was to come off at six o'clock in the afternoon of the twenty-third or twenty-fifth day. The ship would be near the coast for at least a part of two days. If she was within six hours' sail of the land on the twenty-third day out, when Pelham would have the second part of the first dog watch, the rising was to take place then; if not, it was to be deferred till the twenty-fifth day, when the watches were again favorable.

Shuffles communicated with his discontented first officer as often as he could, and unfolded his plans without reserve. Pelham listened, and, still professing his willingness to obey his superior officer, promised to do all that was required of him.

"In your watch, Pelham, you will see that the helm is in the hands of some of our fellows," said Shuffles.

"Certainly," replied Pelham, with more indifference than suited the enthusiastic chief of the enterprise. "By the way, Captain Shuffles, have you laid out any work for Captain Gordon to do?"

"What's the use of talking to me about him now that we are on the very point of accomplishing our purpose?" demanded Shuffles, with deep disgust.

"You can't deny that Gordon is an able fellow, and, as a good commander, of course you intend to give him some important position," chuckled Pelham. "Have you appointed the rest of your officers yet?"

"To be sure I have."

"Have you given Gordon anything?"

"No!" growled Shuffles.

"No? Why, do you think the present captain of the ship will be content to go into the steerage under the new arrangement?"

"He may go into the steerage or go overboard," answered the chief, angrily.

"Accidentally, you mean."

"Pelham, if you intend to be a traitor, say so."

"I! My dear fellow, I don't mean anything of the kind. I am as true as the pole star."

"Have you spoken to the captain about our affairs?"

"Not a word."

"Have you tried him by the signs?"

"I have, and he made no sign," laughed Pelham, who was not much enamoured of the cabalistic claptrap of the Chain.

"Then, of course, he is not a member."

"He must be; he voted," replied Pelham, maliciously.

"How many more times will you say that?"

"Perhaps fifty; perhaps a hundred," answered the fourth lieutenant, coolly. "I shall say it until you are willing to acknowledge the trick you put upon me."

"What trick?"

"O, I know all about it! Didn't you tell Kendall, the captain, and seven or eight others, how to play 'Don't know Beans'?"

"If I did, it was to cheat them when they wanted to know what the beans meant."

"You saw that the fellows threw away the beans, instead of voting for you with them, and you invented your game to make the thing come out right. No matter, Shuffles; I am bound by the compact we made, but I shall persist in regarding Gordon, Kendall, Foster, and others as members. As you made them vote, you are responsible for them. That's all."

"Don't let us quarrel about it, my dear fellow," said Shuffles, in soft, insinuating tones.

"By no means."

"We will have a new election," suggested the chief.

"If we should, I'm afraid all the fellows would want to play 'Don't know Beans.'"

"You shall conduct it any way you please."

"If I did, you would say I cheated you. I agreed to abide by the election, and I shall do so. The fact is, Shuffles, you and I are too smart to play in the same game. I shall stick to the bond. When you order me to do anything, I shall do it," replied Pelham, as he turned on his heel and walked off.

He retreated into the after cabin, where Shuffles could not follow him. At the cabin table, studying his French lesson, sat Paul Kendall.

CHAPTER XIX.

MAN OVERBOARD!

"DO you know how to play 'Don't know Beans'?" asked Pelham, as he seated himself by the side of the second lieutenant.

"Yes; I know how to play it, but it's a stupid game. Shuffles told me how."

"Did he, indeed?"

"There was some fun in it the first time I tried it; but the second time was enough to satisfy me. I don't think there is any sense in it."

"Of course there isn't, Kendall," laughed Pelham. "It was no game at all."

"What are you laughing at?"

"You were sold on that game," added the conspirator, indulging in more laughter than the occasion seemed to require.

"How was I sold? I don't see anything so very funny about it."

"I do."

"Tell me about it; if there is any joke I think I shall enjoy it. You say I was sold."

"You were; and so was I."

"Well, what was it?" asked Paul, impatiently.

"When you gave those fellows the beans that day, you were voting!"

"Voting! Voting for what, or whom?" exclaimed the second lieutenant.

"For Shuffles."

"Did my vote count?"

"To be sure it did; and he was elected to a certain position by your vote and those of seven or eight others who did not understand the trick," replied Pelham, laughing all the time.

"What was the position? I don't understand what you are talking about, and therefore I can't appreciate the joke."

"I'll tell you, Kendall; but you must keep still about it for the present."

"It looks to me, on the face of it, like a dishonest trick. It seems that Shuffles lied to us when he made us believe that we were playing a game. I like a joke well enough, but I don't believe in a fellow's lying for the sake of any fun."

"You are right, Kendall. It was not only a dishonest trick, but it was a mean one."

"What was the position?" repeated Paul.

"Some of the fellows are going to make Mr. Lowington a present of a silver pitcher as soon as we get to some port where we can obtain one."

"Why didn't you tell of it?" demanded Paul. "I should like to join in the presentation, for I don't think there is a fellow on board who likes Mr. Lowington better than I do."

"Yes; but, you see, there's something peculiar about this thing. The contribution is to be confined to those fellows who have been disciplined in one way or another. A good many of us, you know, were mad when Mr. Lowington took our money away; we are satisfied now that he was right. We made him feel rather uncomfortable by our looks and actions, and some of us were positively impudent to him. We purpose to show that our feelings are all right."

"Precisely so!" replied Paul, with enthusiasm. "That's splendid! Mr. Lowington will appreciate the gift when he sees the names of the subscribers."

"Certainly he will."

"But you have no money," laughed the second lieutenant.

"We have put our names down for ten shillings apiece — about thirty of us. When we get into port, we shall tell Mr. Lowington that we wish to present a silver pitcher to a gentleman on board, in token of our appreciation of his kindness, &c., and ask him for half a sovereign each from our funds."

"He will wish to know who the gentleman is."

"We can ask to be excused from telling him."

"I can manage that part of the business for you. Each of the fellows shall give me an order on the principal for ten shillings, to be paid to Dr. Winstock, who will buy the pitcher for you, if you like. He is acquainted in Cork. I will give all the orders to the doctor, and he will get the present without saying a word to Mr. Lowington until after the presentation. Then he will have no chance to object, on the suspicion that the gift is intended for him — don't you see?"

Paul Kendall entered into the project with a degree

of enthusiasm which was rather embarrassing to the conspirator.

"The fellows have been very secret about the thing," added Pelham.

"They must have been, or I should have heard something about it," replied Paul, innocently.

"No one but ourselves has known a thing about it till now. They have formed a kind of secret society, and know each other by certain signs."

"But what was the voting for?"

"For orator of the day."

"For the fellow who is to present the pitcher and make the speech?" added Paul.

"Yes."

"And Shuffles was chosen?"

"Yes, by a trick."

"You mean that no one but subscribers ought to have voted?"

"Precisely so."

"It was a mean trick."

"It was a sort of practical joke upon me, I suppose."

"I don't believe in practical jokes which need a lie to carry them through."

"Well, Shuffles has the position, unless some of you fellows will help me out. I wanted to make the speech, and without the nine votes which you and other outsiders put in, I should have been chosen."

"What can we do?"

"I have a right to consider all the fellows that voted as members of the society. The fact of their voting makes them members.

"I don't know anything about that."

"It's clear enough to me, and in a talk I had with Shuffles just now, he didn't pretend to deny the correctness of my position."

"If he agrees, it must be all right," laughed Paul.

"If you had understood the matter, for whom should you have voted?"

"I don't know; but after the trick Shuffles played off upon you, I should not vote for him."

"Very well; then you can change your vote."

"How shall I change it?"

"Go to Shuffles; and the other eight fellows who voted in the dark must do the same."

"What shall I say to him?"

"You must go to him as a member of the society, and salute him as such."

"I don't know how."

"I'll tell you. When you meet him, scratch the tip end of your nose with the nail of your second finger on the right hand; in this manner," continued Pelham, giving the first sign.

"That's it — is it?" said Paul, as he imitated the action of Pelham.

"Yes; that's right. He will reply by taking the lower part of his left ear between the thumb and first finger of the left hand — so," added Pelham.

"I have it," answered Paul, as he made the motions.

"Then you will scratch your chin with the thumb nail of the left hand, and he will reply by blowing his nose."

"Let's see if I can do all that," laughed Paul, very

much amused at the mystic indications of membership in the secret association.

He made the signs to Pelham, who replied to them, several times, until he was perfect in his part.

"All right. I will remember them," said Paul.

"But you haven't got the whole of it yet. When you have made the signs, and he has answered them, he will say, '*Is* that so?' with strong emphasis on the first word."

"*Is* that so?" repeated Paul.

"Then you will reply, '*That* is so,' with the stress on *that*."

"*That* is so," added Paul.

"Then you must place yourself so as to look directly forward or aft. If you look forward, he must look aft."

"I understand you."

"Now I want to know who the other fellows were that played 'Don't know Beans' that day."

"Captain Gordon was one."

"Will you post him up in what I have told you?"

"I will, and the other fellows who voted for Shuffles, if you say so."

"Thank you. I wish you would. Let them all tell him they desire to change their votes; but have them do it one at a time."

Paul Kendall promised to do what was required of him; and in the course of the following forenoon he initiated "the outsiders who had voted for Shuffles" in the secret machinery of the supposed society, but in fact of the Chain League. Being off duty during the second part of the afternoon watch, he encountered Shuffles in the lee side of the waist.

"Well, Shuffles, we are almost up with the coast of Ireland," said Paul, as he scratched the tip of his nose with the second finger of his right hand, agreeably to the instructions given him by Pelham.

"Yes; and I suppose by Saturday, if the wind holds fair, we shall be off Cape Clear," replied the captain-elect, as he took the lower part of his left ear between the thumb and forefinger of the left hand.

Shuffles did not suppose that the second lieutenant was a member of the league, and pledged to assist in the capture of the ship; but as he had made the sign, probably accidentally, he replied to it.

"There is a prospect of fair weather for some days to come," continued Paul, as he scratched his chin with his left hand, which was the second step towards a recognition in the "Chain."

Shuffles was duly and properly astonished at this exhibition of intelligence on the part of the officer; and it was now quite certain that Paul had joined the league, or that he had obtained its tremendous secrets.

"I hope it will be good weather now during the rest of the passage," added the captain-elect, as he took his handkerchief from his breast pocket and blew his nose, for he was determined to satisfy himself whether or not the second lieutenant was a member of the League.

"*Is* that so?" demanded Shuffles.

"*That* is so," answered Paul.

Shuffles was almost overwhelmed with astonishment to find that one who was a model of fidelity and propriety had actually joined the Chain.

"Shuffles, I voted for you the other day," added Paul.

"I know you did."

"I wish to change my vote."

"Change it!" exclaimed Shuffles.

"Yes; I voted in the dark. I wish now to vote for the other candidate."

"For whom?"

"For Pelham, of course."

"You are too late."

"I think, under the circumstances, that my vote ought to be counted on the other side, even if it reverses the result," said Paul, earnestly.

"Why do you wish to vote for Pelham?" demanded Shuffles, rather because he had nothing else to say than because he was interested in the anticipated reply.

"I don't think it was quite fair for you to obtain my vote as you did."

"No matter for that. Do you think Pelham would make a better captain than I should?"

"A better what?"

"Do you think he will command the ship any better than I shall."

"Command the ship!" repeated Paul, bewildered by this extraordinary question. "I wasn't aware that either of you were to command the ship."

Shuffles, in his turn, was confounded when he found that the second lieutenant was a member of the "Chain" without any knowledge of its objects.

Though he had used all the precautions required by the League, a hint had unwittingly been given to Paul, whose simple integrity rendered him the most dangerous person on board to the interests of such an institution as the Chain.

"Mr. Kendall, may I ask what you now suppose you were voting for?" asked Shuffles, with easy assurance.

"For the orator of the day, of course," replied Paul, who was too free from wiles or arts to make any use of the advantage gained.

Indeed, he was so true himself that he was not suspicious of others; and he did not even perceive that he had obtained an advantage.

"Exactly so," added Shuffles; "for orator of the day; but we don't speak the idea out loud, or call it by its proper name."

"What did you mean by commanding the ship, Shuffles?" laughed Kendall.

"I meant orator of the day. We keep this thing to ourselves," added Shuffles, who had no idea what was meant by his companion.

"Of course; I understand all about that," said Paul, knowingly. "I don't think I had any right to vote; and in my opinion the trick you played on Pelham was decidedly wrong."

"It was merely a joke," answered Shuffles.

"But do you intend to use the advantage you gained by this trick?"

"Certainly not."

"I'm very glad of that."

"It was only for the fun of the thing," added Shuffles, at a venture.

"It may have been funny; but I don't think it was honest."

"I didn't intend to make any use of it," continued Shuffles. "What did Mr. Pelham say to you, Mr. Kendall?"

"He told me all about it," replied Paul.

"Did he, indeed?"

"He said that you, by causing me to vote, had made me a member."

"Just so."

Shuffles did not dare to say much, though it was evident, from the words and the manner of the second lieutenant, that Pelham had not yet betrayed the real object of the Chain. If he had, the captain elect was satisfied he would have been in irons, confined in the brig, before that time.

"I told Mr. Pelham I fully approved the purpose, and would help him out with it."

"What purpose?" asked Shuffles, anxious to know what Paul meant.

"Why, don't you know?"

"Of course I do; but I wish to know precisely what Mr. Pelham told you."

"He will tell you himself," laughed Paul, as he walked aft, in order to afford the other "outsiders" who had voted an opportunity to communicate with Shuffles; for he perceived that they were waiting their turns.

As the second lieutenant went aft, the captain went forward on the lee side of the deck.

"Shuffles!" called Captain Gordon, as the chief conspirator was going forward.

The captain elect turned and walked towards the commander, and touched his cap with becoming respect.

"What do you think of the weather?" demanded Captain Gordon, scratching the tip of his nose.

Paul had instructed the "outsiders" to talk about the weather while they went through with the mystic routine of the signs.

"I think we shall have good weather," replied Shuffles, who, though he was confounded and amazed to be saluted from this quarter with the language of the "Chain," dared not refuse to give the signs, after he had done so with the second lieutenant.

"I wish to change my vote; for I don't think it was fairly given before," said the captain, when he had gone through all the forms of the recognition.

"Certainly, Captain Gordon, if you desire to do so."

Fortunately for Shuffles, the captain did not prolong the conversation; for others were waiting an opportunity to make themselves known to the conspirator. One after another, they saluted Shuffles in the waist, inquiring about the weather, and making the requisite signs. The captain elect was filled with indignation and rage against Pelham, who had played off this trick upon him; but he was compelled to meet all who came, and go through the signs with them, while the "outsiders," scattered about the deck, stood watching the motions with intense delight. He would fain have fled, but he could not leave the deck; and he was afraid that any impatience, or a refusal to answer the signs, would involve him in a worse difficulty.

At last the nine illegal voters had "made themselves known," and having requested that their votes might be changed, Shuffles was released from torture. He was both alarmed and indignant. He had not been able to ascertain what was meant by " the orator of the day:" and he began to fear that Pelham had exposed the whole, or a part, of the real purposes of the League. He was enraged that he had revealed anything. Even the captain and the second lieutenant had made all the signs, and they could not have done so without the assistance of a traitor.

"It's all up with us, Wilton," said Shuffles, as they met near the foremast.

"What is?"

"Pelham has blowed the whole thing."

"No!" exclaimed Wilton, almost paralyzed by the information.

"He has. The captain and several of the officers made all the signs to me just now. We shall spend our time in the brig for the next month."

"Did Pelham do it?"

"Yes."

"That was mean," added Wilton, his face pale with terror.

"He will fall overboard accidentally some day," added Shuffles, shaking his head.

"Don't do that, Shuffles," protested the frightened confederate.

"I will, if I get a chance."

"You will only make the matter ten times worse than it is."

Monroe joined them, and was informed of the desperate situation of the League.

"It's all your fault, Shuffles," said Monroe, indignantly. "I don't blame Pelham."

"You don't! He has told a dozen outsiders how to make the signs, and let them into the secrets of the Chain, for all I know."

"If he has, we may thank you for it, Shuffles. You cheated him, and played a mean trick upon him," replied Monroe. "I wouldn't have stood it if I had been he."

"Pelham is a traitor, and you are another."

"No matter what he is, or what I am. You got all those fellows to vote for you, and cheated him out of the place that belonged to him."

"Did you think I was going to have him captain, after I had got up the Chain, and done all the work?"

"You agreed to leave it out to the fellows who should be captain. They voted, and you cheated," added Monroe. "I've had enough of the Chain; and if any fellow makes the signs again, I shall not notice them."

"Humph! It's a pretty time to talk so, after the whole thing is let out."

"Well, I will face the music, and get out of it the best way I can. I was a fool to join the Chain."

"So was I," said Wilton.

There was no difficulty in arriving at such a conclusion, after the affair had been exposed; and the sentiments of Wilton and Monroe were, or would soon be, the sentiments of all the members of the League. Shuffles realized the truth of the old adage, that rats desert a sinking ship, and he began to feel lonely in his guilt and his fear of exposure. But he could not forgive Pelham for his perfidy, forgetting that each had been treacherous to the other.

In the first dog watch on that day, while Shuffles' heart was still rankling with hatred towards the alleged traitor, the rivals met in the waist, which was common ground to officers off duty and seamen.

"I want to see you, Pelham," said Shuffles, in a low tone.

"Well, you do see me — don't you?" laughed Pelham, who, feeling that he was now even with his rival, was in excellent humor.

"Things are going wrong with us."

"O, no; I think not."

"Will you meet me on the top-gallant forecastle, where we shall not be disturbed?" asked Shuffles.

"That is not exactly the place for an officer."

"You are off duty, and you can go where you please."

"What do you want of me?"

"I want to have an understanding."

"I suppose you think we have too many members — don't you?" asked Pelham, lightly.

"The more the better."

"I'll meet you there."

Shuffles went to the place designated at once, where he was soon followed by the fourth lieutenant.

"Well, Shuffles, what is it?" demanded Pelham, as, with one hand on the sheet of the fore-topmast staysail, he looked over the bow at the bone in the teeth of the ship.

"What is it? Don't you know what it is?" replied Shuffles, angrily.

"Upon my life, I don't know."

"You have been a traitor," exclaimed Shuffles, with savage earnestness.

"O! have I?"

"You know you have."

"Perhaps you would be willing to tell me wherein I have been a traitor," added Pelham, laughing; for he was enjoying the scene he had witnessed in the waist, when, one after another, the "outsiders" had made the signs to his rival.

"You have betrayed the secrets of the Chain."

"Have I?"

"Didn't you give the signs to Paul Kendall, the captain, and half a dozen others?"

"But, my dear fellow, they are members," replied Pelham, chuckling.

"They are not; and you know they are not."

"But, Shuffles, just consider that all of them voted for you."

"I don't care for that."

"I do. You recognized them as members first, and I couldn't do less than you did."

"You are a traitor!" said Shuffles, red in the face with passion; and the word hissed through his closed teeth.

"Well, just as you like: we won't quarrel about the meaning of words," replied Pelham, gayly; for he enjoyed the discomfiture of his rival, and felt that

Shuffles deserved all he got, for the foul play of which he had been guilty on the ballot.

"You pledged yourself to be honest, and stand by the vote, fair or foul."

"Very true, my dear fellow; and I do so. Give me your orders, and I will obey them."

"But you have exposed the whole thing," retorted Shuffles. "What can we do now, when Kendall and the captain know all about it?"

"They don't know any more than the law allows. Besides, they are members. Didn't they vote for you? Didn't they know beans?" continued Pelham, in the most tantalizing of tones.

"Do you mean to insult me?" demanded Shuffles, unable to control his rage.

"Not I. I respect you too much. You are the captain — that is to be — of the ship," laughed Pelham. "The captain, the second lieutenant, and all the flunkies, voted for you; and, of course, I couldn't be so deficient in politeness as to insult one who——"

At that moment Pelham removed his hand from the sheet, and Shuffles, irritated beyond control at the badinage of his companion, gave him a sudden push, and the fourth lieutenant went down into the surges, under the bow of the ship.

As Pelham disappeared beneath the waves, Shuffles was appalled at his own act; for even he had not sunk so low as to contemplate murder. The deed was not premeditated. It was done on the spur of angry excitement, which dethroned his reason. The chief conspirator had so often and so lightly used the language of the League, about "falling overboard accidentally," that he had become familiar with the idea; and, perhaps, the deed seemed less terrible to him than it really was. When the act was done, on the impulse of the moment, he realized his own situation, and that of his victim. He would have given anything at that instant, as he looked down upon the dark waves, to have recalled the deed; but it was too late. Self-reproach and terror overwhelmed him.

"Man overboard!" he shouted with desperation, as he threw off his pea-jacket, and dived, head foremost, from the forecastle into the sea.

His first impulse had been to do a foul deed; his next, to undo it. Shuffles was a powerful swimmer. The ocean was his element. He struck the water hardly an instant after Pelham; and the ship, which was under all sail, making nine knots, hurried on her course, leaving the rivals to buffet the waves unaided.

"Man overboard!" cried officers and seamen, on all parts of the ship's deck.

"Hard down the helm, quartermaster! Let go the life-buoys!" shouted Kendall, who was the officer of the deck.

"Hard down, sir. Buoy overboard," replied Bennington, the quartermaster at the helm.

"Clear away the third cutter!" added Kendall.

The orders were rapidly given for backing the maintopsail, while the courses were clewed up; but the ship went on a considerable distance before her headway could be arrested.

When Pelham went down into the water, he had been injured by the fall; and though he struck out to save himself, it was not with his usual skill and vigor;

for, like his companion in the water, he was a good swimmer. Shuffles had struck the waves in proper attitude, and was in condition to exert all his powers when he came to the surface. He swam towards Pelham, intent upon rendering him the assistance he might require.

"Do you mean to drown me?" gasped Pelham, who supposed his rival had followed him overboard for the purpose of completing his work.

"I mean to save you, Pelham," replied Shuffles. "Can you swim?"

"I'm hurt."

"Give me your hand, and I will support you."

Shuffles took the offered hand of Pelham, who was able to swim a little, and supported him till they could reach the life-buoy, which had been dropped from the stern of the ship when the alarming cry was given.

"Where are you hurt?" asked Shuffles, as soon as they had grasped the buoy.

"My stomach struck the water," replied Pelham, faintly.

The third cutter had been lowered into the water as soon as the ship's headway was stopped, and was now within a few yards of the buoy.

"Will you forgive me, Pelham? I was beside myself," said Shuffles, when his companion had recovered breath after his exertions.

"You have saved me, Shuffles. I should have gone down without you."

"Will you forgive me?" pleaded the penitent. "I did not mean to injure you."

"Never mind it; we won't say a word about it," answered Pelham, as the boat came up.

They were assisted into the cutter, and the oarsmen pulled back to the ship. When the party reached the deck, a cheer burst from a portion of the crew; but Wilton, Monroe, and a few others, believing that Pelham had "fallen overboard accidentally," were appalled at the probable consequences of the event.

Pelham was assisted to the after cabin, where Dr. Winstock immediately attended him. He was not seriously injured; and the next day he was able to be on deck, and do duty.

"How was that?" asked Wilton, when Shuffles had changed his clothes, and warmed himself at the stove, as they met in the waist.

Shuffles looked sad and solemn. He made no reply.

"Did he fall overboard accidentally?" demanded Wilton.

"Don't ask me."

"You jumped in after him, and saved him, they say," added Wilton; "so, I suppose, it was really an accident."

Shuffles still made no reply.

CHAPTER XX.

THE END OF THE CHAIN LEAGUE.

THE fact that Shuffles had plunged into the sea, and labored so effectively for the rescue of the fourth lieutenant, blinded the eyes of " our fellows," who, knowing the penalty of treachery to the " Chain," might otherwise have suspected that he had " fallen overboard accidentally," or, in other words, that he had been pushed into the water by his unscrupulous rival. Wilton, Monroe, and Adler, had discussed the matter, and reached the conclusion that Pelham had been knocked over by the shaking of the staysail sheet, or that he had really fallen accidentally. They had been appalled and horrified by the event; and those who were disgusted with the League were not disposed to betray its secrets; for it was possible, though not probable, that the mishap which had befallen Pelham was an incident in the history of the " Chain."

When a wicked man or a wicked boy exceeds his average wickedness, the excess sometimes produces a moral reaction. A person who tipples moderately may have the drunkard's fate vividly foreshadowed to him by getting absolutely drunk himself, and thus be induced to abandon a dangerous practice. That loathsome disease, small pox, sometimes leaves the patient better than it finds him; and through, and on account of, the vilest sin may come the sinner's reformation.

Shuffles had exceeded himself in wickedness; and the fact that his foul design was not even suspected by any other person than his intended victim did not diminish his self-reproaches. He shuddered when he thought of the remorse which must have gnawed his soul during the rest of his lifetime if Pelham had been drowned. He would have been a murderer; and while so many knew the penalty of treachery to the League, he could hardly have escaped suspicion and detection.

A reaction had been produced in his mind; but it was not a healthy movement of the moral nature. It was not so much the awful crime he had impulsively committed, as the terrible consequences which would have followed, that caused him to shrink from it. It was an awful crime, and his nature revolted at it. He could not have done it without the impulse of an insane passion; but it was dreadful because it would have shut him out from society; because it would have placed the mark of Cain upon him; because the dungeon and the gallows were beyond it, — rather than because it was the sacrifice of a human life, of one created in the image of God.

Shuffles was in a state of terror, as one who has just escaped from an awful gulf that yawned before him. He was not sincerely penitent, as one who feels the enormity of his offence. He was not prepared to acknowledge his sin before God, whose law he had outraged.

When Pelham came on deck, on the day after the exciting event, he greeted Shuffles with his accustomed suavity, and seemed not to bear any malice in his heart against the author of his misfortune. Officers and seamen, as well as the principal and the professors, congratulated him upon his escape from the peril which had menaced him; and all commended Shuffles for his prompt and noble efforts in rescuing him. Pelham dissented from none of their conclusions, and was as generous in his praise of the deliverer as the occasion required.

Shuffles was rather astonished to find himself a lion on board, and at being specially thanked by Mr. Lowington for his humane exertions in saving a shipmate. He was so warmly and so generously commended that he almost reached the conclusion himself that he had done a good thing. He was not satisfied with himself. He was in the power of Pelham, who, by a word, could change the current of popular sentiment, and arraign him for the gravest of crimes. If the fourth lieutenant spoke, Shuffles realized that he should be shunned and despised, as well as hated and feared, by all on board the ship. It was quite natural, therefore, for him to desire a better understanding with Pelham.

The League had fallen into contempt, at least for the present. Even " our fellows " would not have spirit enough to strike the blow; besides, the terrible gulf from which Shuffles had just escaped was too vivid in his mind to permit him to place himself on the brink of another. So far the reaction was salutary.

"When may I see you, Mr. Pelham?" said Shuffles, as they came together in the waist.

"We will visit the top-gallant forecastle again, and see if we can understand how I happened to fall overboard, for really I'm not in the habit of doing such things," replied Pelham, with a smile.

They walked forward together, and mounted the ladder to the place indicated.

"Shuffles, I never paid much attention to the snapper of the toggle before, and never supposed it meant anything in particular," continued Pelham, as he placed himself in the position he had occupied before he went over the bow. "Am I in any danger now?"

"No, Pelham, no!" replied Shuffles, earnestly. "You provoked me so by your cool taunts that I pushed you over before I thought what I was about."

"Did you really mean to drown me?"

"Upon my soul, I did not. If you knew how I felt when I saw you strike the water, and realized what I had done, you would forgive me."

"I have done that already, Shuffles."

"I would have given my own life for yours at that instant, Pelham."

"You saved me, after all, Shuffles. When I went over, I either hit the side of the ship, or struck my stomach on the water, for all the breath seemed to be knocked out of me. I hardly knew what I was about in the water till I saw you. At first I supposed you had jumped overboard to finish your job."

"You wronged me; I would have saved you, if I had been sure of perishing myself."

"You did save me, and I am willing to let that act offset the other."

"I'm grateful to you for this, Pelham. You treat me better than I deserve."

"Never mind it now; we will call it square," replied Pelham, lightly. "How about the Chain, Shuffles? We shall be in sight of land by to-morrow."

"We can't do anything now."

"Why not?"

"How can we? After what has happened, I will not reproach you for what you did. You know how you provoked me. You have exposed the whole affair to the officers."

"Not a bit of it."

"No."

"Certainly not. Did you ever know Augustus Pelham to violate his obligations?" demanded Pelham, with dignity.

"Never before; but the captain, the second lieutenant, and seven others, who would no more join the League than they would steal your pocket-book, went through all the signs with me."

"They all voted too," laughed Pelham.

"I am willing to confess that I played off a mean trick upon you."

"And I have only made myself even with you. I have not betrayed a single secret of the Chain to any one not posted — except the signs. If I had, of course you and I would both have been in the brig before this time."

"I was puzzled to find nothing was said," added Shuffles.

"No one knows anything. The Chain is as perfect as ever. Give me your orders, and I will carry them out."

"The fellows have backed out now."

"Then, of course, we must do the same. I doubt whether we could have carried the thing out."

"No matter whether we could or not: we must drop it for the present. The fellows all suppose they are caught now, and expect every moment to be hauled up to the mast for an investigation."

"They are all safe; at least we can purchase their safety for ten shillings apiece," laughed Pelham.

"Purchase it!" exclaimed Shuffles, mystified by the language of his companion.

"Just so — purchase it," added Pelham; and he proceeded to inform his late rival of the trick he had invented in retaliation for the one Shuffles had put upon him.

"It was tit for tat," said Shuffles.

"I told nothing which would harm either of us, for I am just as deep in the mud as you are in the mire."

"That's true. We must hang together."

"I hope not," replied Pelham, laughing. "We have got into this scrape, and we must get out of it."

"Suppose the captain or the second lieutenant should make the signs to one of our fellows, and he should tell what we were going to do."

"I told all my recruits not to answer any signs now, whoever made them."

"I did the same, when I found the captain knew them."

"Then we are safe; but the silver pitcher must be forthcoming."

"The fellows will all be glad enough to get out of this scrape by paying ten shillings."

"Very well; then every one of them must sign an order on Mr. Lowington for ten shillings, payable to Dr. Winstock," added Pelham.

"They will do it. Are you sure nothing has leaked out?"

"Very sure; there would have been a tremendous commotion before this time, if our real object had been even suspected."

"No doubt of that."

"After all, Shuffles, do you really think we intended to take the ship?"

"I did; I know that."

"I don't believe I did," said the fourth lieutenant. "Nothing seemed exactly real to me, until I went overboard."

"It was more real to me then than ever before," replied Shuffles. "What shall we do with the Chain now?"

"Nothing; we may want to use it again, some time. Let every fellow keep still. When the principal gets his silver pitcher, which the doctor will procure as soon as he can go up to Cork, he will think the members of the Chain are the best fellows on board."

"I think you have sold the whole of us, Pelham,"

continued Shuffles, with a sheepish smile. "Here's the end of the Chain——"

"Yes, and we may be thankful that it isn't the end of a rope instead of a chain," laughed Pelham. "The penalty of mutiny is death."

"I have had no fear of that; it would have been regarded only as a lark. But it is really amusing to think where we have come out," added Shuffles. "We formed the 'Chain' because Lowington was tyrannical; most of the fellows joined it because he took their money from them."

"Precisely so."

"And we are going to end it by giving Lowington a silver pitcher, in token of our respect and esteem!"

"In other words, Shuffles, we have played this game, and whipped out each other, without any help from the principal. It was mean business — I really think so; and while we were trying to overreach each other, the game slipped through our fingers. I am really grateful when I think what an awful scrape we have avoided."

"Perhaps you are right," replied Shuffles, thoughtfully; "but there was fun in the scheme."

"There might have been, if we had succeeded: but it would have been anything but fun if we had failed. Some of us would have found quarters in the brig, and we should not have been allowed to go on shore when we reached Queenstown."

"A fellow won't want to go on shore without any money," growled Shuffles, who was not wholly cured of his discontent.

"Since I went overboard I have been thinking a

great deal of this matter. I have come to the conclusion that Mr. Lowington is not the worst man in the world."

"He is harsh and tyrannical."

"I don't think he ought to have taken our money from us; but I judge him from all his acts, not by one alone."

Pelham seemed to have turned over a new leaf, and to be sincerely sorry for his attitude of rebellion. Shuffles was not to be convinced; he was to be overwhelmed in another manner.

The rivals separated, with their differences removed, and with full confidence in each other. Pelham wrote thirty-one orders on the principal for ten shillings each, in favor of the surgeon, during his off-time on that day, which were to be signed and handed to Paul Kendall. As opportunity occurred, the "situation" was explained to the members of the League; and though many of them growled at the idea of giving a present to Mr. Lowington for taking their money from them, not one of them refused to sign the orders; none of them dared to refuse.

In due time Dr. Winstock had possession of all these little drafts, amounting in the aggregate to fifteen pounds, ten shillings, which would purchase quite a respectable piece of plate. Paul Kendall was the happiest student on board, for the presentation heralded the era of good feeling. The League was virtually dead for the present, if not forever. The inherent evil of the organization, with the bickerings and bad passions of its members, had killed it — the turtle had swallowed his own head.

The weather continued fine; the routine of ship's duty and the studies went on without interruption. On the twenty-fourth day out, at three bells in the afternoon watch, a tremendous excitement was created on board.

"Land on the port bow!" shouted one of the crew, who had been stationed on the fore yard-arm as a lookout.

All on deck sprang into the rigging, to get a sight of the welcome shore. It looked like a fog bank in the distance; there was really nothing to be seen, but the fact that the ship was in sight of land was enough to create an excitement among the boys.

At three bells, in the first dog watch, the land was distinctly visible. It was the Island of Dursey, and was now seen on the beam, while other land appeared in sight ahead. It was Sunday, and all hands were at liberty to enjoy this first view of the new continent. The boys thought the land looked just like that they had last seen on the shore of the western continent, and perhaps some of them were disappointed because everything looked so natural.

The officers and crew were impatient to make their destined port; but the wind subsided as the sun went down on that quiet Sabbath day on the ocean. The ship hardly made twenty miles before daylight in the morning.

At eight o'clock, on Monday, when Paul Kendall had the deck, the Young America was off Fastnet Rock, and not more than half a mile from it. It is about ten miles from Cape Clear, and is a solitary rock rising out of the sea, on which a lighthouse is located. The water around it was covered with small boats engaged in fishing. The port watch were all on deck, and the scene was full of interest to them. The people whom they saw belonged to another continent than that in which they lived. All was new and strange to them, and all were interested in observing the distant shore, and the objects near the ship.

At one bell in the afternoon watch, when the Young America was off Gally Head, all hands were piped to muster. Mr. Lowington, on taking the rostrum, said that he had received a petition signed by a majority of the officers and crew.

"A petition to go ashore, I suppose," said Shuffles to Pelham.

"I think not," laughed the fourth lieutenant, who appeared to know what was coming.

"Young gentlemen," continued the principal, whose face wore an unusually pleasant smile, "a few days since you were all filled with admiration at the noble conduct of one of your number, who saved the life of another at the peril of his own."

"Want to go ashore, Shuffles?" whispered Pelham.

Shuffles was too much confused to make any reply; he did not know whether he was to be praised or blamed.

"I have received a petition, requesting me to appoint Robert Shuffles second lieutenant of the ship, in place of Paul Kendall, resigned," added Mr. Lowington.

Shuffles was overwhelmed with astonishment, and a large proportion of the students received the announcement with hearty applause.

"Young gentlemen, I have only to say that the

petition is granted. I ought to add, however, that no officer will lose his rank, except Mr. Kendall, who, at his own desire, will take the vacant number in the steerage, now belonging to Robert Shuffles, promoted. I take great pleasure in granting this petition, because the request is honorable to you, and shows a proper appreciation of the noble conduct of your shipmate. But let me add, that you should divide your admiration between the one who rescued his friend from death, and him who voluntarily resigned his honorable position in the after cabin, in order to make a place in which merit could be acknowledged and rewarded. Nothing but a matter of life and death could have induced me to vary the discipline of the ship. Young gentlemen, you are dismissed from muster."

"Three cheers for Paul Kendall!" shouted one of the boys.

They were given.

"Three cheers for Robert Shuffles!" added Paul; and they were given.

"Mr. Shuffles will repair to the after cabin, where he will be qualified, and take his position at once."

"Mr. Lowington, I must decline Mr. Kendall's generous offer," interposed Shuffles, who was actually choking with emotion.

"This matter has been well considered, Shuffles," replied the principal; "and as it is the desire of a large majority of your shipmates that you should accept the position, I think you had better do so."

"There isn't a student in the ship who desires it so much as I do," added Paul, with generous enthusiasm. "You know I told you I would like to be in the steerage, for I have always been an officer."

"Allow me till to-night, if you please, to consider it, Mr. Lowington," replied Shuffles, as he grasped the hand of Paul.

"Certainly, if you desire it."

Shuffles was overwhelmed by the magnanimity of Paul and the kindness of the principal. At that moment he would have given everything to be such a young man as the second lieutenant; to be as good and true, as free from evil thoughts and evil purposes, as he was. A light had dawned upon the rebel and the plotter which he had never seen before. Goodness and truth had vindicated themselves, and overwhelmed the guilty one.

"Mr. Shuffles, I congratulate you on your promotion," said the chaplain, extending his hand.

"I cannot accept it, sir," replied the repentant malcontent. "I would like to speak with you alone, Mr. Agneau."

The chaplain took him to his state room in the main cabin; and there, Shuffles, conquered and subdued by the kindness of his friends, confessed the terrible crime he had committed — that he had pushed Pelham overboard.

The chaplain was confounded at this confession, but still more so when the self-convicted conspirator revealed all the secrets of "The Chain." Shuffles mentioned no names; he took all the guilt upon himself.

"I am astonished, my dear young friend," said the

chaplain. "Is it possible the life you saved was imperilled by your own violent passions?"

"It is true, sir," replied Shuffles, hardly able to control his feelings.

"Then I think you had better not accept the promotion that has been offered to you."

"I will not; I would jump overboard first. I am willing to be punished; I deserve it."

"Shuffles, you have almost atoned for your errors by confessing them; and your courageous conduct, after you had pushed Pelham into the sea, proves that you sincerely repented that act. Shall I tell Mr. Lowington what you have said?"

"Yes, sir; let him know me as I am; let him despise me as I deserve," replied Shuffles, wiping away a genuine tear of repentance.

Mr. Agneau talked to the penitent for two hours; and finally he prayed with him and for him. If never before, the moral condition of the culprit was now hopeful, and the chaplain labored earnestly and faithfully to give him right views of his relations to God and his fellow-beings.

"Paul," said Shuffles, when he met his generous and self-sacrificing friend in the waist, after the conference in the state room, "I am the meanest and vilest fellow on board."

"No, you are not!" exclaimed Paul.

"I would give the world to be like you."

"No, no! You wrong yourself, and overdo me."

"I have confessed all to the chaplain, and you will soon know me as I am, Paul. I will not take your place in the cabin. Your kindness and generosity have overcome me. You have convinced me that doing right is always the best way."

Paul did not know what to make of this remarkable confession; but, after supper, all hands were piped to muster again, the ship being off Kinsale Head, nearly becalmed. The chaplain had informed the principal of the substance of Shuffles' confession. Mr. Lowington laughed at "The Chain League," the signs and the passwords, and regarded the mutiny as a matter of little consequence. He did not believe that Shuffles, or his followers, had really intended to take the ship. The project was too monstrous to be credible. The fact that the conspirator had attempted the life of his companion was a grave matter, and it was treated as such. Mr. Agneau was entirely confident of the sincerity of the culprit's repentance. Shuffles had refused to take the proffered promotion, which was abundant evidence that he was in earnest.

The penitent was sent for, and repeated his confession to the principal. He did not ask to be exempted from punishment; but he did ask to be forgiven. He was forgiven; but when the crew were piped to muster, all the particulars of the intended mutiny were exposed to the astonished "outsiders." Paul understood it now. Mr. Lowington ridiculed the mutiny; but he spoke very seriously of the consequences of insubordination.

"Young gentlemen, Shuffles has not mentioned the name of a single student in connection with this silly conspiracy; he has asked to be excused from doing so. I grant his request, and I hope that all who have engaged in the affair are as sincerely sorry for their connection with it as he is. Under the circumstances, Shuffles will not be promoted. Young gentlemen, you are dismissed."

"Shuffles was a good fellow to keep us in the dark," whispered Sanborn to Wilton.

"Keep still," replied Wilton. "We are lucky to get out of the scrape on any terms."

So thought all of them; and it was certainly magnanimous on the part of the chief conspirator to be willing to assume all the guilt, and suffer all the punishment. There was enough of good in Shuffles to save him from the evil of his nature.

"Paul, there is one more thing I must tell you," said Shuffles, that evening, while the ship lay becalmed off Kinsale. "You remember when I told you about the gambling in the steerage?"

"I do."

"I was deceiving you then. I only exposed the fellows in order to make trouble. I knew that the students would be closely watched, and the rules more strictly enforced, which would make them mad."

"What did you want to make them mad for?"

"So that they would join the League."

"Well, you did a good thing for the ship and for the fellows, if your motives were not good," replied Paul. "It was good out of evil, any way."

"I don't think half so many fellows would have joined if Mr. Lowington hadn't taken their money from them."

"Have you seen any gambling since?"

"Not a bit of it, Paul."

"I am glad to know that."

"One thing more; you know all the members of the League, Paul."

"I?"

"Yes; you have their names on the orders, for ten shillings each."

"So I have; but we will make a general affair of the presentation, and that will cover up the whole of them."

"Thank you, Paul. You despise me as much as I like and respect you."

"I don't despise you, Shuffles. You have done wrong, but I respect you for undoing the evil you had meditated. We are all weak and erring, and we can't afford to despise any one. On the contrary, I like you," replied Paul, giving Shuffles his hand.

"You treat me better than I deserve, Paul; but if you are my friend, I shall be all the better for it; and I hope you will not be worse."

The end of the conspiracy had been reached, Before the ship came to anchor in the Cove, every boy on board had drawn his order on the principal for ten shillings, and the members of the League were veiled beneath the mass of names.

At sunrise, on Tuesday morning, the ship had a gentle breeze; and at three bells in the forenoon watch, she was off Roches Point, with the Union Jack at the foremast-head, as a signal for a pilot. On this exciting occasion, the studies and recitations were suspended, to enable all the students to see the shores, and enjoy the scene. The pilot made his appearance, gave Mr. Lowington the latest Cork papers, and took charge of the ship. The honest Irishman was not a little surprised to find the vessel manned " wid nothing in the wide wurld but by's;" but he found they were good seamen.

The Young America ran into the beautiful bay through the narrow opening, with Carlisle Fort on the starboard and Camden Fort on the port hand. The students were intensely excited by the near view of the land, of the odd little steamers that went whisking about, and the distant view of Queenstown, on the slope of the hill at the head of the bay. They were in Europe now.

"All hands to bring ship to anchor!" said the first lieutenant, when the ship was approaching the town.

The light sails were furled, the port anchor cleared away, and every preparation made for the mooring. Then the orders to let go the topsail sheets, clew up the topsails, and haul down the jib, were given.

"Port the helm! Stand clear of the cable! Let go the port anchor!"

The cable rattled through the hawse-hole, the anchor went to the bottom, the Young America swung round, and her voyage across the ocean was happily terminated. Three rousing cheers were given in honor of the auspicious event, and when the sails had been furled, the crew were piped to dinner.

And here, at the close of the voyage, we leave the Young America, with her officers and crew wiser and better, we trust, than when they sailed from the shores of their native country. They were now to enter upon a new life in foreign lands; and what they saw and what they did, on sea and shore, during the following weeks, will be related in "SHAMROCK AND THISTLE, or *Young America in Ireland and Scotland.*"

www.ingramcontent.com/pod-product-compliance
Lightning Source LLC
Chambersburg PA
CBHW031852220426
43663CB00006B/594